Of Bridges

Of Bridges

A POETIC AND PHILOSOPHICAL ACCOUNT

Thomas Harrison

The University of Chicago Press Chicago and London

The University of Chicago Press, Chicago 60637
The University of Chicago Press, Ltd., London

Published 2021
Paperback edition 2023
Printed in the United States of America

32 31 30 29 28 27 26 25 24 23 1 2 3 4 5

ISBN-13: 978-0-226-73529-0 (cloth)
ISBN-13: 978-0-226-82649-3 (paper)
ISBN-13: 978-0-226-73532-0 (e-book)
DOI: https://doi.org/10.7208/chicago/9780226735320.001.0001

The University of Chicago Press gratefully acknowledges the generous support of the Humanities Division and the Department of European Languages and Transcultural Studies at the University of California, Los Angeles, toward the publication of this book.

Library of Congress Cataloging-in-Publication Data

Names: Harrison, Thomas J., 1955– author.
Title: Of bridges : a poetic and philosophical account / Thomas J. Harrison.
Description: Chicago : The University of Chicago Press, 2021. | Includes bibliographical references and index.
Identifiers: LCCN 2020032941 | ISBN 9780226735290 (cloth) | ISBN 9780226735320 (ebook)
Subjects: LCSH: Bridges in literature. | Bridges in art. | Bridges—Social aspects. | Bridges—Religious aspects. | Bridges—History.
Classification: LCC PN56.B78 .H37 2021 | DDC 818.6/08—dc23
LC record available at https://lccn.loc.gov/2020032941

♾ This paper meets the requirements of ANSI/NISO Z39.48-1992 (Permanence of Paper).

CONTENTS

ILLUSTRATIONS

Plates (following page 134)

Figures

Introduction

Many good books have been written about bridges—about their technological functions, the legends attaching to them, their representations in art and literature—but few examine just how we experience those structures. What exactly do we have in mind with bridges, when we build them or cross them? What makes us think of one thing as a bridge but not another?

Wherever we turn we find ourselves connected—to our families, careers, and the paths that we travel. The twenty-first century finds us stretched out more than ever, plugged into seemingly unending networks and matters of concern. On the one hand this condition presents unprecedented opportunities for interaction and cooperative democracy; on the other it creates an openness difficult to control, evoking cries for more borders and deep retrenchments. The more connected we are, the more we become prone to an anxiety of access. What promises to produce connection often does not. And then, with all these external bridges, what bonds do we forge inside, in the inner world of subjectivity? Though bridges are the very issue of our time, we have not thought hard enough about what they are, and what they need to be.

From one perspective, they appear to be transcendent and angelic inventions. Literature presents them often in that light. "When Allah the Merciful and Compassionate first created this world," writes the Nobel Prize–winning author Ivo Andrić, "the earth was smooth and even as a finely engraved plate. That displeased the devil who envied man this gift of God. And while the earth was still just as it had come from God's hands, damp and soft as unbaked clay, he stole up and scratched the face of God's earth with his nails as much and as deeply as he could." The ravaging work of the devil created ravines and rivers, cleaving fissures between God's creatures. In response God sent down angels to spread their wings over these chasms, allowing humans to cross them and live in harmony. "So men learned from the angels of God how to build bridges, and therefore, after fountains, the greatest blessing is to build a bridge and the greatest sin to interfere with them."[1] Bridges were a divine gift to repair diabolical ruptures.

From another perspective, however, nature has perfectly good reasons for her unfordable rivers and unscalable mountains, and only diabolical forces dare span them, meddling with the order of nature to appease the wishes of men. That is precisely how we lost Paradise, according to the poet John Milton. Once, he tells us, the world of humans only depended on Heaven, from which it hung happily like a pendant at the end of a chain. Satan changed that perfection in one fell swoop. Groping his way from Hell to earth through the darkness of Chaos, he then engineered a bridge in his tracks. Over it he sent his children Sin and Death, the world's first "immigrants," who brought rivalry and discord, pride and unappeasable desire into the life of humans. The insular Milton had little good to say about bridges in *Paradise Lost* and channeled much of his hostility into an attack on the master bridge-builder of his time—the *pontifex maximus* or pope of Rome, whose ties to the British Isles were then thought to be a considerable problem. Centuries before Milton, however, even humble Catholics in Europe had taken to calling bridges in perilous mountain passes "bridges of the devil" (*ponte del diavolo* and *pont du diable*). Their grotesque and tottering spans seemed unnatural, arrogant, and dangerous.

Depending on the end from which it is looked at, the construction of angels can appear to be that of devils. The same might be said about the distinction between material bridges and spiritual ones. The first material bridge was probably a log lowered over a stream, enabling humans to forage more widely for food. Constructions in stone achieved more lasting and far-reaching results. The one that has been in longest continuous use, reports Guinness World Records, is in my birthplace of Izmir, Turkey: the Pont des Caravans (Kervan Köprüsü), constructed around 850 BCE. Some say that Homer himself crossed it as a boy. For nearly 3,000 years this Caravan Bridge experienced the same "constant succession of trains of camels, horses, mules, & donkeys" that Herman Melville observed at the site in his journal entry of December 20, 1856. Here westbound caravans reached the end of the longest and most important trade route of the ancient world: the Assyrian Route, stretching 2,500 kilometers from the imperial capital of Susa to the port of Smyrna, as Izmir was called for centuries. To deliver its merchandise to boats plying the Mediterranean, however, the Assyrian Route had to overcome one final small obstacle on its way: the narrow Meles River at the outskirts of Smyrna. It was over this river that the single-arched, slab-stone Caravan Bridge was laid, and where it still stands.

The tiny bridge was of inestimable importance. It furnished a link between two massive geological masses—the land and the sea—which humans traveled by road and boat. In the millennia that have passed since 850 BCE, the socioeconomic importance of that crossing has increased exponentially. On three colossal suspension bridges, 380,000 vehicles now cross each day between the continents of Europe and Asia due north of Izmir.

Spiritual bridges are less conspicuous but no less critical. Some are religious, tying believers to realms beyond visible creation, their connections maintained by worship and ritual. The first chapter of this book, "The Great Bridge-Building of God," examines a number of variants, from the rainbows of Native Americans to bird bridges between astral divinities in Chinese and Japanese legends. Other bridges are literary, carrying readers into a world of ideas. Many of these also appear in this book, where one chapter in particular, "Word Bridges," focuses directly on the question of prosaic and poetic expression. It argues that the newer and more deliberate such expression is, the more extensively it binds words in metaphorical relations (the word "metaphor" originally meaning carrying over one thing to the place of another). Bilingual and interlingual writers eventually emerge from the process and are examined separately in the chapter "Sea Bridges and Selves," where the transcultural space of the Adriatic Sea suggests that seemingly simple and straightforward expressions of self essentially sidestep the entire problem of intellectual negotiation.

Musical bridges lie in the same general vicinity as literary ones, forging and strengthening communal bonds. Blues music acts as a case study in "Musical Bridges," crossing genders, races, and continents in back and forth motion. That chapter begins by situating music within a general phenomenology of hearing, a sense drawing the absent near and allowing bodies to register their subjectivity through voices. *Of Bridges* contains discussions of several other bridges of this sort, in ethical, affective, and philosophical variation.

Ultimately, however, the distinction between material and spiritual bridges is as shaky as the one between godly and fiendish ones. The bridges of commerce and war have affected human thinking more decisively than the writings of Plato and Kant. Rome's massive stone bridges propelled not only battalions into Europe but the entire ideology of that *caput mundi*, or Capital of the World. The chapters "Sea Bridges and Selves" and "Bridge Brothers and Foes" point up the extent to which sociohistorical conditions of cultural contact underlie and often challenge collective positions. Contested and shared territories here include the Balkans during the age of the Yugoslavian wars and during considerably longer periods of troubles between Ottoman Turks and their Christian neighbors. Another chapter, "Bridged Disconnection," tells of how material bridges were destroyed in World War II, making way for the erection of Cold War walls, to be followed by the bridge-building efforts of the European Union, an alliance recently put on the defensive but still bolstering its influence, with other great competing nations, through the construction of megabridges both material and symbolic. Every functioning bridge serves material and spiritual purposes at once.

We could go a step further and say that cultures themselves are bridges, composed of thousands of linking structures. The philosopher Friedrich Nietzsche allegorized the situation in an image of human life as a rope stretched over an abyss. On one side stands nature in the raw and on the other an idea of how the species wants that nature to be. Humanity—both artifact and architect of culture—is no less the rope, woven out of multiple tense strands, than the passage across it. It is not that we choose this tightrope walk; no doubt we would prefer a fixed and firm place to its tottering suspension. And yet we have no choice. Connected at the very core of our being, and unable to operate in isolation, we are agents of bridge-existence. We can only choose how best to manage our connections. How narrow or broad should our bridges be? How many should we build, and to serve what destinations? Those are the questions we encounter on our *pons asinorum*, or "donkey's bridge," as medieval thinkers called the critical passage required by a problem. The bridge-crossings we make depend on the readings we give of the bridge we are on. "Living on the Bridge" sees this point of transition as a final abode, producing affective unions among transients seeking alms and shelter.

The art historian John Ruskin advised us to develop the art of "reading a building as we would read Milton or Dante."[2] He left a model for this manner of reading in *The Stones of Venice* (1853), inspiring two generations of readers to recognize ideas in form. If no full-fledged reading of bridges per se emerged from the post-Ruskin era, a short essay of 1909 gave an example of how one might proceed. It was the six-page "Bridge and Door" (1909), an interpretation of the very form of bridges by the philosopher Georg Simmel. His essay gives us a model for architectonic understanding that can easily be expanded beyond the formal features of the material structure of a bridge to its historical determinations, its cultural associations, and its symbolic connotations, as elaborated in conceptual, figurative, and metaphorical schemes. A brief summary of Simmel's essay can show how the form of a bridge points in these directions.

Bridges, roads, doors, windows, and walls have this in common, Simmel observes. They all connect spaces and keep them separate. They are different, however, in their affective and intellectual repercussions. They bear distinct existential effects. The door poses a barrier that is dynamic and dramatic. It allows for inward and outward motion. And this is clearly not the case with a wall. Yet precisely *because* a door can be opened and closed, writes Simmel, it creates "a stronger feeling of being shut out than does a mere undifferentiated wall." One could say, poetically, that the wall "is mute, but the door speaks." When we exit a door we activate our freedom to overcome limits, embracing potentially unlimited direction. The choice of where to go is ours to make. When we step onto a bridge, by contrast, we commit to a single direction. While bridge-movement is reversible, there is "a total difference of intention between going in and going out of a door."[3]

The door's inside-outside division is different again from that of windows. A window creates only a partial opening from internal to external space. It also exists "for looking out, not for looking in," for which reason curtains are usually placed on them (except in the proverbial case of Holland, where curtainless windows declare that the dwellers of this country have nothing to hide, or that the country includes no Peeping Toms). Given that one crosses a window only through one's gaze, it lacks the "profound and foremost significance of the door" (68).

A road links more extensive spaces than window or door, and in a much more definitive fashion. Only humans have the ability to build roads, believed Simmel, who didn't have the benefit of later studies in animal cognition. Animals regularly cross even greater distances than humans, he notes, "and often in the most clever and difficult ways"; but for them the points of departure and arrival remain separate. By establishing a path between two places, early humans accomplished a radical and truly decisive symbolic feat: They tied a place of origin to a place of destination. Here, as in much else that they do, they show themselves to be creatures who "cannot unite without separating" (66, 69). Even by thinking of two places as separate, we join them in thought.

The overcoming of topographical separation reaches its zenith in a bridge. A bridge, unlike a road, overcomes not just a passive separation of space but an active and dramatic cleft of nature—a body of water or gorge. The bridge is more imaginative, ingenious, artificial, and abstract a construction than others, which is why it frequently appears picturesque and occasionally even surreal. A bridge generates conceptual and aesthetic effects beyond its practical ones. It gives *visible form* to the idea of union, highlighting a human supplementation of nature. It bears a "less haphazard relationship to the banks that it unites than does the house to its land and foundations, which are hidden underneath it." A road is consubstantial not only with its site of departure and arrival but with the entire space in between. In its conspicuousness, a bridge draws opposite banks of a river into "a singleness that is of a completely spiritual kind." It makes "movement cohere into a solid creation" (67, 69). Windows, doors, roads, and walls do not produce this impression of felt connection. A bridge calls to mind the fabricational work of humans.

Thus, in a few bold strokes, Simmel's essay traces a phenomenology of architectonic structures. It attunes us to the figurative effects that these structures have on human cognition, encouraging us to explore further implications. We then become prepared to notice, for example, the effect of walls in representations, as in one of the most extraordinary stories ever told—Melville's "Bartleby, the Scrivener." The scrivener, or clerk, works on Wall Street, where he spends most of the day staring at the wall of a building opposite his window. He even behaves like a wall. Each time the lawyer who has employed him asks him to fulfill an assignment, he answers, "I'd prefer not to." Before coming to this position, Bartleby worked in the postal service's Dead Letter Office. What did he do there? He replied to letters mailed to people now deceased by saying, "I am sorry to say that Mr. So and So has passed away. . . ." Thus Bartleby works around the wall separating sender from receiver. By the end of Melville's narrative Bartleby himself is discovered dead beneath a wall at "The Tombs," a monicker for the city's Halls of Justice. The conclusion, associating walls with the institutions of justice, also lets us understand how the rhetoric of walls finds its way into political discussions, as Wendy Brown illustrates in her book *Walled States*, exploring how citizens confront the reality or the fantasy of rendering their nation great by immuring it from neighbors.

Political, psychological, and literary discourse just as easily invokes bedrooms, hallways, basements, and attics. Franz Kafka draws exceptional attention to windows, fascinated *not* by the casual gaze outside them but by their capacity to provide surveillance. Kafka's windows turn seen subjects into objects of monitoring. They are portals through which characters are followed as they stroll down streets.

As these examples suggest, the significance of architectonic structures lies to no small degree in their conceptual and cultural elaborations. A geospatial exposition of bridge-form like Simmel's invites us to investigate social, historical, and intellectual articulations of that form. That is where form burgeons into figure, developed into the representations of literature, painting, and philosophy, discursively expanded into myths and legends. If the door speaks where the wall is mute, the bridge speaks louder than both. It is more prone to symbolization.

A book appropriately titled *Figure del ponte* by Alberto Giorgio Cassani provides groundwork for this more extended level of bridge study where the connectors become symbols or figures.[4] The conversion, in fact, is all but automatic: Form becomes figure the moment a bridge reveals more than meets the eye—and it almost always does. For example, after annexing Crimea in 2014, Vladimir Putin tied that peninsula to Russia by way of a bridge. If a bridge ideally suggests reciprocal connection—a bond of equals—then Putin's bridge perverts that form. It is a pseudo- or mock-bridge, turning Crimea into an appendage of its dominant neighbor. That is to say, bridges can serve aggressive, invasive, appropriative intentions as well as reciprocal relations; some even function in the manner of walls, as will be discussed in the chapter "Bridged Disconnection."

Symbolic overtones are carried by hundreds of historical bridges. For example, the material purpose of the Golden Gate Bridge was to relieve ferryboat traffic over the San Francisco Bay. But its deeper and more spectacular effect was to unify technology and nature at the continental end of American civilization. Unintentionally, the bridge also invited suicide, an association it now has difficulty shaking. It created the ancillary effect of displaying the sublime contradiction between human smallness and the vast ocean before it. "The Bridge as Gallows" as well as this book's first chapter speculate on bridge-junctions to realms beyond, whether dark to the mind or vividly imagined.

It is likely that more stories have been told about bridges than about anything else built by human hands. Each bridge has at least one tale to tell. The Bridge of Arta in Greece is said to have walled up a live human being in its foundations to fortify it against the onslaught of waters. The Morandi Bridge in Genoa, a remarkable technological feat at the time (1967) which enabled millions of Italians to travel the freeways of Liguria, collapsed barely fifty years after it was built, taking nearly four dozen lives with it. The event fed into two widespread notions: the precarious nature of bridges, especially those that are technologically daring, and the dereliction of public institutions proverbially associated with Italian states. Each bridge has not just its story, but also its history.

By means of these associations, bridges take on the aspect of a concrete subset of more abstract phenomena like transcendence, risk, and so on. The "bridge" as a notion enters figures of thought and speech. "Build bridges, not walls!" Concerned with communicating rather different lessons, earlier generations were more prone to saying, "Don't burn your bridges!" or "We'll cross that bridge when we get to it" or

"That is water under the bridge."[5] The conceptual assumptions of these expressions are perfectly clear: Bridges suggest transition and cooperation, efficient and expedient coordination, openness and reciprocity. What is more difficult to recognize are the more extensive and eloquent developments of bridge-concepts in literature and art; in sites where they operate invisibly; in the failure to draw clear distinctions between bridge-like connections and mere contacts or interactions.

At this higher or more subtle level, phenomena analogous to physical bridges are constructed through moral commitments, affective ties, imaginative and intellectual relations. They are fastened by theoretical and ethical belief. Of course, at some point everything in the world is a bridge, including the waterways and the skies through which we fly—but only on the condition that we construe them as such, which is apparently not the case with fragmented, localized approaches to the same spanning skyways. It takes bridge-thinking to grasp how the discharge of one nation's sky carries over to the other side of the globe. Bridge-thinking also means active crossing of conceptual, cultural, and historical divides. A thought acts as a bridge when it lays foundations in foreign lands. Technologies and social institutions do the same, often modifying their functions as they reach the other point of landing. Some bridges even lead nowhere, like a *pont où nul se passe*: their practical and emotional objectives never reach their destination, perhaps mainly because the destination was not properly thought out to begin with.

These are some features of bridges that I will explore in the chapters to follow, each built out of a divergent set of particular historical cases and art-critical interpretations. A few additional features and principles can round out this introduction.

Bridges take shape within a topology of separation. They presuppose geological or geocultural borders, some overreaching divisions between nations. The Suchiate River between Guatemala and Mexico is one, though under current political conditions it is a crossing that most find easier to make by raft. The Han River estuary between North and South Korea—which almost no one now crosses in any manner—is another.

Bridges counteract, resist, or overcome the dynamics of the divisive element, be it water or air. They bind territories that remain disparate, albeit joined. A bridge allows only limited interaction. It does not neutralize the differences between the shores and peoples that it links. It creates no synthesis, but rather a locked couple: a vital experience of being-together.

Establishing rapport, a bridge itself transcends the differences it joins. It is a third space or term between them, a passageway by which we move between bordered things. It calls attention to that junction of visibly disjointed places. The philosopher Martin Heidegger put his finger on some aspects of this issue in an essay that has received its fair share of philosophical attention ("Building Dwelling Thinking"), and so did the analytical psychologist Rosemary Gordon.[6] Bridge-connections themselves are critical matters for thought.

Bridges must be solid—not fleeting and instable like many connections in our virtual, liquid, and digital world. In crossing a bridge we do not glide over water or step over stones. The supports or piers of a bridge are driven deep into a riverbed. Liquid flows offer no supports for bridges. Imagine if the city of Rome altered its main features every five or ten years, not perduring in fixed architectural forms to which one could return. What is designed to be here today but gone tomorrow gives us little on which to build. "Interruption, incoherence, surprise are the ordinary conditions of our life," noted poet Paul Valéry a century ago, dismayed by the new challenges of mental discontinuity.[7] The humus of boredom, eventually soliciting extended concentration, is more likely to produce connections that last. And "things are great," said Longinus two thousand years earlier, "because of their connection with others so ordered with them as to make a firm structure." To inhabit a city like Rome or Bologna is at least to be bridged with the past, dissuaded from forgetting. There are also, of course, impermanent bridges—retractable ones, drawbridges, bridges that are burned—but we gauge them by reference to a rule. The passages we create between spaces entail understandings of those spaces.

A bridge gets us elsewhere—without cutting us off from where we start. It accesses a place from which we can return. (Again, this is true in principle if not always in fact: over the Bridge of Sighs in Venice one entered a prison usually not to come out again, except as a corpse.) A bridge is not a portal to multiple pathways, not a gateway, rhizome, network, or interface. Though many phenomena that we experience can be bridged, the more that are, the fewer bridge-experiences remain. A hyperconnected world is a labyrinth.

To step onto a bridge is to follow a destination that remains partially unclear. Even so, a glimmering goal impels the move. We cross bridges with a sense of purpose. Road trips are more prone to improvisation. Sailing is open. The end of a bridge beckons like a sign, or better a symbol, indicating latent content in something manifest, beyond a current condition that has come to look incomplete and that pushes us to the bridge to begin with. A bridge is not just a symbol, but the symbol of symbols, a means to a region holding hidden significance.

On a bridge we move from the familiar toward the strange. Its setting is itself the strange—a strange no-place of transit, the space of a gap, of relationship and having-in-common. The move onto the bridge challenges us to come to terms with a different condition. Creative writing does much the same, carrying us from familiar and matter-of-fact knowledge to new understandings. Reading reverses the motion, bringing discoveries back from the strange to the commonplace. Something similar happens when we listen, decoding sounds and purposes that land at our ear, in a process described in "Musical Bridges." Traveled to and fro, the spaces of listening, reading, and writing are the spaces of thought. We travel them, too, in imagining, recollecting, and deciding the future.

Some crossings yield bridge-events. Those with collective effects can be world-historical; most, in the span of a lifetime, are microhistorical: the crisis of love lost, a death in the family, emigration to a new country, a change in career. These critical events turn one life-form toward another. That new subjective field does not replace the previous one, however. It ties itself to it. Experiences are turned into bridge-events when one embraces the *yon* to which they point.

Deeply determining, bridge-events leave neither joined element the same as it was before. They are two-way junctures, like the sculpture *Between Memory and Oblivion* by Paolo Delle Monache, placed at the border of land and water (fig. 0.1), where it gazes like a subject in both directions, memory carrying forward a past partially sealed by oblivion. A bridge provides a structure for dual motion. But just as no one steps into the same river twice, so the land to which you step back is different from the one you left. A once seemingly simple situation now looks complex.

Bridges mediate but they do not fix the terms of mediation. They pose the challenge of just how to negotiate differences. "My friends are my *rivals*; we dwell on opposite banks of the stream," wrote Henry David Thoreau in his journal on January 16, 1853.[8] Was he speaking of friends as rivals or of rivals as friends? The relationship can be maneuvered either way. The tension of the relationship remains open. Nietzsche registers the problem in personal terms:

> There was a time in our lives when we were so close that nothing seemed to obstruct our friendship and brotherhood, and only a small footbridge separated us. Just as you were about to step on it, I asked you: "Do you want to cross the footbridge to me?" —Immediately, you did not want to any more; and when I asked you again, you remained silent. Since then mountains and torrential rivers and whatever separates and alienates have been cast between us, and even if we

Figure 0.1. Paolo Delle Monache, *Tra memoria e oblio / Between Memory and Oblivion* (2004). Bronze, 285 × 90 × 70 cm.
Courtesy of the artist

> wanted to get together, we couldn't. But when you now think of that little footbridge, words fail you and you sob and marvel.[9]

A disillusioned young György Lukács wonders whether the features of the bridge established between rival-friends do not limit the terms by which they behave. Ethics, he writes, "is a bridge that divides us; a bridge over which we come and go and always arrive back at ourselves, without ever encountering each other."[10] Considering that ethics suggests a tendency to act on behalf of others, Lukács's worry may be counterintuitive. But ethics is also a normative discipline, often solidified in dogma, dictating a particular manner of human interaction. Its principles are notoriously stressed by the most complex and singular human experiences, leaving us in the lurch in times of conflicted allegiance. Divisions bridged are not thereby canceled; some are in fact accentuated. A solution to differences is promised or disappointed by the exchanges enabled by the bridge itself.

These are some skeletal ideas distilled from the study that follows. Many more arise from the concrete cases brought into view. For the opportunities and challenges created by each bridge transcend the very principles that held sway before that bridge was constructed. Each bridge, in offering a new solution, creates a new problem.

CHAPTER 1

The Great Bridge-Building of God

As long as you catch only what you throw yourself,
all is mere skill and meaningless gain;
only when you suddenly become the catcher of a ball
thrown at you by an eternal teammate,
to your very center, with a precise
skillful swing, in one of those curves
from the great bridge-building of God:
only then is knowing how to catch a virtue . . .

—RAINER MARIA RILKE, "SOLANG DU SELBSTGEWORFNES FÄNGST"

Rainbow Lovers

We begin with the transcendent space of bridges—the distances into which they reach. Bridges in the sky, and others linking Heaven to earth, present unity as an imagined or ideal scenario. They also bear witness to one of the oldest human tendencies, explaining visible events by reference to invisible ones, spiritualizing key events in lived experience. Before being established scientifically, unity is an ideal transposed or projected elsewhere. Celestial bridges give tenuous and nebulous form to rare, momentaneous combinations. They possess filigree-fine textures like rainbows or stars. Some crystallize into mythological and religious belief.

One of the most unusual bridges in the heavens, or the firmament as one used to say, is perfectly temporary. It is built to accommodate the embrace of two immortal lovers on one single night on the seventh day of the seventh month of the year. Tanabata-tsumé lives on the left side of the Milky Way—a great river in Heaven—and Hikoboshi, her husband, on the right. If the weather on the seventh day of the seventh month is not too rainy, making the great river unfordable, magpies and crows spread their wings across the galaxy to permit one divinity to cross and spend the short night with the other. A similar opportunity will not recur for at least another year, and sometimes three or four, provided the skies are clement.

The predicament provokes profound grief in the couple that lives only for this day: "Though for a myriad ages we should remain hand-in-hand and face-to-face, our exceeding love could never come to an end. (Why then should Heaven deem it necessary to part us?)"[1] Why indeed?

This poem about the astral divinities was written in Japanese before the year 760 and is based on a Chinese story two thousand years older. It is passed on to us in English by the scholar Lafcadio Hearn, who notes that every year for centuries similar poems were written by hundreds of common people to commemorate the special union of the couple. Why then, if their "exceeding love could never come to an end," did Heaven think it necessary to part them? After all, Heaven also condoned their marriage. The implied answer of the poem gives scant comfort, presenting something like the plausible simplicities one offers to children. It involves the way things are and must be, and in particular the unmovable boundaries of economic and filial responsibility, which the love of the couple disrupts. The context for their love is key, and is provided by Hearn's translation as follows.

One day Tanabata, the lovely daughter of the great God of the Skies, fell in love with a humble but handsome peasant leading an ox in front of her house as she wove garments for her father. Out of kindness her father overlooked their difference in social status and granted Tanabata her wish to take Hikoboshi as husband. All went well until "the wedded lovers became too fond of each other, and neglected their duty to the god of the firmament, the sound of the shuttle was no longer heard, and the ox wandered, unheeded, over the plains of heaven." To remedy the situation the celestial father separated the two, sentencing them to live apart from each other on different sides of the Milky Way. He allowed them to see each other only one night per year when "the birds of heaven make, with their bodies and wings, a bridge over the stream; and by means of that bridge the lovers can meet." This arrangement assured that the rest of the time they would fulfill their social duties. No matter how long the astral lovers are stopped from meeting, "their love remains immortally young and eternally patient; and they continue to fulfill their respective duties each day without fault—happy in their hope of being able to meet on the seventh night of the next seventh month."[2]

The beauty of this legend is celebrated not only by dozens of *tanka* variants that Hearn translates, but by his poetic conclusion, its evocative associations revealing him to be a writer of the late nineteenth-century:

> [In] the silence of transparent nights, before the rising of the moon, the charm of the ancient tale sometimes descends upon me, out of the scintillant sky—to make me forget the monstrous facts of science, and the stupendous horror of Space. Then I no longer behold the Milky Way as that awful Ring of the Cosmos, whose hundred million suns are powerless to lighten the Abyss. . . . And heaven seems very near and warm and human; and the silence about me is filled with the dream of a love unchanging, immortal—forever yearning and forever young, and forever left unsatisfied by the paternal wisdom of the gods.[3]

While confirming the conflict between spiritual order and bodily Eros, this fable still humanizes cold and silent space. The very recognition of the stars and the Milky Way gives a transcendent space to human action, a "pole" or dimension by which to measure it. The supernatural dimension itself looks like life on earth, where lovers are divided by their duties. The bridge of birds is an expression of devotion, an homage of creatures to the principle of bringing together, offsetting the immeasurable, dividing expanse. Their bond of beating bodies and wings is all the more stirring for its delicacy. It acknowledges what must be eternally divided, but what remains together in its dividedness. The divine exceptionality of this cooperative work intensifies its value, countermanding an otherwise intolerable interdiction. This bridge in the sky is not just a union of earthly things, but a reprieve from isolation that is earned through commitment, restraint, and patience. It is an ephemeral reparation of an unalterable condition.

Other bridges in the sky are just as fragile and respectful of ephemeral contact. The uncommon occurrence of the rainbow, or *arcus caelestis*, has frequently been seen as a connection between the domains of mortals and divinities. Its droplets of water, air, and light forge no less conditional a formation than a bridge of birds. More conspicuous than this, a rainbow appears to be even more evanescent. In diverse cultures it creates a miraculous conduit between earth and sky. In the *Prose Edda*, a thirteenth-century collection of tales of Norse mythology, an enthroned figure called High explains to the disguised king Gylfi that the rainbow is a bridge formed by the gods to reach our world below. Consisting of three colors, it has extraordinary strength "and is built with art and skill to a greater extent than other constructions."[4] Elsewhere the

Figure 1.1. Max Brückner, *Walhalla* (1896). Scenography of *Twilight of the Gods* from *The Ring of the Nibelungs* by Richard Wagner. Chromolithograph on paper, 23 × 28.

Norse rainbow bridge is called Bifröst and Asbrú (Bridge of the Gods); all gods but Thor ride their horses across it daily. Since Bifröst may well mean "shimmering path" or "the swaying road to heaven," some scholars have identified that heavenly phenomenon with the Milky Way itself—the same thoroughfare that the great love of Tanabata-tsumé and Hikoboshi traversed.[5] By the late nineteenth century, the idea of the rainbow as passageway to the realm of the gods had become popularized by Wagner's *Das Rheingold*, in a scene where the supreme Wotan leads his fellow divinities to a newly constructed home called Valhalla. Numerous illustrations show the great castle of the gods tied to the universe by way of a rainbow bridge (fig. 1.1). The Wagnerian scenario builds on the Norse story about this "hall of the slain" (Valhöll), to which flying Valkyries lead valorous warriors who met their death in battle and make them their lovers. There the heroes prepare for an ultimate battle (the Ragnarök) which will destroy the entire earth and launch a new cosmic beginning.

The most tenuous of all bridges to the eye, the rainbow is also an emanation: a numinous transmission of meaning and energy. The ancient Greeks saw its iridescent arch as the pathway of the winged goddess Iris, carrying messages from gods to mortals. She was the lesser and alternative messenger of the Olympians; the main one was Hermes, from whom we develop the word "hermeneutics," the scrutiny of intellectual bridges that are crossed in all acts of understanding, tying culturally and historically positioned recipients to the signs they need to interpret.[6] The disclosive, heaven-opening rainbow also marks the resolution of the cataclysm in the tale of Noah, announcing the attainment of a new accord between God and the creatures of the earth. Not incidentally it announces a different respect for fleshly existence than the Almighty had previously shown in unleashing the flood (Genesis 9.13–17). The rainbow is a tenuous covenant of metaphysical understanding, a fleeting accord, stressing the rule of a generally opposite condition. It signifies emergence and contact. Epiphanic, it shows the coming into view of the other bank.

Supernatural Rock Bridges

Similar sympathy is achieved by other stories about rainbows, accompanied by a similar sense of frailty. On the American continent rainbow bridges testify to an embrace between terrestrial and everlasting life which is just as tenuous as the one in Norse mythology. One is an online cemetery for pets called Rainbows Bridge [*sic*], which for a fee lets grieving masters choose not only virtual tombs but the season beneath which their pets will lie in perpetuity within them.

The Rainbow Bridge in Utah, the longest natural arch span in the world, possessed deeply theological connotations before being recast by white migrants as a national monument in 1910 (fig. 1.2). If Native Americans repeatedly defended it against touristic uses and abuses, it is because they deemed Rainbow Bridge a sacred meeting ground of mortals and the immortals they call Holy People. Even so, they failed to forestall the federal government's decision to flood the Holy People of the canyon with the waters of the Glen Canyon Dam in 1966. The Navajo Nation and four other Native American tribes succeeded in little more than getting signs posted at the nearby Rainbow Bridge requesting that tourists and visitors not approach or walk directly beneath this formation. Not only is it metaphysically unnatural to pass under a rainbow, but this particular one is believed by the Navajo to be an access point for underworld spirits. The American tribes also received a concession that the ages-old trail to the bridge not be paved over, so that the movement of spirits to and from the site would not be restricted.[7] Some miles away, within the complex called Natural Bridges, lies another rock arch that the Hopis call *Sipapu*, "the place of emergence," viewing it as the gateway of their ancestors' first worldly arrival.[8]

Accounts of the Rainbow Bridge in Utah, or Rock Arch as the Navajo call it (*tsé naa Na'ni'ahi*), are collected in a book of oral history compiled by Karl W. Luckert. These indigenous accounts identified the arch with a rainbow from the very moment the Navajo first alighted upon it, around 1863, when fleeing the army of Kit Carson. They saw the arch

Figure 1.2. Rainbow Bridge, Utah.
Courtesy of Tom Till

as a Rainbow Person, an incarnate divinity, or a combination of twin spirits who sprang to life there, or on Navajo Mountain slightly to the north, to protect the tribe from American soldiers. Medicine man Floyd Laughter recounts that when these two spirits wanted to make their way back to their father the Sun, they did so by climbing onto a rainbow. Another Navajo singer relates that he personally alighted on Rock Arch by way of rainbow travel.[9]

Native American mythology inspired a very different singer, part Cherokee, to imagine similar forms of sky travel in several of his compositions, some performed at the concert called Rainbow Bridge on July 20, 1970 in Hawaii. The gods of Hawaii, too, are believed to descend to earth on rainbows.[10] It was one of Jimi Hendrix's last performances, staged next to the theological entrance to worlds beyond: the volcano called the House of the Sun and the abode of a demigod on the island of Maui. The concert and its name, Rainbow Bridge, were sponsored by a New Age planetary meditation cult elaborating spiritual implications of the Gaia hypothesis, according to which organic life actively interacts with its inorganic surroundings. Hendrix's extraordinary imagination led his music to elaborate other terrestrial-spiritual references to the rainbow. The seven colors of the song "Axis Bold as Love" (1967) are personified as separate human emotions that "keep holding me from giving my life to a rainbow like you." The term "Axis" designates "an all-knowing mystic who provides a bridge between the real and the spiritual worlds."[11] Hendrix had been traveling that bridge for some time, from which he saw more than one angel. He dubbed the musical ensemble that performed with him at Woodstock in 1969 "Gypsy Sun and the Rainbows." His band members were the Rainbows and he was the itinerant Sun.

One can only imagine what Hendrix might have made of the tales about rainbow journey transcribed by Luckert. In one, two wandering mortal women happen on a place of water divinities. The spirits reject them and send them back home on a rainbow. This brings them down near Navajo Mountain and then petrifies into the Rock Arch discussed above. In another, Bear Man and Big Snake Man travel to the easternmost reach of the continent until they come on a mountain with water flowing *upward* along its sides. At its peak the mountain turns into Cloud, gathering all the water together into the world's source of rain. Once up on Cloud, Bear Man and Big Snake Man return home by way of a rainbow. This rainbow also hardens at the point of their descent to earth.[12] Although it permits travel, and links human and divine, there comes a point when the rainbow petrifies. Then the world as we know it ends.

Near Rainbow Bridge lies Rainbow Canyon, bordered by the Head of the Earth where mortals and gods lived in harmony long ago in the blessed company of multiple animal peoples. Eventually the gods, or Holy People, withdrew and preferred to live in isolation, some retreating to windswept caves carved out of the canyon rock, others embedding themselves in colossal, monolithic stone sentinels monitoring and protecting the hallowed grounds of the canyon. But not even these gods, the stories report, will be able to stop Rainbow Bridge from collapsing one day, like the Norse Bifröst, raining universal disaster on the heads of both faithful and faithless humans. There is no way of telling what this catastrophe (or for that matter the Norse Ragnarök) will look like. One might imagine it through the eyes of Wassily Kandinsky as a cosmic battle between spirit and matter, a clash that the painter articulated in both his treatise *Concerning the Spiritual in Art* and paintings like *Composition IV* (plate 1). Beneath Kandinsky's horses rearing tall on the left, among lances of battle, adjacent to a peak as tall as Navajo Mountain, a rainbow recedes into the horizon, signaling perhaps a covenant lost.

Figure 1.3. Amanohashidate, Miyasu Bay, Japan.

Sirat, Chinavad, and Pontifex Maximus

The rainbow is one visible link between material and immaterial worlds. A Japanese creation story tells of another, claiming in the eighth-century chronicle *Tango Fudoki* that Heaven was originally linked to the earth by *Ama no Hashidate,* a bridge enabling the gods to come and go at their pleasure. One day, while everyone was sleeping and no one watching, that bridge collapsed into the sea. Geologically it now forms the spectacular three-kilometer-long isthmus to the west of Kyoto (fig. 1.3). With comparable concern for the gap separating the divine from the earthly, Japanese architects design arched bridges to usher worshippers into the precinct of the gods at the threshold of Shinto shrines (plate 2). The bridges purify the souls of those crossing over.

The vermilion-lacquered Sacred Bridge depicted by Yoshitoshi (fig. 1.4) leads to the tombs of three deities. Also known as the Snake Bridge of Sedge, and said to have materialized out of two serpents cast over the gorge by a god in the year 766, the bridge that he depicts and that we still see standing was actually built in 1636 by the same shōgun Iemitsu that Yoshitoshi represents in the print. For centuries the bridge remained off limits to all but aristocrats, samurai, and members of the court.

Other religions warn those who would be saved of a bridge laid over the miseries of Hell which each soul must traverse to reach the afterlife. Called Sirat ("way") in Arabic, it is thinner than a hair and sharper than the edge of a sword. The righteous "will cross the bridge as quickly as the wink of an eye, some others as quick as lightning, a strong wind, fast horses or she-camels [while others] will fall down into Hell."[13] The Islamic image of the Sirat derives from the Zoroastrian bridge called

Figure 1.4. Tsukioka Yoshitoshi, *Tokugawa Iemitsu and Ii Naotaka on the Sacred Bridge at Nikkō* (1878).

Chinavad ("the connecting link"), leading more directly to the other world. On this bridge, at the end of time, angels will stop all transiting souls to receive a strict account of their actions on earth and determine their deserved destination.

The Christian Middle Ages abound with images of a bridge crossing fire, over which departing souls will come to their final resting place. Narrow and slippery to those who have sinned, it is broad and secure for the righteous. We find variants of the bridge in the dialogues of St. Gregory, the visions of St. Paul, Alberic, and Tundale, the narrative of

Figure 1.5. *Last Judgment* (late fourteenth century). S. Maria in Piano, Loreto Aprutino. PescaraPost (www.pescarapost.it)

Zosimus, and Germanic and Celtic traditions straight up to the purgatorial Brig o'Dread described in the eighteenth-century *Like-Wake Dirge*.[14] A dazzlingly detailed Italian fresco of the late 1300s (fig. 1.5) incorporates a bridge at the scene of the Christian Last Judgment, wide at its base and narrowing sharply at the top. "With the help of angels, elect souls manage to cross over, others fall inexorably into the current below. Demons downstream await."[15] Norse mythology assigns a bridge to the departing dead called Gjallabrú, covered and "thatched in glittering gold." Instead of crossing Hell, this one leads straight to it, where the unrighteous, however, were not punished. The Norse Hell was the abode of shivering, pusillanimous souls who met their end through inglorious disease or old age.

Even in the context of these distinguished mythological traditions, the most imposing of all bridges between life and the afterlife is a purely conceptual one, albeit supported by powerful institutions. It is the connective path provided by the vicar of the Catholic Church—the *pontifex maximus*. This appellation, inscribed on dozens of monuments in Rome, alludes to the spiritual passage that the church provided from fallen and carnal existence to everlasting salvation. *Pons* + *facere* = the making of bridges. The *pontifex*, *pontefice*, or pontiff, is a builder of bridges, and *pontifex maximus* is the "master bridge-builder," constructing the bridge of all bridges to Heaven. Just as Peter, the first pope, guards the gates to Heaven, so his descendants grant the structure by which to get there.

No bridge in the sky possesses the solidity and massive strength of the great bridge forged by the leaders of the Roman Church. Not only was it founded on the rock of Peter; it was supported by the political institutions of the Roman Empire. Before Christians ever existed, the *pontifex maximus* did. He headed up the committee of high priests—the pontiffs—composing the Roman Collegium—the highest spiritual authority in the state, charged with interpreting and overseeing the religious rituals, laws, and traditions of the land. The function of this *Collegium Pontificum* was to mediate between the rights of the Roman gods and the duties of men, bridging the two claims on life, and occasionally also to proclaim doctrine, or "pontificate."

Not incidentally, and this is what seems to have been indicated by the etymon *pons*, or bridge, in their original title, the members of the Collegium oversaw the upkeep of those sacred passageways over water that were material bridges, principal of which was the venerated Pons Sublicius over the Tiber.[16] Once Julius Caesar became the official head of the Collegium in 63 BCE, the title *pontifex maximus* became customarily applied to the supreme authority in the state—the reigning Roman emperor—and was relinquished only by the Emperor Gratian in the late fourth century CE (and probably *because* he was Christian, for by this time the title *pontifex* was being used by those to whom it was more appropriate: priests of Gratian's own faith).[17] At that point the title *pontifex*, spiritual leader, named bishops, and *pontifex maximus* the prime bishop among them, or pope. That was one way in which the faith of the peace-loving Jew of Nazareth conquered the Roman Empire. As Christianity became the state's religion it made use of the political institutions of the *caput mundi*, Rome absorbing the alien new faith into its existing traditions and operating the monotheistic creed with the machinery of its system.

How fundamental the maintenance of material bridges may have been to the activities of the Roman Collegium was debated before Jesus was even born. For example, an early head pontiff insisted that his title had nothing whatsoever to do with the prosaic task of maintaining bridges, but rather indicated the capacity to do *everything*, or to establish the very bounds of human potential (*posse* + *facere* = *pontifex*).[18] His account did not find many subscribers. What resounds more persuasively today is the etymological origin of the root *pons*. Before there even was a Roman bridge to maintain, the word *pons* meant "way, road, path, or passage." *The American Heritage Dictionary of Indo-European*

Roots gives the meaning of *pontifex* as "he who prepares the way." This then becomes compatible with the later views of architects like Leon Battista Alberti and Andrea Palladio who saw bridges as extensions of roads, suggesting that road building in central Italy was necessarily synonymous with bridge-building, providing "fixed points to indicate the direction of roads otherwise vaguely defined in open and sparsely inhabited country."[19]

The root of *pons* is the Vedic Sanskrit *pánthāh* and comes to yield that cognate of the Latin stem which is *pontos* (sea) in Greek. The Greeks were no bridge-builders; they made their crossings by sea. The notion of *pánthāh* is thus where the most ancient source of the *pontifex*'s function is to be sought. It names not merely a passage from one point to another, but one marked by hardship, uncertainty, danger, and unpredictability.[20] The implications of the word were magisterially presented in 1944 by Doña Luisa Coomaraswamy's study of analogues in Asiatic texts such as the *Rigveda* (c. 1700–1100 BCE). A more recent study of the tie between *pontifex* and the Vedic *pathikrt* suggests that the paths made passible by the *pontifex* were "treaded by the gods to take part in a sacrifice and, inversely, treaded by the sacrifice itself," or by human rituals to gain the gods' attention.[21] By the Christian era this had clearly become the function of the Catholic pontiff. The passage the head priest opened—and whose validity was contested by the reformer Martin Luther—was a perilous route to God Almighty which could be crossed only through the tutelage of the Roman Church.

The Underworld, In and Out

Of course, there was more to Luther's objection to this church than a disagreement over what it took to reach Heaven, and this touches on another connotation of *pontifex*. The broader target of Luther's polemic was the excessive "pontification" of the Vatican: the bridging of its spiritual function with a political one. This amounted to a fusion of the political institutions of the Roman Empire and the program of Christianity which the papacy had achieved from the very start, many centuries earlier. The simultaneously secular *and* religious claims of the Roman Church had always been of concern to political subjects, and especially rivals of Rome, since Henry IV's famous capitulation to the pope's authority in Canossa in the year 1077. That was the historical bridge that had been built by the popes and that was formalized in the influential (but counterfeit) imperial decree known as the Donation of Constantine, giving the pope power not only over Rome but over the entire western part of the Roman Empire. Even Dante Alighieri, who as a Guelph was an ostensible supporter of the papacy, turned against such aggrandizement of religious authority when Pope Boniface VIII absolutized it in his Papal Bull of 1302, proclaiming "that it is absolutely necessary for salvation that every human creature be subject to the Roman Pontiff." The gospels inform us, the bull announced, "that in this Church and in its power are two swords; namely, the spiritual and the temporal" and, "with truth as our witness, it belongs to spiritual power to establish the terrestrial power and to pass judgment if it has not been good."[22] In other words, all roads lead to Rome, and the bridges of the pontiffs built and reinforced such roads. Those bridges did not only make the religio-political bond possible; they reaffirmed Rome's central, imperial administration of spiritual and practical affairs throughout western Europe. *Ubi papa, ibi Roma*: Wherever the influence of the pope extends, there reaches the power of the capital city.

What Dante thought of Boniface's bridge is clear enough from his attack on the temporal ambitions of the papacy in his *De Monarchia* of 1312–13. In fact, it is already implicit in an apparently innocuous simile of *The Divine Comedy* where Dante compares two thick lines of sinners in Hell to the two-way traffic on the bridge leading to the Vatican during the Jubilee Year of 1300, masterminded by Pope Boniface:

> Nel fondo erano ignudi i peccatori;
> dal mezzo in qua ci venien verso 'l volto,
> di là con noi, ma con passi maggiori,
> come i Roman per l'essercito molto,
> l'anno del giubileo, su per lo ponte
> hanno a passar la gente modo colto,
> che da l'un lato tutti hanno la fronte
> verso 'l castello e vanno a Santo Pietro,
> da l'altra sponda vanno verso 'l monte.

> Along its bottom, naked sinners moved,
> to our side of the middle, facing us;
> beyond that, they moved with us, but more quickly—
> as, in the year of Jubilee, the Romans,
> confronted by great crowds, contrived a plan
> that let the people pass across the bridge,
> for to one side went all who had their eyes
> upon the Castle, heading toward St. Peter's,
> and to the other, those who faced the Mount.[23]

This occurs in canto 18 of *Inferno,* the circle of fraud, which makes more mention of the word "bridge" and its synonyms than any other part of the *Comedy*. What appeared so scandalous to many about the Jubilee Year was that it granted pilgrims to Rome a plenary indulgence for their sins: complete remission of the punishment they normally warrant, including the need to expiate them in Purgatory. Dante was no Protestant reformer, but he had comparable reservations about these indulgences, especially when put to the service of economic and political ambition. The very comparison between infernal sinners and believers thronging to Rome for salvation casts a pall on the pope's great Jubilee. More seriously, it impugns the temporal uses of the religious *pons* on the part of a leader like Boniface, with his imperial designs for the *caput mundi*. Dante stumbles on the place prepared in Hell for this simonist pope in the very next canto: Boniface will be buried head-first along with other sellers of spiritual goods. There Pope Nicholas III, who already inhabits this trench, declares that not long after Pope Boniface joins him (in 1303, when Boniface is destined to die) a man even "uglier in deeds" will be thrust into the very same grounds. That is *pontifex maximus* Clement V, guilty of stretching the pope's political bridge as far as Avignon, France, who moved the spiritual capital there in 1309 in order to fornicate with kings (*Inferno* 19.79–114).

Before the Christian conquest of Rome, the passage from bodily existence to eternal salvation was not so rectilinear—nor the Great Beyond so accessible—as some pontiffs made it seem. The ancient Romans and Greeks considered the spaces of the living and the dead to be separated by broad and all-but-impassable bodies of water. No interaction or communication was permitted between those two, just as no particular theological confession—no precise "way," path, or method of worship—could guarantee safe passage from here to there. The fluvial separation between the two orders of being was utterly resistant to a bridge. So absolute was the boundary of earthly existence—the river Styx—that every solemn oath of the Olympian gods had to be pronounced in its name. Virgil called it the "irremeable" Styx (*irremeabilis*), for you could pass over it but never come back (*ir*, "no," + *remeare*, "come back"). The Styx and its tributaries the Acheron, the Cocytus, the Flegethon, and the Lethe could be crossed only on a boat steered by the ferryman Charon, and only on the condition that he found you suitable. You rowed and he steered. And woe, Dante was to discover when he reached the banks of the Acheron, if ever Charon felt the weight of a live, palpitating body attempting to sneak over to the nether realm. He would lash out at the imposter with implacable fury.

The classical underworld tolerated no breach by manmade structures.

The unfordable waters enclosing it resisted the return of the dead souls, protecting the living from their dreaded incursions. It is perhaps for this reason that Italic towns generally situated their cemeteries on the far side of streams.[24]

Hence T. S. Eliot took inordinate poetic license in *The Waste Land* when, alluding to Dante's *Inferno,* he imagined London as the underworld and envisioned hordes of the dead coming over London Bridge:

> Unreal City,
> Under the brown fog of a winter dawn,
> A crowd flowed over London Bridge, so many,
> I had not thought death had undone so many.[25]

To be sure, these corpses designate benumbed clerks making their way to the financial district of the great metropolis. But the mise-en-scène of the dead crowd crossing over the city's main bridge is inappropriate, despite the learned allusion to the medieval poet. Eliot would have done better to have these lifeless souls pressing together on the other side of London Bridge, in the square in front of the church of St. Mary Woolnoth, staggering in the direction of the Bank of England.

The prohibition against crossing from one side of the Styx to the other was so great that none but the most godly of mythical heroes could accomplish such a feat. Heracles crossed the Acheron to capture the many-headed Cerberus; Orpheus passed over to reclaim Eurydice; Theseus and Pirithous embarked on a mission to abduct Persephone. And yet all that these living adventurers succeeded in doing was to affirm the *impossibility* of bringing the dead back to life. The *catabasis,* or descent into Hades, remained an extraordinary exception to the incommunicable separation between the two realms.

If Norse, Qur'anic, and Zoroastrian bridges to the underworld aimed to assure an expeditious exit from life, the lack of a bridge in classical antiquity was designed to offset the risk of return on such two-way structures. The Chinese bridge across the Styx, the Nai-ho-k'iao, gets around this problem. It leads the dead away from the Tenth Court of the underworld after the souls have drunk a special broth of oblivion. As they approach the other shore the deceased are hurled "into the foaming torrent beneath, where they are wafted towards the Four Continents, there to be reborn as men, animals, birds, fishes or insects" (fig. 1.6).[26]

Even so, select heroes of the descent into Hades crossed the border between those material and spiritual realms which their cultures were so intent on guarding. In a ritual called the *nekyía,* geared to obtaining counsel, both Odysseus and Aeneas reached Hades to commune with

Figure 1.6. *The Nai-ho-k'iao Bridge*. From Henry Doré, *Researches into Chinese Superstitions*, vol. 7, second part, 298.

their predecessors. By establishing this channel of communication, they tapped into the wider ontological contexts for life on earth, activating the bridging operations of knowledge itself. The very abyss between life and death made connections between them necessary—by way of religion, mythology, philosophy, and ritual. Ancient intelligence bridged known and unknown worlds also through poetry, painting, and sculpture, through necromancy and divinations of natural mystery like medicine and science. Interactions between the ontologically distinguished realms did occur after all: they were already evidenced by the anthropomorphism of the pagan divinities, who lived in and among humans, and whose wishes were translated to mortals by oracles and prophets, conveyed by rainbows, or communicated directly in the animistic and Shamanistic traditions of non-European cultures.

With or without a material bridge, Aeneas, Odysseus, and Gilgamesh crossed into the netherworld and reported back to the living. No lesser a hero in this distinguished company was Dante himself, whose line it is that T. S. Eliot imaginatively applies to the near-zombies on London Bridge: "I had not thought death had undone so many." Dante pronounces these words as he seeks admittance to Hell at the banks of the Acheron and is overwhelmed by the sheer number of souls amassed there. These hordes of the dead, however, will never get ferried to Hades. Outside the boundaries of the underworld proper, they are eternally excluded from Hell no less than Paradise, for in life they never had the courage to assume a moral position that could earn them either place. They will never be properly dead because they were never properly born to begin with. Their procession through Eliot's London ignores this spiritual paralysis, making light of the crossing.

The Cross and the Bridges of Hell

Dante's own journey through Hell, Purgatory, and Paradise is a more extended journey for counsel than any in Virgil's *Aeneid* or Homer's *Odyssey*. His trip aspires to share knowledge of worlds beyond with worlds to come. Soon after he is ferried across the Acheron by Charon, Dante recalls not Aeneas or Odysseus but the supreme precursor of the *catabasis*: the undamned and undead outsider to Hell, Jesus Christ. In his journey called the Harrowing of Hell (apocryphal, but accepted as church doctrine in 1215), Jesus is described as descending to the underworld in order to rescue virtuous dead pagans—those who, never having known Christ or received his glad tidings, needed special dispensation to enter Heaven. Jesus's journey between his death and resurrection was therefore a bridging operation, on the occasion of his own Passover—from life to death and from this death to a life eternal.

Virgil, Dante's guide, mentions this Harrowing of Hell just as soon as the two are inside the gates of the underworld. Virgil had been there to witness its effects. He elaborates on the event in canto 12, noting that the coming of Jesus was preceded by an earthquake of cosmic proportions. Dante's early readers would have recognized the allusion to the belief that the crucifixion provoked a massive earthquake, splitting the high temple of Jerusalem and pouring souls out from their graves to haunt the holy city (Matthew 27:51). The splitting of the graves is a poetic literalization, for the agent of this *catabasis* is only apparently dead, coming back to life, ascending to eternity after a brief and deep descent.

Though the pagan Virgil does not understand the reasons for this global earthquake, he fully registers its spiritual import:

> da tutte parti l'alta valle feda
> tremò sì, ch'i' pensai che l'universo
> sentisse amor, per lo qual è chi creda
> più volte il mondo in caòsso converso
>
> . . . on all sides the steep and filthy valley
> had trembled so, I thought the universe
> felt love (by which, as some believe, the world
> has often been converted into chaos)
>
> (*INFERNO* 12.40–43)

The pagan idea of chaos being produced by love (a doctrine of Empedocles) undergoes a change in the Christian Dante, who sees Hell itself—the disordered landscape in which the pilgrim and Virgil are roaming—as ruled by the higher intentions of metaphysical love. So, in fact, it is written over the gates of his Hell: even this underworld was created by "primal love" (*Inferno* 3.6). The effects of the seismic emanation of love on the devastations of Hell become clear as the *Inferno* proceeds.

A later discussion stipulates that the earthquake provoked by the crucifixion destroyed all bridges there in Hell where everyday fraud is punished. And this is poetically appropriate, for fraud creates the appearance of human bridges while destroying them. To destroy the misleading bridges is to make their false promise apparent. The bridge-breaking force of Christ's death becomes perfectly evident when Dante reaches the fifth trench of the underworld. There, in canto 21, he finds that the bridge that should have carried him and Virgil across a ravine has collapsed. The setting has personal significance for Dante: He is coming on the very spot in Hell that punishes people accused of the same crime for which he was banished from Florence: barratry, or the corruption of public office. In the absence of bridges over this trench, the voyaging Dante risks being stranded where his detractors believed he belonged. Here, to reinforce this impression of peril, Dante-the-author creates closer calls with danger for his journeying self than anywhere else in Hell, with the devils repeatedly catching him unawares. This unusually extended episode in *Inferno* finds Dante and Virgil particularly vulnerable.

This canto begins with the two in a state of uncharacteristic relaxation. As they stroll on the top of a ridge, they discourse freely about things that the author claims do not concern his *Comedy*, moving effortlessly from bridge to bridge:

> Così di ponte in ponte, altro parlando
> che la mia comedìa cantar non cura,
> venimmo; e tenevamo 'l colmo, quando
> restammo per veder l'altra fessura
> di Malebolge e li altri pianti vani;
>
> We came along from one bridge to another,
> talking of things my Comedy is not
> concerned to sing. We held fast to the summit,
> then stayed our steps to spy the other cleft
> of Malebolge and other vain laments;
>
> (*INFERNO* 21.1–5)

The easy feeling is only a setup. Dante's remark about discussing matters off-topic is a tongue-in-cheek way of suggesting that the journeyman *believes* that his current situation has nothing to do with him, while instead it does. Before he and Virgil are able to progress from one passageway to another, the devil Malacoda announces news of a broken bridge ahead and alludes to its Christological cause:

> Poi disse a noi: "Più oltre andar per questo
> iscoglio non si può, però che giace
> tutto spezzato al fondo l'arco sesto.
> . . .
> Ier, più oltre cinqu' ore che quest' otta,
> mille dugento con sessanta sei
> anni compié che qui la via fu rotta."
>
> To us he said: "There is no use in going
> much farther on this ridge, because the sixth
> bridge—at the bottom there—is smashed to bits.
> . . .
> Five hours from this hour yesterday,
> one thousand and two hundred sixty-six
> years passed since that roadway was shattered there."
>
> (*INFERNO* 21.106–114)

The devil has a demonic precision of memory. It reaches back 1,266 years plus a day (to the crucifixion), allowing scholars to calculate that this moment in Dante's journey through Hell occurred at 7:00 a.m. on Saturday, April 9, 1300. Yet the devil's precision does not carry forward, for now he misleads Dante and Virgil into believing that there is *another,* intact bridge beyond the broken one before them. When they reach that supposedly serviceable bridge it is not there. At this precise point, where Dante is most threatened by demons, the missing bridge risks arresting his forward passage. Through these obstructed bridges, Hell makes a dramatic attempt to "cut off the road of salvation" to its visitor.[27]

Dante's difficulties in passing through the grounds of cantos 21–24 become clearer by comparison with a place of equally poor footing. There was uneven terrain also in canto 12, and it too was due to the death of the Savior. Significantly it leads Dante to make creative use of the impassable landscape. Threatened by a monstrous Minotaur on a cliff, he darts down from the ledge along a landslide of rubble produced by that same crucifixion. The positive suggestion of Dante's escape is this: The Christ-induced destruction of passage has opened an alternative route: "the rock is shattered so / that it permits a path for those above" (*è sì la roccia discoscesa, / ch'alcuna via darebbe a chi sù fosse* [*Inferno* 12.8–9]).

According to Christian theology, the death of Jesus marks an absolute break in the history of the world and thus in the available itinerary of souls. The broken way that Dante faces in canto 12 and later in the Malebolge follows directly from a fact—the crucifixion of the Savior—without which no passage of the soul to salvation can occur. Shattering every accepted pathway from mortal to infinite life, this event proclaims the need for an altogether different type of crossing or bridge. And that is the Way of the Cross, more arduous in nature than any previously conceivable road. Said otherwise, only *by way* of the broken crossing can Dante move forward; the landslide of Christ's martyrdom grants Dante a means to slide to safety. In the face of the fallen bridges that he later encounters at the sixth trench of the Malebolge (*Inferno* 21–24), the pilgrim does something comparable: He climbs *out of* the trench upon the stone debris left by the broken bridges of swindlers (*Inferno* 23.133–38). The ruins of such swindler-bridges provide a ladder (like the body of Satan when Dante, with divine backing, exits Hell in canto 34.76ff.).

The life and death of Christ, that bridge between man and God, bear witness to an ontological chasm between practical principles of earthly existence and others leading to everlasting life. The crucifixion is the only bridge that can span this chasm. On this bridge—on this belief and faith—Dante must make his arduous way, making progress in and by means of its cataclysmic fatality. The debris of material, sophistical, self-interested bridges is the basis for the soul's transcendence.

So studied are these figures for the bridge-destroying-and-recreating Way of the Cross that Dante focalizes them all into a single image facing him before he escapes the perils of his trenches: the stupefying sight of a writhing and crucified man pinned down to the road before him. The victim is the person most immediately responsible for Jesus's crucifixion, the high priest of the Sadducees, a Jewish sect of the time of Jesus, which did not believe in the afterlife. It was Caiaphas who, the night before Christ's Via Crucis, made his people understand that, if they did not put the Nazarene to death, they risked losing their own followers. Note the nature of his argument: It was not that Jesus *deserved* his death, but that his execution was *practically* ordained in order to save the accepted faith (a reasoning reprised in Dostoevsky's tale of the grand inquisitor). For eighteen years Caiaphas was the high priest of the supreme Jewish court called the Sanhedrin. The Greek term for his office in that passage of the Gospel according to John (11:49–50) which describes his dealings with Jesus is *archiereus*, rendered *pontifex* in the Latin Vulgate, and *princeps sacerdotum* in the Gospel according to Matthew.

Dante describes the infernal punishment of the *pontifex* in terms that make him the opposite of the Savior:

> "Quel confitto che tu miri,
> consigliò i Farisei che convenia
> porre un uom per lo popolo a' martìri
> Attraversato è, nudo, ne la via,
> come tu vedi, ed è mestier ch'el senta
> qualunque passa, come pesa, pria."

> "That one impaled there, whom you see,
> counseled the Pharisees that it was prudent
> to let one man—and not one nation—suffer.
> Naked, he has been stretched across the path,
> as you can see, and he must feel the weight
> of anyone who passes over him."

(*INFERNO* 23.115–120)

Caiaphas is crucified horizontally in such a way that each hypocrite passing through this trench in Hell has to tread over his bleeding body (fig. 1.9). His cross acts as a bridge—but the *false bridge* of these hypocrites' expedient morality. In that respect it is the very opposite of Christ's vertical, broken-bridge cross. The crucifixion of Caiaphas is a travesty of the holy one (and, indeed, his teaching backfires, for by dying Christ only gains more followers). To do what is *expedient* is a temptation to those without honesty, but must be shunned by those seeking salvation. The quake of the Cross advocates a more radical crossing.

The route to eternal salvation must take place under the auspices of precisely that Cross—along the broken way of Christian faith. The Caiaphas incident serves as a reminder that no practical bridge—no procedure, *methodos*, or "way"—can tie earthly existence to everlasting life. Between them there can be only a paradoxical crossing, in and by way of forgiveness for losses and love, figured in the man-God-on-the-cross. The breakdown of all expedient and hypocritical bridges in Hell points to another bridge to life eternal, a bridge less "hypothetical" (posited beneath our feet, like the cross of Caiaphas) than "metathetical" (posited *beyond* the given). That is the meaning of the figure of Jesus as a means of passage: "I am the way, the truth, and the life: no man cometh unto the Father, but by me" (John 14:6).

The image of the salvific bridge of the cross is articulated in other critical Christian texts that can be summarized in four brief examples. "Our Lord was trampled by death, and turned to tread a path beyond death. . . . Praise to you who suspended your cross over death so that souls could pass over on it from the place of the dead to the place of life." So writes St. Ephrem the Syrian (306–73 CE) in his "Homily on our Lord." The same dividing-joining cross had already been presented as the Way in the Acts of John 99: "This Cross [*stauros*, stake] . . . is that which fixed all things apart by the Word." The paradoxical implications of this cross presented an insuperable intellectual problem for Jews and Gentiles, St. Paul reported: "Jews demand signs and Greeks look for wisdom, but we preach Christ crucified: a stumbling block to Jews and foolishness to Gentiles" (1 Corinthians 1:22–23). Centuries later St. Catherine of Siena (1347–80) reflected at length on this passageway of the cross. "I have made a Bridge of My Word, of My only-begotten Son," the Eternal Father spoke unto the saint, "that you, My children, should know that the road was broken by the sin and disobedience of Adam [and] that this Bridge reaches from Heaven to earth, and constitutes the union which I have made with man. This was necessary, in order to reform the road which was broken."[28]

Blake's Infernal Bridges

William Blake, noting that Dante clusters his discussions of bridges precisely here, between cantos 18 and 24 of the *Inferno,* makes much of this bridge motif in illustrating *The Divine Comedy* between 1824 and 1827. Indeed, he composes a visual essay on them in his visual rendition of the eighth circle of Hell. Blake's bridges of Hell are not broken, however. They are more solid and more constricting than Dante would have wanted them to be.

The Seducers Chased by Devils (fig. 1.7) presents the landscape where panders and seducers are punished as a lake overarched by two natural rock bridges. Where does this idea of water come from? Dante's scene does not contain it. Blake apparently constructs it out of a simile in which the poet likens the topography of the ten trenches of the Malebolge to concentric and connected moats around a castle (*Inferno* 18.1–39). In his illustration Blake highlights two massive rock bridges in the middle, presenting them to the desperate and drowning sinners in the water as the only means of escape, a chance to grasp at solid rock and breathe air. Flying fiends chase the sinners away from these routes.

Blake's illustration of the swindlers burning in a lake of boiling pitch in canto 22 contains a similar backdrop. *The Devils, with Dante and Virgil, by the Side of the Pool* references the sinners described by Dante as lying

Figure 1.7. William Blake, *The Seducers Chased by Devils* (1824–27). From *Blake's Dante: The Complete Illustrations to the Divine Comedy,* plate 32.

Figure 1.8. William Blake, *The Devils, with Dante and Virgil, by the Side of the Pool* (1824–27). From *Blake's Dante*, plate 40.

on the bank partially submerged like frogs (*Inferno* 22.26–29). To the aqueous scene Blake adds four natural bridges (fig. 1.8). Flames shoot up from the lake as far back as the horizon. The bridges, which might suggest escape, only arch back down, returning the would-be fugitives to their punishment. Leading nowhere, the bridges seal their doom.

The entrapment is more symbolic in the illustration of *The Hypocrites with Caiaphas*. A thick and barren bridge, more graphically imposing than the previous ones, divides the scene of the high priest's punishment from the airy space of the spirits above. Beneath this frame the first hypocrite, in a row of many all clad in the false modesty of cloak and cowl, steps onto the shorter axis of Caiaphas's crucifixion-pathway (fig. 1.9). The rock bridge above Caiaphas emphasizes the ontological difference between the suffering beneath the bridge and the mobile arena above. This bridge, too, fails to link spheres of interest. It acts as a separating zone.

Blake's own understanding of Caiaphas as "the dark preacher of Death, / Of sin, of sorrow & of punishment," illuminates the entrapping function of this bridge.[29] The high priest of Jerusalem was a prime representative of what Blake thought of as "Natural Religion": institutional belief, more intent on meting out punishment than promoting forgiveness. Caiaphas, notes Albert S. Roe, is "the epitome of the Natural Man as opposed to Jesus, the man of Vision and Imagination. As

Figure 1.9. William Blake, *The Hypocrites with Caiaphas* (1824–27). From *Blake's Dante*, plate 44.

such he is bound down to this world without hope of redemption and becomes inevitably a victim of its cruel tortures."[30] Blake thought of imagination as the faculty that freely crosses boundaries, as religion, art, and poetry properly do. Hellish bridges instead are the deadly, heavy, dysfunctional markers of the expedient mentality of Caiaphas, turning back on themselves, tracing closed circles, trapping subjects forever. They stress the *false promise* of organized, Natural Religion: that if you take one particular step here it will get you there.

The Hell of Blake is self-enwrapped, opposite to the world-bridging function of Christ and the imagination. Blake in fact suspected that the entire text of Dante's *Divine Comedy* was vitiated by the same thirst for punishment, borne down, rather than upward, by the will to assign consequences.[31] The illustrations of *Inferno* 18–24 give us a vision of institutional religion's anti-bridge-building. Blake's two most eloquent bridges reinforce the immobility in question. *The Devils under the Bridge* glosses *Inferno*'s canto 21 on corrupted public officials. *The Pit of Disease* imagines the falsifiers of cantos 29 and 30. Both further the notion that sin traps its subjects in a condition from which they fail to break free. Blake *petrifies* these sinners, immuring them in bridges to nowhere.

In the first illustration (fig. 1.10) the steepest of the arches is cemented entirely out of human bodies and pieces of bodies. These dismembered limbs and spirits form a rocky landscape of spiritual inertia,

Figure 1.10. William Blake, *The Devils under the Bridge* (1824–27). From *Blake's Dante*, plate 34.

suggesting that the human imagination could have put these heads, feet, and ears to better use. Fiendish torture is wreaked on souls swimming helplessly in the waters beneath the pseudobridge.

The Pit of Disease. The Falsifiers (fig. 1.11) builds bases of arches out of all-but-lifeless human forms, collapsed and crushed. Beneath Dante and Virgil, who cover their noses from the rising stench, two alchemists are propped back to back in the cavity of one arch, the bottoms of their bodies turning scaly and fishlike. They will never bring about the change they sought through their witchcraft, but are perennially condemned to scratching their scabs (*Inferno* 29.73–84), walled into bridges of waste. Dark arches behind them presumably supply more definitive tombs for nonmoving human spirits. The bridge-building of God never reached their ears. As Rilke's poem heading up this chapter suggests, these miscreants caught nothing but what they threw themselves, pursuing a life where "all is mere skill and meaningless gain."

The No Longer and Not Yet of Hermann Broch

Blake was not the only post-Dantean writer to engage in original meditations on this topic of true and false bridges to eternal vitality. A century after Blake's illustrations came the long novel by Hermann Broch called *The Death of Virgil* (1945). The interest that it shows in Dante's guide Virgil makes it stand as another companion piece to the *Comedy*.

Figure 1.11. William Blake, *The Pit of Disease. The Falsifiers* (1824–27). From *Blake's Dante*, plate 58.

The Death of Virgil—viewed as a magnum opus by readers like Hannah Arendt and George Steiner but by others as "a strong candidate for the least readable alleged masterpiece in the European canon"[32]—presents an extended monologue by Virgil on his death bed. There he attempts to come to terms with the great space between life and death and expresses his wish to burn his great secular epic, the *Aeneid*, for failing to address that space. The very words of the dying poet, writes Arendt, are a "kind of bridge with which Virgil tries to span the abyss of empty space between the no longer and the not yet."[33] The *no longer* designates Virgil's ending life, along with the ending era of Roman antiquity. The *not yet* names the future after this death, and most importantly the cultural turn of Europe to Christianity, on the cusp of which Virgil stands (dying in 19 BCE). Between Romanity and Christianity lies a chasm that Arendt believes retroactively bridged by Broch's philosophical meditations, just as she deems the novel to be a stylistic bridge between the narration of things past in Proust and futural perspectives in Kafka. Most centrally, however, the extended reflection of Virgil presents human existence as a condition in which "we forever 'stand on the bridge that is spanned between invisibility and invisibility.'" The intellectual challenge that Broch set himself in this work is to understand how the mind can inhabit and articulate "the abyss that yawns . . . between life and death."[34]

The dying Virgil considers his manuscript marred by belief in a colossal error: the idea that world history manifests its own intentions, an idea that issued into the *Aeneid*'s apotheosis of the state and the imperial rule of Virgil's friend, Emperor Caesar Augustus. As Virgil dies he begins to believe that only otherworldly realms can provide a solid foundation for political rule and for a responsible tale of the tribe. Spiritual salvation can never be properly served by creations of beauty and art, constrained as they are within known worlds of appearance and forms. The ultimate achievement of art would lie in something more like a language of religion, adumbrating unknown realities of life beyond death. And this is something that Virgil's *Aeneid* has not even attempted.

Alarmed by Virgil's plan to destroy his opus, Caesar Augustus visits his dying friend and tries to dissuade him. Virgil, who appears (as in medieval interpretations of his *Eclogues*) to sense the imminent arrival of Christ, indicates to the emperor that humans have the need for a savior which neither state nor conventional religion can fulfill. Nothing rational informs either that need or the operations of the savior who would fulfill it. That savior must be a pure principle of love, an exemplification of sacrifice, a receptacle for an unreciprocal, metaphysical "pledge" and "perception." The messianic event would open a transcendent realm of truth beyond the worldly one, bearing hidden responsibilities. No doubt the penitent writer's new attitude to political empire reflects Broch's own despair at the moral and intellectual scandal of the Nazi reign unfolding during the years of the book's composition (1937–45). The book speculates that invisible bridges of human meaning, forged in the manner of Christ's paradoxical teachings, need urgently to be found.

One of those bridges links Virgil in friendship to the secular emperor, a man unable to understand this line of reasoning. Finally he vents his rage at Virgil in deeming the alienation and division between the friends to be final and irremediable. That is precisely the type of broken connection that Virgil believes can be mended in the space of the "no longer" and "not yet." When does this invisible bond between friendly foes become clear to the poet? It happens at the very moment Augustus accuses the work-burning poet of resentment against the ruler, of egotism and unavowed will to power. In other words, the invisible bridge comes into sight when Virgil stands accused of a sin in that religion for which he senses the need: selfishness, envy, and resentment toward those who possess more; tacit lust for power. That is when Virgil relents and bequeaths his epic to Caesar, acknowledging that it is impossible to make the work say what the author wanted; that piety creates bridges precisely where intellectual connections fail. At this moment it appears to the poet as though there were

> an invisible firm ground showing within the invisible realm, that invisible firm ground from which invisible bridges could be flung again, human bridges to humanity, chaining one word to another, one glance to another, so that word, like glance, should again become full of meaning, human bridges of meeting.[35]

This invisible ground within an invisible realm, about which little else can be said, is what overcomes the breach between Augustus and Virgil, closing the distance between secular, political philosophy and a rationally indefensible principle of love. Virgil, for Broch as for Dante, points to the bridge of that saving force, guiding souls from the "no longer" of pragmatic pagan life to the "not yet" of its death to come. That is the Virgil who is reputed to have lit the way toward the new religion for his fellow poet Statius, who thanks him as follows in Dante's *Purgatory*:

> "Facesti come quei che va di notte,
> che porta il lume dietro e sé non giova,
> ma dopo sé fa le persone dotte,
> quando dicesti: 'Secol si rinova;
> torna giustizia e primo tempo umano,
> e progenïe scende da ciel nova.'"
>
> "You did as he who goes by night and carries
> the lamp behind him—he is of no help
> to his own self but teaches those who follow—
> when you declared: 'The ages are renewed;
> justice and man's first time on earth return;
> from Heaven a new progeny descends.'"
>
> (*PURGATORY*, 22.67–75)

Broch's book attempts to cross the limen of that dark night of death. The unbridgeability of the Styx becomes the basis for the broken way. If Broch's Judaism and his secular aestheticism had not stood in the way, *The Death of Virgil* might have explicitly claimed that from the absence of bridges leading into life beyond death there emerges another invisible bridge adumbrated in the sacrifice of the Nazarene. That is one act in the great bridge-building of God which is imagined with variations by religions the world over.

CHAPTER 2

Living on the Bridge

Akbar's Bridge

Several years after the bloody partition of India and Pakistan in 1947, a reviewer of *The World Is a Bridge* urged people to remember that

> there once was a time of peace and understanding between Hindus and Muslims. In the 16th century the Mughal emperor, Akbar, by his own attitude and effort, achieved this harmony within his realm. During his life Hindus and Muslims lived contentedly side by side, and throughout his cities craftsmen of both religions labored to erect buildings of Hindu and Muslim architecture.[1]

Confronted with the turbulent aftermath of this cataclysmic event—"when the work of Akbar was undone by the greatest schism India has known"—Patricia Natirbov nostalgically evokes different conditions in that land under the rule of a great joiner of cultures. The enlightened Emperor Akbar (1542–1605) was remembered not only for his conquests but especially for seeking to reconcile the theological and ethnic differences dividing the communities making up his state. His imperial palace sponsored debates among sages drawn from throughout Asia. Their mission was to research and report on beliefs that Muslims, Hindus, Roman Catholics (Jesuits), Sikhs, and Cārvāka atheists held in common. Akbar suspected that cultural variations in thinking would yield shared truths, a speculative ambition that had precedents in the age of the Florentine Medici and of the Ottoman sultan, Suleiman the Magnificent. Scholars call it syncretism. It eventually grew into the nineteenth-century liberalism of Europe and the United States.

Akbar's support for multicultural, theoretical bridges warrants extended study, particularly in the context of political efforts to cross ethnic and ideological divides like those discussed in the pages of the chapter "Sea Bridges and Selves." However, the constructive work of the emperor is dampened by another hunch of his that philosophical and moral comprehension of life on earth ultimately serves no practical purpose. A motto reflecting this attitude appears over a grand gateway on the imperial grounds of a city that Akbar built, and it pronounces a cautionary statement to all who enter: "Isa [Jesus], Son of Mary, said: The world is a bridge, pass over it, but build no houses upon it. He who hopes for a day, may hope for eternity; but the world endures but an hour. Spend it in prayer, for the rest is unseen." Life, in this view, is a mere act of transit, warranting no lasting affective investment, no constructive material labor. Our short time on the planet is best spent preparing for what is to come after the journey. Comprehension and the management of life are engulfed in blindness.

This is the overt recommendation of Akbar's epigram, attributed to Jesus of Nazareth and taken from the holy scriptures of Islam. Its figurative meaning is more elaborate. The saying compresses the vast rotundity of the globe into a narrow, rectilinear passageway. It slices a thin sliver of time out of eternity and makes that the context of human action (the span of an hour). If life is a bridge, then this one is a mere point of contact between Hannah Arendt's "twofold nowhere, from which we suddenly appear at birth and into which almost as suddenly we disappear in death."[2] Akbar's statement suggests that if there is any such thing as "being" in an absolute and permanent sense, it remains unseen at the far end of our living platform. Before our eyes lies only a foundationless life, which we experience shortsightedly, where we would best not build a house.

The words of the epigram say nothing about where this bridge starts or where it leads. But we can take a hint from where the motto is positioned. It appears above a *portal*—over the High Door (Buland Darwaza), the tallest gateway on earth, at the top of a steep climb of forty-two steps. The portal opens onto the City of Victory (Fatehpur Sikri) commissioned by the same emperor Akbar. The gateway is 176 feet high and 110 feet wide, crowned by pillars, chhatris, and a dozen domes, providing passage to an immense courtyard uniting a complex of religious, residential, and official pavilions. All act as an antidote to the short bridge on which we seek life's accommodation. Here stands the 165-meter-wide Masjid Mosque near a marble mausoleum. Here too is a reflecting pool, and (ironic in this context) a harem capable of housing 5000 wives—bridges, as it were, to the next generation, though far more than any person should ever have desired!

It is said that Akbar built the walled city to honor the holy hermit Sheikh Salim Chishti, who is interred in the mausoleum. Historical fate apparently wished that this sumptuous City of Victory would itself bear dramatic witness to the ascetic wisdom of both Chishti and Jesus, for it was abandoned just a few years after it was built. The reasons for this remain dim, but the desertion of these quarters has its symbolic cogency. The ghost town has now, for five hundred years, paid iconic tribute to the stark indifference of the suprahistorical. Its adamantine architectural structures have given durable form to evanescence, proving that even the most transcendent and ambitious human constructions serve no worldly purpose. What stands tall at Fatehpur Sikri is not life but monumental demise. How should we understand the message of this great, commemorative site? Is it that the only intelligent response to time is time-weathering work? That work of this kind—discouraged by the motto on the gate!—can somehow compensate our passing? Or is this different from "occupational" work (like building a house), and rather a more commemorative type of work, meant to recollect the idea of life instead of to serve that life?

Bridge-life is inscribed on a door opening onto a sacred court and putting us in the presence of an engineered home of life-in-death: a mausoleum. That mausoleum is contrasted by the harem, its emptiness denouncing lust and procreation. Akbar was a collector of literature and art from far reaches of his empire, famed for tolerance and liberal thinking. He did not cite words from his own prophet Mohammed on the gate to his city. He quoted the reported words of an eternally living bridge, the one tying Mohammed to his monotheistic ancestor Abraham: the prophet's forerunner Jesus, who had passed that way before. Jesus provided Akbar with continuity. But why did the emperor choose this motto over another? Why, when he gave ample evidence of great feats of cultural construction, would Akbar warn us to build nothing over the course of our earthly sojourn? There are not enough links between his time and ours to yield the answers. We can only make deductions from the grand, multidimensional "performance" of the Fatehpur Sikri itself, which combines architecture, word, and symbol to suggest that the *only* type of construction we should concern ourselves with are not houses but monuments. And yet monument building is not the way of lowly, everyday mortals.

The House the Bridge Built

At the time of Jesus it made eminent sense not to build houses on bridges. Allowing for a few Roman and Chinese exceptions, bridge engineering of the age was decidedly unstable. Even today bridges hardly offer adequate support for buildings. Yet inhabited bridges have existed for centuries. Several, like the Ponte Vecchio, are still standing. There were once more than a hundred such bridges in Europe, frequented with more pleasure than ordinary streets. There is a tie, after all, between living and bridging, between functioning, making connections, and constructing purposes. Considering that the bridge Akbar has in mind is human experience conducted between birth and the grave, one can only wonder what kind of people would *not* build houses on it? Life is given purpose by tying phenomena together. Practical, reciprocal, and communal attachments fend off precarious experience—just as decisively as mosque or mausoleum.

With apparently no thought of Akbar, the American writer Thornton Wilder defends those attachments. Knowing that the statement would raise eyebrows, he introduced guests to his mansion as "the House the Bridge built."[3] The perplexity of his guests opened the way to his punch line: This sumptuous house was built on the profits that Wilder made with his novel *The Bridge of San Luis Rey*. Wilder's word bridges, he meant to say, had been converted into mortar. Before writing that Pulitzer Prize–winning novel he was only a modestly salaried schoolteacher.

Flying in the face of Akbar, Wilder's witticism suggests that houses can indeed be built on or by means of bridges. It suggests that the irrational permutations of life can produce better dwellings. His novel had already shown the way to this accomplishment, for its central ethical concern was this: What kind of house can be built on life's precarious, bridge-like foundations? The answer emerges whenever one reflects on bridges as places of dwelling.

Wilder's novel *The Bridge of San Luis Rey* (1927) approaches this problem by elaborating a meditation on a question that arises when a calamity catapults five guiltless people to their deaths from a bridge in Peru. The same question inspires another book years later, *Quella volta sul ponte*, a compilation of local reflections on the collapse of the great Morandi Bridge in Genoa on August 14, 2018, killing forty-three people. Why do some persons come to such a fateful end? Have they done anything to deserve it? In Wilder's novel it is Brother Juniper, an unassuming Franciscan friar, who attempts to understand the five deaths in Peru from a bridge dedicated to the only canonized king of France, the crusader St. Louis IX. Was there any relationship between these victims? Something they shared, which could explain why they were persecuted precisely there at that point in space and time, on July 20, 1714?

The question, in other words, is whether their fate amounts to a *destiny*, or whether it can be read as a justifiable event. To find an answer, Juniper reconstructs the motivations of the five unfortunate travelers, the ethos by which they lived. Did hidden guilt bind them to the end of their *own* living bridge? Could a sympathetic, scientific, inquisitive mind—say a novelist—unearth an explanation, achieving a sense of why the bridge of life is mysteriously brought to ruin?

For Juniper, the fateful bridge of San Luis Rey inspires a quest for an intellectual bridge between act and consequence, between free will and a "guided world," in which no sparrow falls without good reason. The bridge this thoughtful Franciscan seeks to understand is one linking decisions taken by individual agents to an omnipotent and cosmic mind.[4] Unfortunately after six years of research the friar comes up empty-handed, unable to relate what happens on earth to the transcendent plans of God. "The discrepancy between faith and the facts is greater than is generally assumed," he sighs, in understated despair (99). The religious authorities are unmoved by this confession of ignorance: They burn Brother Juniper at the stake. His unacknowledged crime lies in his very attempt to comprehend the ways of God. And so Wilder's novel ends.

Despite the failure of Juniper's research, the book leaves us with one consolatory conclusion to ponder. If any bridge exists at all between divine and human action—a pattern, as it were, of destiny—it is one that cannot be rationalized. Whatever bridge this might be, it does not tie the fortunes of the living to their ethical merits. What survives or follows, however, is a quite different bridge, and it is constructed between people, composed out of affective attachments. The resulting human connection is described in the last sentence of Wilder's novel, culling a lesson from the perplexing meditations that have reached no satisfactory end: "There is a land of the living and a land of the dead and the bridge is love, the only survival, the only meaning" (107). We, the bridge-crossers, suspended between two imponderable points, must build this tie ourselves, extending it toward those who have gone before and those who are still to come. On it

> Lost centuries of local lives that rose
> And flowered to fall short where they began
> Seem now to reassemble and unclose,
> All resurrected in this single span[5]

Philip Larkin wrote these lines in a poem to inaugurate the Humber Bridge in his adopted hometown of Kingston upon Hull in 1981. There, on the platform of a bridge, lives that have been solitary and scattered can "reassemble" and "unclose" like resurrected flowers. The poem, one of the last that Larkin wrote, concludes that "Always it is by bridges that we live." The upshot of Brother Juniper's study of lives cut short is similar: The only lasting and true human ties are affective ones, even if not always consolidated in time. The friar discovers that all five characters who fell from the Bridge of San Luis Rey were immensely important to others, but most did not recognize it until after the fact.

That affective bridge is built on a bridge between two eternal, invisible points, in the absence of a transcendent, metaphysical bridge, in a lack of connection between life and death, with no comprehensible relationship between personal behavior and cosmic fortune. Little joins the finite, material world to the absolute spaces of Akbar but this bridge, making those who are alive gravitate toward those who aren't, in the kinship of shared fate. This is a non-Akbarian bridge, spanning that schism between life's short hour and perpetual eternity which the intellect is unable to do.

Resigned as the conclusion of Wilder's novel is, it stresses the efficiency of this love. The last page pictures rows on rows of sick people consoled by the Abbess Doña Clara in a shelter:

> She talked that night of all those out in the dark . . . who had no one to turn to, for whom the world perhaps was more than difficult, without meaning. And those who lay in their beds there felt that they were within a wall that the Abbess had built for them; within all was light and warmth, and without was the darkness they would not exchange even for a relief from pain and dying. But even while she was talking, other thoughts were passing in the back of her mind. . . . "[S]oon we shall die and all memory of those five will have left the earth, and we ourselves shall be loved for a while and forgotten. But the love will have been enough; all of those impulses of love return to the love that made them. Even memory is not necessary for love. There is a land of the living and a land of the dead, and the bridge is love, the only survival, the only meaning." (107)

Connections established on bridges, by means of bridges—in the *absence* of bridges—are the bridges in question. A Croatian legend relates how the magnetic pull of two lovers walled into the piers at the opposite banks of the Old Bridge at Mostar holds the bridge together.[6] How else should mortals cope with the dire realities of the Qur'anic Jesus's short bridge except through such connections? If life, as his motto says, is a temporary passage between two nowheres—and in itself is nothing—then what else can one build on that bridge except a house to share?

Love Flowing and Locked

The allegiance manifested by sharing a house is occasionally pledged by locking emblems of love to bridges. It is a gesture that spread in the last fifteen years from Rome's Ponte Milvio, some claim from the Most Ljubavi, or Bridge of Love, in Vrnjačka Banja, Serbia, to the Pont des Arts in Paris and to other parts of the world. Inspired by the example of a couple in the film *Ho voglia di te* (dir. Luis Prieto, 2007, based on a novel by Federico Moccia), young Romans flocked in droves to write their names with magic markers on a lock they then attached to a lamppost of Ponte Milvio, flinging the keys into the river. From 2008 on, the love-locked Ponte Milvio gave tangible validation of indissoluble, multiplicitous love, becoming so laden with weight that tons of metal had to be cut away from the bridge to keep the lampposts standing (fig. 2.1).

The bridges of memory did not prove as strong as the ritual practice, however, forgetting how many centuries Ponte Milvio was reputed to be a site of the most fleeting erotic encounters, taken up on the spot. One generation after Jesus, Tacitus informs us that this bridge was "famous for its nocturnal attractions."[7] This aspect of romance is not figured into the gesture of locking love together forever. As a matter of fact,

Figure 2.1. Locks on the Ponte Milvio, Rome.
Renatonee / Wikimedia Commons

the character who introduces the gesture in Moccia's novel *lies* when he tells his girlfriend that it represents an ancient and bona fide tradition. Thus the couple in the book engages in a counterfeit ritual, and young Romans copy them. Then others around the world copy the new Romans. Studies of young lovers who have installed locks on Ponte Milvio reveal that most stay together less than six months.[8]

Yet it is perfectly clear that the love that moves them outlasts each contingent occasion. Affective bonding is deeper than any pledges made in its name. The tension between the two is staged in a poem by Guillaume Apollinaire that celebrates enduring human affection in a world of transience. With an ebb and flow impossible to render in another language, "Le Pont Mirabeau" (1912) responds to Akbar in a manner comparable to Thornton Wilder and lovers the world over. The scene this poem evokes on a bridge includes more than the act of a single hour against a background of immovable time. It pictures a permanent performance above waters that even themselves are incessantly changing:

LE PONT MIRABEAU

Sous le pont Mirabeau coule la Seine
Et nos amours
Faut-il qu'il m'en souvienne
La joie venait toujours après la peine

Vienne la nuit sonne l'heure
Les jours s'en vont je demeure

Les mains dans les mains restons face à face
Tandis que sous
Le pont de nos bras passe
Des éternels regards l'onde si lasse

Vienne la nuit sonne l'heure
Les jours s'en vont je demeure

L'amour s'en va comme cette eau courante
L'amour s'en va
Comme la vie est lente
Et comme l'Espérance est violente

Vienne la nuit sonne l'heure
Les jours s'en vont je demeure

Passent les jours et passent les semaines
Ni temps passé
Ni les amours reviennent
Sous le pont Mirabeau coule la Seine

Vienne la nuit sonne l'heure
Les jours s'en vont je demeure

MIRABEAU BRIDGE

Under the Mirabeau Bridge there flows the Seine
And our loves
Must I recall how then
After each sorrow joy came back again

Let night descend bells end the day
The days go by but still I stay

Hands joined and face to face let's stay just so
While underneath
The bridge of our arms shall go
The weary wave of eternal gazes

Let night descend bells end the day
The days go by but still I stay

All love goes by as water to the sea
All love goes by
How slow life seems to me
How violent the hope of love can be

Let night descend bells end the day
The days go by but still I stay

The days the weeks pass by beyond our ken
Neither time past
Nor love comes back again
Under the Mirabeau Bridge there flows the Seine

Let night descend bells end the day
The days go by but still I stay[9]

The flow of the Seine carries away days and loves, with all joys and pains. Contrasting that flow is the bond of this poem's "we," here standing face to face, though whether in an eternal present or a locked past, we cannot say. The bridge formed by "our" clasped hands overarches the fluvial, all-dissipating current. The speaking "I" endures and recurs beyond the togetherness of the lovers, figuring maybe the only final stability within all this change, consciously recalling the plural and indefinite loves that come and go *comme cette eau courante*. "The days the weeks pass by beyond our ken / Neither time past / Nor love comes back again." Loves pass irrecuperably. Yet they also return—in the subjective space of this poem, in memory and verbal articulation. The bridge once built by the lovers' connection continues to last in a poem bridging readers and lovers across time. The speaker's plea for night to come and close the day recurs with the relentless beat of a clock, in a litany as unending as the river itself. It calls for an end—to the violence of hope. The returning refrain, *Vienne la nuit sonne l'heure*, reiterates commitment to the coming together, redeeming the passage of time.

A less limpid poem commemorates the very same bridge in Paris in a graver and more complex way. Those familiar with the biography of the poem's author, Ingeborg Bachmann, will recognize the bridge as the location from which her lover and fellow poet Paul Celan leapt to his death in 1970. The act occurred nearly twenty years after her poem alluded to suicides from that bridge:

> Pont Mirabeau . . . Waterloobridge . . .
> Wie ertragen's die Namen,
> die Namenlosen zu tragen?
>
> Von dem Verloren gerührt,
> die der Glaube nicht trug,
> erwachen die Trommeln im Fluß.
>
> Pont Mirabeau . . . Waterloo Bridge . . .
> How do the names bear
> to bear the nameless?
>
> Stirred by those lost,
> Whom faith could not bear up,
> the river's drumbeat awakens.
>
> ("DIE BRÜCKEN," LINES 6–11)

Figure 2.2. Le Vieux Moulin, Vernon, France.
Spedona / Wikimedia Commons

How can the names Mirabeau and Waterloo bear—not only accept, but support, pay tribute to—the nameless ones, whom "faith could not bear up"? Celan also leapt namelessly, leaving no note, his body never found. Bachmann's scene is the same as Apollinaire's, but the drama has transitioned from love to death, from the solitude of the poetic subject to his annihilation. Bachmann's poem links the disappointments of bridge-union to the loneliness of the spot where the union occurs:

Einsam sind alle Brücken,
und der Ruhm ist ihnen gefährlich
wie uns . . .

Lonely are all bridges,
and fame is as dangerous for them
as it is for us . . .

(LINES 12–14)

The emptiness of those unifying structures is what induces some to build a house in the middle (fig. 2.2).

Affective Bridges

Bridges extend a promise to overcome separation. In some films they allow individual desperation to be transformed into redemptive

Figure 2.3. Arroyo Seco Bridge (Colorado Street Bridge, 1913), Pasadena, California. Steve Lagreca / Shutterstock.com

attachment. An early dramatization occurs in Charlie Chaplin's *The Kid* (1921), at the Arroyo Seco Bridge in Pasadena, the world's first curved cement bridge (fig. 2.3). Before reaching this bridge, built just a few years before the film, a young mother gives birth but is abandoned by the infant's father. That broken connection gives way to a second as she, in turn, abandons the newborn in an empty car. Instantly she regrets her decision and returns to the car to find that it has been stolen. Frantic, she takes herself to the Arroyo Seco Bridge, preparing to leap from its parapet. Suddenly a small child clutches at her skirt, evoking in her mind her infant's pleas. This contact mends the breach. The mother eventually rediscovers her child, who has been well tended in the meantime on the margins of society by Chaplin's tramp. Indeed, the film ends happily. The bridge affirms its unifying function.[10]

Romantic comedies in particular use bridges to advance the despair-into-happiness theme. Two homeless persons, with no place to seek shelter, find each other to cling to on the Pont Neuf in *The Lovers on the Bridge* (*Les amants du Pont-Neuf*, dir. Leos Carax, 1991). In another French film, *The Girl on the Bridge* (*La fille sur le pont*, dir. Patrice Leconte, 1999), a girl is on the point of jumping off a bridge when a professional knife-thrower offers her a somewhat less lethal prospect: to be the live target of his blades. Eventually the two separate, but by the film's conclusion the girl discovers her knife-thrower climbing onto an Istanbul bridge to cast himself into the Bosphorus. She reaches him just in time to assure their future together.

The Bollywood production *Anjanna Anjaani* (dir. Siddharth Anand, 2010) features *two* suicidal protagonists ready to jump off the same bridge at the same time, and they proceed to make several additional botched efforts to end their lives. Ultimately they admit that they will be far happier simply by vowing to love themselves and each other more. (Bridges have served similar functions in the lives of Hollywood actors, as with Richard Burton and Elizabeth Taylor, who connected houses with a bridge across a street in Puerto Vallarta. Frida Kahlo and Diego Rivera devised a similar arrangement in Mexico City.)

Bridge-bindings less smooth than the ones in these three films are also more interesting. Bachmann's poem "Die Brücke" refers not only to the Mirabeau Bridge but also the Waterloo Bridge, reputed to be the last stop on the road for socially unassimilated women by the time Thomas Hood published a poem on that subject in 1844 ("The Bridge of Sighs").[11] Bachmann's poem is from 1952, before the release of the third film adaption of the well-known drama by Robert E. Sherwood, *Waterloo Bridge* (1930). Sherwood's play lent itself well to the cinematic imagination. It opens with the prostitute Myra picking up a naive soldier called Roy on that London bridge toward the end of World War I. Not recognizing Myra's profession, Roy falls in love. The question posed for the audience is whether Myra will conceal the truth or confess to Roy that she is a streetwalker and risk losing her honest man.

Transposed to the screen, the resolution of Sherwood's narrative varies with the mores accompanying the respective productions. The first film (*Waterloo Bridge*, dir. James Whale, 1931) respects the tragic outcome of the play. Myra confesses her "fallen" situation and Roy assures her that this changes nothing in the nature of his commitment. However, minutes after he leaves the bridge to return to the front, German bombs explode. The camera tracks in to frame Myra's dead body on the Waterloo Bridge. This deviant woman, unlike Chaplin's, will not be redeemed.

The commercially more successful *Waterloo Bridge* of 1940, starring Vivien Leigh and directed by Mervyn LeRoy, sanitizes the tale. In deference to Hollywood's new Motion Picture Production Code (1934–68), charging movies to deliver properly edifying messages to the American audience, it presents Myra as a respected ballerina who falls into prostitution only after believing that her Roy has been killed in battle. When

Roy does return alive, she prefers death to scandal. Myra pays just as dramatic a price here for her deviance as in the previous film. The next, 1956, film version of *Waterloo Bridge* (*Gaby*, dir. Curtis Berhardt, with Leslie Caron) gives itself even more poetic license, the bridge turning into an unequivocal forger of human union and moral progress. It reunites ballet dancer turned prostitute and then virtuous wife with her man in a reciprocal arrangement of good fortune.

Only the 1940 film has the merit of using that figure of encounter and unification which is the bridge to underscore the tenuousness of human ties. Accordingly it begins twenty years after Myra's suicide, with Roy alone at the bridge, in analogy to the poem by Apollinaire. The film then flashes back to the lovers' meeting at the same place during the war and proceeds to construct their story, showing how the relationship developed, how Myra mistakenly believed Roy to be dead and made her new living, and how, even after seeing him return, she preferred to die. As the elder Roy recalls his loss on that bridge, the film's soundtrack plays the famed song about the recollection of separation, "Auld Lang Syne." The social, moral, and psychological strictures of the age allowed neither Roy nor Myra, nor the film's producers, to construct a bridge on the bridge.

The motif of bridge as locus of potential union undergoes a more startling subversion in an episode of the omnibus film *Paris vu par . . .* (*Six in Paris*, 1965) called *Gare du Nord* and directed by Jean Rouch. Here a man is on the point of jumping from a Parisian bridge when he is approached by a woman whom we have already seen as trapped in an unhappy marriage. A few words suffice to establish a deep and reciprocal sympathy between them, both realizing that this other person can give them precisely the type of relationship they need. The man invites the woman to drive away with him into a mysterious realm that he explains will nourish love. The woman Odile holds back, not mustering the courage to act on spontaneous intuition. "This morning," the man declares, "I decided to die. Then I met you. You are my last chance. I thought nothing could interest me anymore. Then I saw your smile." Odile still makes no move to cross over to him. The man jumps to his death, the bridge failing to bring them together.

Another that emphatically separates lovers while beckoning to their union appears in Luchino Visconti's 1957 film adaptation of Dostoevsky's "White Nights." A man called Mario, out of place in a town that also lacks distinguishing features, cautiously approaches a delicate, apparition-like woman weeping on a bridge. There Natalia waits to be reunited with a man to whom she had promised herself one year earlier.

The film reconstructs elements in their prior attachment, in which the man appears decidedly sinister. With no sign of this mysterious lover ever returning, Natalia (Maria Schell) and Mario (Marcello Mastroianni) develop a deep and passionate relationship over the course of the following days. This fledgling love has everything to be said for it. The film makes it appear much more convincing than the attachment between Natalia and the older stranger that we have seen in flashbacks. But just when the new couple decides to seal their commitment, the silhouette of the forbidding former lover appears on the distant bridge in the background. Thick snow falls down from this white night. Weeping with emotion, Natalia runs from Mario to embrace the stranger.

The story is melodramatic, but it suggests that attachments like the one between Mario and Natalia arise without apparent reason or purpose, without justification or preparation, and can only be cherished as such: "May you be blessed for the instant of happiness that you have given me, for it is not little, even in an entire lifetime," Mario says, as he too weeps. The closest bond one can build on the frail bridge of feeling reveals itself here to be nearly as insubstantial as Akbar's city of the dead. The attachments housed on bridges in these films are for those who lack them: single mothers and motherless children, tramps (Chaplin) and prostitutes, estranged wives and husbands. The characters in *White Nights* have no more dependable social grounding than they.

Aliquis de Ponte

Bridges both narrow and wide, both on clear and snow-filled nights, provide shelter for the homeless. In older times, when bridges favored pedestrian traffic, prostitutes sold a semblance of love to passersby on them; they withdrew beneath them. Famous for these wares, one bridge in Venice is still called Ponte delle Tette, or Tits Bridge. There, beginning in the sixteenth century, female prostitutes exposed their breasts as a marketing ploy. Homosexuality at this time had grown so rampant that it dramatically impacted the livelihood of these women, estimated to have composed 10 percent of all females in Renaissance Venice, or 20 percent of all women of sexual age. Facilitated by cross-dressing at nighttime, homosexuality was made punishable by decapitation, which apparently did little to curb its practice. To lure men back to the heterosexual fold, women sat with their legs hanging out of the windowsills above the Ponte delle Tette with their breasts exposed, giving palpable evidence of the ostensibly real deal.[12] While it is not clear how well this strategy worked, Ponte delle Tette gives one example of how unsanctioned sexual acts make the best of a tough situation, often on and beneath bridges.

The Italian idiom *sotto i ponti* designates homelessness no less than sexually illicit encounters. Both are bridged with nonchalance in a famous French song of the 1910s called "Sous les ponts de Paris":

> Beneath the bridges of Paris at nightfall, all sorts of beggars sneak into hiding places, happy to find their bed. Drafty Hotel, where the prices are low. Perfume and water cost almost nothing, my marquis, beneath the bridges of Paris. Julot meets Nini at the factory exit. How goes it my redhead? Today there is a party. Take this bouquet, some sprigs of lily, not much, but it's all my riches. Come with me, I know a place where we don't even need fear the moonlight. Beneath the bridges of Paris at nightfall, without enough to pay for a room, a happy couple comes to love in secret.

Transience and prostitution converge less casually in another composition, where the liminality of the bridge makes it impossible to achieve the appurtenances of social identity. Prakash Jadhav's poem "Under the Dadar Bridge" stages an encounter between a woman from the Dalit class and her beggar son who furiously demands to know who fathered him. What were his identity, his religion, his ties with the world? The son receives only embittered answers from his diseased and abused mother, mired beneath the Mumbai bridge where many die "in the bastard gutter which / has links with high-class sewage water." She cries to her son:

> "You are not a Hindu or a Muslim!
> You are an abandoned spark of the
> World's lusty fires.
> Religion? This is where I stuff religion!
> Whores have only one religion, my son.
> If you want a hole to fuck in, keep
> Your cock in your pocket!"[13]

Untouchables and transients continue still today to throng over and under the Dadar Bridge. "The foxes have their lairs, and the birds have their nests," as St. Francis liked to repeat, "but the Son of man hath not where to lay his head." St. Francis, like Diogenes of Athens, voluntarily embraced such a condition, while millions of others have no choice in the matter. When Gustave Doré visited London in 1869 he was overwhelmed by its squalor and by the teems of its poor populating the East

Figure 2.4. Gustave Doré, *Asleep under the Stars* (1872). From Doré and Jerrold, *London: A Pilgrimage*, 179.

Figure 2.5. Gustave Doré, *Outcasts: London Bridge* (1872). From Doré and Jerrold, *London: A Pilgrimage*, 149.

End and the city's bridges. With something of the consolatory spirit of St. Francis, he imagined these generations to be protected by heavenly spirits, brightened by the light of the stars (fig. 2.4). One sketch of these outcasts on London Bridge incorporates the watchful guardianship of a colossal angel (fig. 2.5). Other illustrations highlight the illuminating

Figure 2.6. Gustave Doré, *Under the Arches* (1872). From Doré and Jerrold, *London: A Pilgrimage*, 185.

sky seeping under the bridge where transients huddle (fig. 2.6). Often Doré stresses the inner dignity of the bridge dwellers (fig. 2.7).

Indigent people have been so ubiquitous on the world's pedestrian bridges that the ancient Romans had a euphemism for them: *aliquis de ponte*, a bridge-dweller, someone from a bridge. Contemptuous of the miserly fare presented at a Roman dinner party, the satirist Juvenal exclaims, "Why, even a bridge-dweller would refuse an invitation to such a meal!"[14] In Parisian slang pimps and pickpockets used to be called *officiers du Pont-Neuf* (officers of the Pont Neuf) and *avant-coureurs* (precursors) *du Pont-Neuf*. They were officers simply in laying down the only "laws" that were operative on the bridge. In French as well as Italian *finir sous les ponts* means finishing one's life without a penny.[15] On and around bridges, those without homes could receive alms by day and shelter by night. Platforms over which multitudes are compelled to pass give vagrants a strategic spot to station, pressing face-to-face encounters with their fellows. On bridges as on subways everyone is put eye to eye. "The law in its wisdom allows both the rich and the poor to sleep under the bridge," Anatole France is quoted as saying. His actual words say rather the opposite: "the majestic equality of the law . . . prohibits the wealthy as well as the poor from sleeping under bridges," but the misquotation better conveys the *inefficiency* of laws to enforce

Figure 2.7. Gustave Doré, *A Cold Resting Place* (1872). From Doré and Jerrold, *London: A Pilgrimage*, 177.

comportment on bridges, whose radically egalitarian space permits few interdictions.[16]

The Holy Drinker

An author as familiar with the bridges of Paris as Anatole France envisioned them as sanctified spaces effacing the class difference between the indigent and the rich. Joseph Roth lived in the precinct of Paris's bridges during the final years of his life, where he was reduced to economic and drunken straits not far removed from those of his protagonist in "The Legend of the Holy Drinker." He is the clochard Andreas, whose name comes from *andros*, or "Man" in a generic sense, and he is a holy and homeless imbiber of wine. The story is worth examining in detail for the conclusion it reaches.

One morning, as he shakes off his slumber after a night beneath a bridge, Andreas encounters a well-heeled man climbing down from the quay to the riverbed. The man inexplicably gifts Andreas the sizable sum of 200 francs, asking only that he repay the debt one day by making an offering to a church. Although Andreas is very grateful, and has every intention of managing this money wisely, he ends up squandering the sum on wine. He does the same thing with another 1000 francs that inexplicably fall into his lap some time later. Within three weeks he again has hardly a sou left in his pocket and believes there is nothing left to do but "to entrust himself to god, to the only god he believed in. So he went down the familiar steps, back down to the Seine, to the home of all the homeless vagrants."[17] The space beneath the bridge is the informal home of Andreas's god.

As Andreas descends to the river, the rich man is coming up again to the quay and gives him another 200 francs. Andreas recognizes his benefactor and exchanges nearly the same words as on the first encounter. He apologizes for not having an address where he can be contacted to repay his debt. "'I too have no address,' replies the gentleman, 'and I too may be found under a different bridge every day'" (3). Apparently Fortune, like the majesty of the law, does not distinguish between rich and poor—except that this man *does* have money, and chooses to live like the poor, in conditions to which they are compelled, and he offers them a portion of his privilege.

The gentleman now suggests a reason for his generosity. After reading about the life of St. Thérèse de Lisieux, a popular French saint of the final decades of the nineteenth century, he has converted to Christianity. Was he Jewish, like Roth himself? The story does not tell us. The man repeats his request: at his convenience Andreas can make good on his debt by donating it to a particular church that contains a statue of St. Thérèse. This "little Thérèse," as she was affectionately termed, became a nun at age fifteen and by the time of Roth's writing (1939) was one of the most loved saints in all the Catholic Church, considered the intercessor of those who suffer.

One night, as the story proceeds, she visits Andreas in a dream, looking exactly as he imagines his own daughter to be—or rather how she might look, for he has no daughter. Roth's narrator does not tell us why this saint belongs in this story nor why Andreas has such difficulty paying back his debt. Could it be because in the grand scheme of things, no one is ever free of debt? Or because Andreas is as unwilling to sacrifice his wine as was his author? Roth, a deteriorating alcoholic, and profoundly shaken by the anti-Semitic turn that his native Austria took during the 1930s, took his own life in Paris one month after completing this story—his last.

The drinker Andreas is an immigrant too, from Poland, and we learn that the French state had ordered his deportation before he became homeless, indeed forcing him into that homelessness. The last month of his life sees mysterious gifts of cash raining down on him in such a way as to restore his sense of dignity and to spur him to regain control of his life. Each Sunday he sets off for the church containing the saint's shrine, determined to repay his debt. If he never gets there, it is apparently only because he is naturally committed to self-forgetfulness, sacramentally nourished by symbolic wine.

On the story's final Sunday Andreas tries once more. Waiting for the right moment to approach the church from a bistro across the street, he encounters a young girl in this unlikely setting. Her name is Thérèse and she is dressed in sky blue: "as blue as only the sky can be, and then only on certain blessed days" (47–48). Andreas identifies her as the saint, his creditress. He believes that the little saint has finally come to him. After she gives him a hundred franc bill, Andreas collapses onto the floor. He begs the waiters to carry him into the church in the company of the girl, where he thrusts about in his pocket for the money he owes and cries, as he dies, "Miss Thérèse!"

A redemptive grace envelops the final experience of Andreas. It concludes the story's celebration of the holy liberality of those like him—like the poor in spirit of the Gospels—who are blessed precisely in recognizing their own destitution. In his last weeks of life Andreas squanders the few resources he has "believing himself to be fortune's spoilt darling" (43) and returns faithfully to the secure home of the clochards beneath the bridge. If this story possesses the enigmatic clarity of a mystical fable, it defies the utilitarian argument that life gives just rewards to those who work to achieve them. Andreas may be too drunk to distinguish the difference between a long-deceased saint and a palpably living young girl, as he repays his debt to *her* rather than to a statue in a church, or rather to her in the presence of the statue. The "little Thérèse" of the nineteenth century may well have resembled this young girl who enters the bistro on the fourth Sunday of every month, just as she resembles the imagined daughter that Andreas never had. Both, in this parable, are incarnations of the saint just as Andreas, in his fallenness, is Man favored by Fortune. Without building one, he possesses a house on the bridge.

Under the Overpass

Roth gives us an account of time spent beneath a bridge, in the absence of security elsewhere. If this experience produces holy abandon, glimmers of analogous conversion can be found in other places, even in popular songs. “Under the Bridge” by the Red Hot Chili Peppers, on the album *Blood Sugar Sex Magik* (1991), recounts how the singer of the Los Angeles group was repeatedly drawn to a ghetto downtown to obtain not alcohol but speedball, a concoction of heroin and cocaine. By a logic that remains just as unspoken as the one in Roth’s story, the descent beneath the bridge pulls the singer into sympathy and union with the city. At the scene of the bridge he comes to feel “like my only friend is the city I live in.”

The song sold a million copies by striking a chord in the souls of alienated, metropolitan youths the world over. As the lyric writer Anthony Kiedis later commented, the real casualty of this descent into the world of drugs was not his sober self but his affective relationship with a single treasured friend—a “love” that he forgot. The forgetting was consubstantial with the descent. The underbelly of the city repaid the loss of that single love with a love for the city, together with which he now cries to be taken “to the place I love.” The three different loves—for the woman, the city, and for a place where the two might be unified—are fused with the bridge downtown.

On the same day that this song was issued as a single (September 24, 1991), Nirvana, another celebrated rock band of the decade, released its own song about bridge-refuge. “Something in the Way” harks back to the time Kurt Cobain spent under the Young Street Bridge in Aberdeen after dropping out of high school (fig. 2.8). The story tells that he came home one day to find his belongings packed up and left outside the house by his mother, at which point the bridge became his destination. If “alternative rock crashed into the mainstream” with the album on which this song appears, *Nevermind*, then the crash occurs in this, the album’s conclusive song, where something comes “in the way” of social belonging.[18]

“Underneath the bridge,” sings Cobain, “the tarp has sprung a leak,” and the animals that he traps become his pets. He lives “off the grass” and off what drips down from the bridge above him, reckoning that “it’s OK to eat fish” because they “don’t have any feelings.” The short lyrics of the song are as puzzling as any from Nirvana because there is so little to go on: one verse and a chorus repeated. The tarp may be the singer’s covering for physical protection, just as the fish, grass, and trapped animals may name his nutrition but may also be euphemisms for substance

Figure 2.8. Young Street Bridge, Aberdeen, Washington (1956).
Popturf.com / Flickr

abuse. All that is definitive in the song is its repetitive, harmonic fall from Em to C without variation, producing the impression of a spatial distinction between the platform of the bridge above and the makeshift dwelling beneath it. "Underneath the bridge," the opening words, also emphasize the contrast between the place where Cobain took shelter and the vector of transit above it.

This hidden underbelly is a collateral effect of the bustle on the bridge—beneath, outside, and immaterial to it. The support for the passage of cars becomes a roof for shelter; the motion it enables produces a place for immobility. The "place-action" above is underscored by a "non-place/non-action" below. The bridge separates those engaged in productive industrial processes from another group of people who, as an earlier song puts it, are "down by the river . . . along with lovers, buggers, and thieves." These words, from the Standells' "Dirty Water" (1966), portray dwellers of the Charles River in Boston as profligate outsiders.

Nirvana's song identifies "something in the way" of life on the move, something that *gets* in its way, ignored or denied beneath it. When compared with the homeless who sleep exposed in doorways or on sidewalks, transients beneath a bridge appear discrete, unassuming, and self-hiding. They take refuge from the business and buildings above, often absconding with like-minded fellows. They possess neither worldly commitment nor the otherworldly commitment advanced by Akbar. The vagrant and homeless fringe-members of society associated with bridges take up a dialectical relationship toward constructive, pragmatic life.

More Than Transit

The bare life of bridge-living embraces the tenuous ties of life on earth that so worried the emperor Akbar. But bridges have also supported houses built in solid and collective ways. The centrality of bridges to towns is reflected in the names of communities that developed where rivers were forded: Cambridge, Oxford, Alcántera, Innsbruck, Frankfurt, Fiume, Mostar (meaning "keepers of the bridge"). The banks of rivers, where estuaries flow out into the sea, provide food and sources of livelihood. Bridges have critically facilitated trade routes. Hostels, campgrounds, and fairs huddle around them.

The practical function of bridges is to transfer humans and their wares from one side of a river to another. They become permanent structures in order to serve needs of residence, with the support of social and institutional practices. In medieval Europe many bridges were supervised and managed by the church. Chapels were given a prominent position upon them (fig. 2.9). Frequently they were outfitted with defensive towers (fig. 2.10) and eventually mills, shops, and dwellings.

Figure 2.9. St. Ives Bridge, Cambridgeshire, England (fifteenth century), including two floors added to the chapel in 1736 and removed after 1930. Undated postcard.

Figure 2.10. Pont Valentré, Cahors, France (1350), with its fortified towers.
Velvet / Wikimedia Commons

Figure 2.11. Old London Bridge in the sixteenth century, the city's only river crossing until 1769.
Classic Image/Alamy Stock Photo

In the Middle Ages each bridge in Rome had at least one watchtower.[19] Most of the bridges in Europe's major cities were inhabited, putting to use the advantage of proximity to the water. The original London Bridge was one of them (fig. 2.11).

The wooden bridge at the Rialto, Venice, lined with rows of shops and rebuilt several times over the centuries, was replaced in 1591 by the one we see there now. Its designer, appropriately named Antonio da Ponte, won the commission over the better-known Andrea Palladio. Palladio's rejected design was even more ambitious than Da Ponte's and would have granted the city space for an entire forum (fig. 2.12). Even the Ponte Sant'Angelo, Leon Battista Alberti tells us, was covered in the early fifteenth century. "The beams of its roof were supported by twenty-four marble columns; it was covered in bronze, and marvelously decorated."[20]

Paris housed the largest concentration of France's thirty inhabited bridges, including the busy Pont au Change (fig. 2.13) where money changers and goldsmiths plied their trade. The very first bridge in Paris *not* designed to carry shops and houses over the Seine was the aforementioned Pont Neuf (1607), though even it was originally planned to do so. *How Paris Became Paris,* by Joan DeJean, outlines some of the civic functions this hospitable bridge succeeded in serving with its singular "officers," leveling social differences, hosting street performances, public readings of the news, and political demonstrations.

Populated day and night, such bridges have been with us for centuries. Over a series of incarnations the Galata Bridge crossing Istanbul's Golden Horn has hosted entire neighborhoods (fig. 2.14). The longest and oldest wooden bridge in China, the Wan'An (fig. 2.15), allegedly built a thousand years ago, hosts a temple at one end and a center for village life along its platform. For centuries the Khaju Bridge in Iran (fig. 2.16) has featured octagonal pavilions at its center for public meetings and originally a teahouse. The covered bridge in Lovech, Bulgaria, designed by the famed Kolyu Ficheto, destroyed in 1925 but recently reconstructed, hosts fourteen shops (fig. 2.17). The many covered bridges in North America offer travelers an opportunity to shelter and rest. Lovers are said to post billets on them, in a strategy drawing isolated subjectivities together, as popularized by the film *The Bridges of Madison County* (1995). The Wakefield Covered Bridge (Pont Gendron) in Québec, often topped in snow, is one (fig. 2.18).

Before vehicular mass transit became the lay of most lands, bridges operated as nerve centers of collective life. On the Sokolović Bridge, writes Andrić in his historical novel *The Bridge over the Drina* (1945), "the life of the townsmen flowed and developed. . . . In all tales about personal, family or public events the words 'on the bridge' could always be heard. Indeed on the bridge over the Drina were the first steps of childhood and the first games of boyhood." Anything but a symbol of transience, Andrić's bridge at Višegrad yielded the only stable point

Figure 2.12. Andrea Palladio, second model for the bridge at Rialto (1569). Drawing by Francesco Corni.

Figure 2.13. Nicolas-Jean-Baptiste Raguenet, *La joute des mariniers entre le Pont-Notre-Dame et le Pont-au-Change* (1751). Oil on canvas 47 × 83.5 cm.
Musée Carnavalet, Paris

of reference for the vicissitudes of the town it united, its narrative nexus. Of hundreds of river municipalities like this one could say, "The town owed its existence to the bridge and grew out of it as it from an imperishable root."[21]

Another distinguished bridge forms the hub of civic life in a city of the same former Yugoslavia (fig. 2.19). There two footbridges, splaying

Figure 2.14. Old Galata Bridge, photograph from 1895.
Wikimedia Commons

out at angles, combine with an earlier stone arch bridge. The Triple Bridge of Ljubljana, designed by Jože Plečnik in 1929, adds ribs to the city's main pedestrian zone. Such spots on the water are more than urban landmarks; they weave together a fabric for social interaction. And city planners in recent decades have built an increasing number of them to enhance our Akbarian passage, footbridges for amblers to congregate and saunter, to play music and dance, and to converge in communal activity. The Ponte della Musica (fig. 2.20) and its companion Ponte della Scienza in Rome were devised with this in mind, despite still standing virtually empty. Rationales for their competing designs pitched ideas for the bridges as "a square suspended above the water," providing the "catalyst of a set of events"; or as a "door to a space of exposition," establishing a "new locus of centrality . . . wending its way around the central void dedicated to the river." Designers spoke of alternating "introverted" and "extroverted" stretches of theatrical space, offering not only a "natural observatory," but also a "bridge-square, bridge-theater, bridge-market."[22] Competitions for pedestrian bridges in London in 1996 and 2009 yielded just as interesting results, accompanied by pleas to increase this type of urban planning on the model of inhabited bridges of the past.[23]

New nonvehicular bridges reduce the colossal ambitions of twentieth-century projects to construct inhabited bridges throughout

Figure 2.15. Wan'An Bridge in Pingnan County, in southeast China's Fujian Province, constructed in the Northern Song Dynasty (960–1127) and rebuilt several times since. Reputed to be the oldest and longest wooden bridge in the country (98.2 meters). TAO Images Limited / Alamy Stock Photo

cities of the world, often connecting them in networks between one metropolis and another: the skyscraper-bridges in New York and over the San Francisco Bay planned by Raymond Hood, Hugh Ferris, and Louis Christian Mullgardt in the 1920s; bridges designed by Kenzo Tange to host airports across the Tokyo Bay (1960); the envisioned transformation of Paris into a Spatial City by Yona Friedman (1958–59) and his later plans for bridge-cities; the Marin County Civic Center (1962) of Frank Lloyd Wright, completed after his death.[24] In the 1970s an entire university campus in Calabria was built on a nearly mile-long bridge-highway, with three vertical floors, designed by the Vittorio Gregotti group (figs. 2.21 and 2.22).

Considerable institutional investment has fueled the "reinvigoration and rebranding of established cities [through] small, boutique, art installation-type bridges,"[25] producing dramatic results like the Zhangjiajie Glass Bridge and Lucky Knot Bridge in China (both 2016), the Henderson Waves Bridge (2008, fig. 2.23), the Citadel Bridge in the Netherlands (2015), the London Millennium Footbridge (2000), the Kurilpa (2009) and Webb (2003) bridges in Australia, the Golden Bridge in Vietnam (2018), the Ponte del Mare in Pescara (2009, fig. 2.24), and numerous elite structures by Santiago Calatrava. Several of these bridges carry explicit semiotic intent. Names such as Peace Bridge, affixed to Michele De Lucchi's structure in Tblisi (2010) and Calatrava's in Calgary (2012, fig. 2.25), suggest that the symbolic

Figure 2.16. Khaju Bridge, Isfahan, Iran (1650).
Alireza Jahaveri / Wikimedia Commons

Figure 2.17. Covered Bridge, Lovech, Bulgaria (originally 1874).
Eola / Wikimedia Commons

Figure 2.18. Wakefield Covered Bridge, Québec, Canada (1915). Burned down by arsonists in 1984, rebuilt and opened in 1998.
Alastair Wallace / Shutterstock.com

Figure 2.19. Triple Bridge, Ljubljana, Slovenia (1842–1932).
sduraku / Shutterstock.com

purposes of these bridges are often as strong as their practical ones. A particularly striking one was designed by Cecil Balmond and named after an ill-fated pair of lovers. They were Crown Prince Pedro of Portugal and Inês, the lady-in-waiting of the prince's wife, with whom Pedro fathered four illegitimate children (fig. 2.26). Pedro's father King Alfonso was hardly as enamored by the affair and had Inês murdered in 1355. Unable to forget her, the desperate Pedro exhumed the dead Inês, dressed her up, and married her postmortem. Commemorating

Figure 2.20. Ponte della Musica, Rome (2011).
Nicola Cerroni / Wikimedia Commons

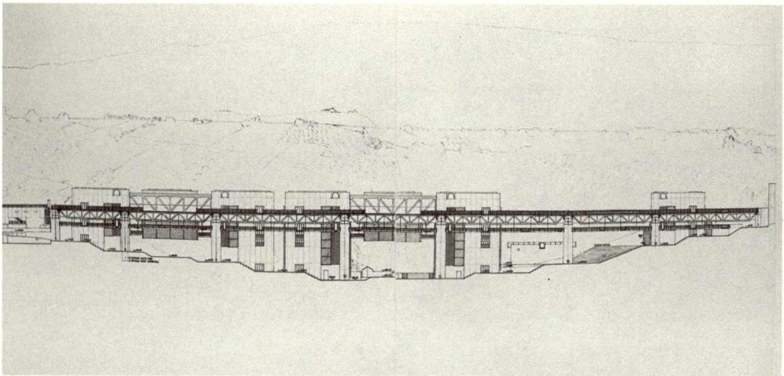

Figure 2.21. University of Calabria, Arcavacata (1973–1981), detail of plan. From Vittorio Gregotti, *Il progetto per l'Università delle Calabrie e altre architetture / The Project for Calabria University and Other Architectural Works*, ed. Italo Rota and Gabriella Borsano (Milan: Electa International, 1979), 9–10.

the tragic relationship, the Pedro e Inês Bridge (2007) is referred to as the bridge that doesn't meet: It is composed of two contiguous walkways on parallel but separate axes.[26]

Much is to be said for the imaginative technology of the new footbridges and the reflective ambulation they foster. Their most conspicuous feature is their conceptual audacity, shifting the crosser's

Figure 2.22. University of Calabria. Photograph by Alessandro Lanzetta, for the project *L'Italia raccontata attraverso l'architettura,* financed by the Direzione Generale Creativa Contemporanea del MiBACT.

Figure 2.23. Henderson Waves Bridge, Singapore (2009).
Nostpedestry / Shutterstock.com

attention from pragmatics to aesthetics, eliciting active perception and feeling. Rather than serving pressing needs of transit, they aim to create another cognitive space for humans, slowing motion itself down to become a topic of contemplation. Their visual drama dominates city skylines and prominently imposes itself on riverscapes. At an additional remove from pragmatics lie perilously suspended thrill-bridges.

These eye-catching bridges elaborate principles that dwellers experience in more traditional and extensive ways in bridge-cities like Venice and Amsterdam, where city life is woven around the water and in intervals between one stretch of land and another. The new pedestrian

Figure 2.24. Ponte del Mare, Pescara, Italy (2009).
mauri3001 / Wikimedia Commons

Figure 2.25. Calgary Peace Bridge, Canada (2012).
Pxhere.com

structures aim to produce a comparable loosening and bending of rigid civic structures. Up to this point they present opportunities for practices that are not fully operative outside contexts of leisure and that cannot become so without massive overhauls of the daily life-structures of urban economy. Many are not truly inhabited, so to speak. Until city

Figure 2.26. Pedro e Inês Bridge, Coimbra, Portugal (2007), designed by Cecil Balmond. © Cecil Balmond, 2003

planning catches up, they remain inspirational, constituting something of the non-place of their ostensible opposites: megabridges of megastates that connect spaces without granting the socially and psychologically integrative action that needs to accompany them. One can only hope that these imaginative bridges will eventually accrue definitively living purposes, allowing houses, so to speak, to be built on them.

CHAPTER 3

Musical Bridges

The Span of Sound

Stringed instruments resonate thanks to a bridge—a small elevated piece of wood over which vibrating cords, of different gauges and stretched to achieve different tensions, are spanned. Plucked, bowed, or strummed, they emit tones that can be coordinated into music. The word "bridge" also names a transition from one melody, theme, or key to another in a musical composition, effecting an excursus away from the main section of a work. This bridge, or "bridge passage," in popular songs brings alteration or modulation, coordinating two elements.

Music does quite the same thing with human subjectivity, conveying listeners to another space of mental attention. It draws them into the place of a span. In fact sound itself is a bridge, even before being manipulated into aesthetic form. The acoustic registry of our ears is an echo chamber, where each tone connects and rings. Acoustic bridges are potentially infinite in number and variation; too many at once will produce noise. They tie us to miniworlds of natural and social activity often evoked by a single sound.

Sound is our tie to the invisible. It penetrates walls, seeps through floors, rings over rooftops and mountain peaks. It brings notice of distance, which hardly can be said of the other four senses. If we close our eyes and concentrate on the sounds reaching our ears, we sense the individual location of each, transmitting contours and textures of living activity. Close by the warble of a bird on a branch rings out, three houses away the blunt sounds of a hammer, the engine of a car receding a kilometer further on. Nearest of all rings the clatter of the writer's keyboard, punching out letters translating such sounds into words. Sonorous events emanate from places that are often visually indeterminate. They enter the hearing and subside. The listening mind gathers together a vibrating world of particulars each with its own being, timbre, and scale.

Sights, and the things they represent, do not radiate in that way. They occupy a unified, coextensive place. Sounds instead arrive singly and oblige us to *bridge* them, or compose them into the multiply connected terrain we inhabit. Sight, penned in by space, is obstructed by physical barriers like walls, tree trunks, and people. It depends on light. It is exclusive, limited by the direction of our eyes. Sound surrounds and engulfs us. It is multiplicitous and is not easily shut out. Vision is a painted and completely filled canvas; hearing is more like a white canvas containing splashes of color. We perceive sounds against the background of that canvas, or silence. Vision is like a face mask drawn around the eyes; hearing is more like a celestial sphere through which acoustic stimuli shine like stars. To focus on components of a visual picture we simply shift our attention, scanning one detail and then another. Sounds are instead layered, producing harmonies or dissonance. They have an insistent agency. We can shut our eyes, but our ears remain open.

Sound draws the absent near. It emerges often from places unseen, across broad and otherwise untraversable spaces. The perception of invisible things allows for imagined, offscreen realities, which help us make sense of what lies bluntly before us. Those invisible realities belong to our horizons of action, to which we are implicitly connected in everyday practice and explicitly through thinking, writing, recollecting, and building. Sound is an indispensable link to that offscreen space, filling narrative gaps in the stories we tell.

Sound affirms distance between us and its source. Visual presence, writes Jean-Luc Nancy, "is already there, available, before I see it, whereas sonorous presence *arrives*." It contacts the listening subject, from which it signals its difference even while making connection. In listening we strain "toward a possible meaning, and consequently one that is not immediately accessible." We stand "on the edge of meaning . . . as if the sound were precisely nothing less than this edge, this fringe, this margin."[1] That edge is really more like a bridge on which subjective-objective movement occurs. "Listening to the ringing of a bell is moving inwardly to an outward activity," writes David Burrows. Listening to *others*, adds Simone Weil, is putting oneself in their place.[2] Listening consists in a two-way process of reference, from the sign to its origin or cause, and from the stimulus of that sign to an action within the subject.

The copresence created by these bridging effects is particular to hearing. Hearing is like being touched, notes Burrows again, "except that the touch of sound does not stop at the skin. It seems to reach inside and to attenuate [the distinction] between here and there, [and] the biologically still more basic one between within and without." Instead of producing the pure and simple presence of touch, auditory sensations convey a presence of presence, "a relationship *to* self, or . . . a presence *to* self."[3] This is similar to the kind of referral that Hannah Arendt associates with the act of thinking, where the reflecting subject perceives itself as perceiving.[4] Looking or watching does not normally involve this transcendental relation, no matter how neurologically moved the mind is by visual events (in fact, the more moved the seeing mind is, the less it experiences its own experiencing). This space of referral, connection, or relay is nothing less than the operational space of the self, so long as we not consider the self an entity or subject, but rather a process, as a relationship to self. If the technology of vision is developed at staggering rates each day, courting infinitely high definition, the experience of sound grows ever more muddled, confused, and suffused, downgraded in quality. Today one can hardly even understand people on telephones.

When perceived as musical—and this means demanding focused attention—the presencing relationship of sound is intensified. Coming *toward* me on a sonorous bridge, musical perception is "both phenomenally proximate and immediate," writes Thomas Clifton, "because I have first voluntarily erased the barriers between myself and it. . . . There is no longer a dichotomy between my space and musical space. . . . Being in a musical space means that . . . I dwell in it."[5] That is why modern philosophers from Schopenhauer to Nietzsche and Adorno think of human nature as turning "toward music as toward its own sublimity—toward its *metaphysics* . . . (Schopenhauer called it 'will'; the 'will to live,' that is to say, being as desire rather than being as reason)."[6] Being as "will" or "desire" involves a tending toward, a mobile tension, a spanning of ego and other in which experience, understanding, and human interaction unfold.

The Acoustic Imagination

The poet Giacomo Leopardi belonged to that company which saw sounds as bridgers of distance. He was particularly intrigued by sounds that were disembodied, clarifying material absences. The process entailed the same principle of "acousmatics"—of hearing without seeing—which was put to such good effect by Pythagoras when he found that his students understood him better when he lectured from behind a veil. The strategy forced them to focus on his words alone, and reflect on their implications. Registered separately from their physical sources, sounds, voices, and songs require heightened interpretive attention.

Voices provide indexes of bodies—implying subjectivities, desires, and willed intentions. The complexity and frequency of their use in nature appear proportionate to the intensity of animals' social relations, most prominent in species that live in pairs (90 percent of birds, for instance), which consolidate their contact through auditory pathways. Voices ring out at a threshold between creature and world. They communicate data not revealed by a merely present or self-evident body, Burrows argues. They grant that body a means by which to make an appeal. In every voiced exchange, partners "are at once apart . . . and together in a new synthetic place, the location of their sympathetic resonance in common."[7] In the voice of an out-of-sight body one hears, or overhears, a vital world.

A voice links the emitter and the receiver of sound in a spirit or concern transcending both. Leopardi jots down a note to remind himself to ponder just how the sound of a voice can conjure up considerations

> of the plurality of worlds and the nothingness of us and this earth, and of the greatness and power of nature, which we measure with its torrents, etc., which amount to nothing on this globe, which is a nothing in the world, and is reawakened by a voice calling me to dinner, from which it then seemed that our life and time and celebrated names and all of history, etc. were a nothing.[8]

Leopardi is speaking of a banal call of a family member summoning the young poet to supper, penetrating his solitude from an excluded and ignored place outside it, and confirming his own intuition of the boundaries and limitations of physical being. The call introduces palpable evidence of a separate reality into the listener's here and now, which his thoughts had dispelled as he studied, another reality that in turn dispels the reality of the poet's *own* imaginings. That voice's independence of a visible body suggests too that being, however one is to define it, *also* consists in transcendent will, desire, and spirit.

Another disembodied voice also recalls the limits of material being:

> My sadness at hearing the night song of country people passing in the late evening after some festivity. Infinity of the past that came into my mind, as I thought back to the Romans, so fallen after such clamor, and to the many events now past that I compared sorrowfully with that profound quiet and silence of the night, which it took the prominence of that peasant's voice or song to make me realize.[9]

The singing of this unseen person connects with time not present but past, even infinitely past, with once analogously sounding events, even clamorous ones like marching armies, which on the day that Leopardi jots down this note are as imperceptible as the stillness of night. Such a song, he remarks elsewhere, can even give a sense of the very source of being, like "the beginning of the world (which I would have liked to put to music, poetry being unable to express these things and so on), imagined in hearing the song of that mason."[10] Only the mind can imagine the source of the mason's song. Or rather, the mind *cannot* imagine it, for it lies beyond the reach of visual and conceptual representations, and can only be expressed by music. It involves the coming-to-life of things out of nonphysical, prehistorical time, a process in which existence itself comes into being. And no word or conceptual image can render this advent of presence.

Leopardi's meditations on sound and voice suggest a series of relays. First the voice acts as a sign or index of an absent body. Then it indicates a larger, unquantifiable reality. Finally it implies the operations of the human understanding itself, translating vague events into recognizable forms. Leopardi's voice is thus the antithesis of the embodied voice that interests the philosopher Adriana Cavarero, which embeds meanings, intentions, and speech in palpitating and corporeal life-situations. Leopardi's voice calls to mind the conversion, through perception and understanding, of concrete body-spirit situations, activating movement brought *into* the ear *back out* to the source of the heard sound, a source ultimately carried away by space and time—pointing across a bridge to the ontological context *of* that sound.

Only thanks to such a voice can one imagine the silence into which sounds sink, the boundless horizon enclosing the world we perceive. Leopardi's most famous poem identifies this voice with the invisible wind. On hearing it storm through the plants, he writes in "The Infinite,"

> . . . io quello
> Infinito silenzio a questa voce
> Vo comparando: e mi sovvien l'eterno,
> E le morte stagioni, e la presente
> E viva, e il suon di lei.[11]

> . . . I compare that
> Infinite silence to this voice;
> And recall the Eternal, and the seasons
> That are dead, and the one that is present
> And living, and the sound that she makes.

The present season's sound in the wind enables a cognitive comparison with what has no voice at all. The act of comparison is imaginative action. It makes a metaphorical crossing from acoustic perception to imperceptible infinity. It transcends a definite and delimited datum (the voice) to contemplate what is inassimilable to that datum—the place from which it comes and to which it returns, creating a back and forth passage (*vo comparando*: "I go comparing; I institute a relationship"). The acoustic imagination activates philosophical speculation, producing reflection on missing and abstract bodies, and on relationships between known and unknown. The acoustic imagination compensates for vision's shortcomings, sounding out feelings and ideas beyond the body.

Sound Bridges in Film

Sound as used in the art of film fills analogous gaps. It brings absent phenomena into the visual space of the screen, helping thereby to produce a story. Before the technology of cinema acquired the ability to synchronize sounds with flickering screen pictures (in the "talkie"), film experience was limited to the observation of photographic images, projected in such rapid succession as to give the impression of movement (and usually accompanied by musical performance). To tell stories often meant inserting intertitles, filling in the audience about nonrepresented causes and clarifying screen actions. Once images could be coupled with recorded sound, their communicative possibilities were enhanced. Screen actions were endowed with an extravisual, phenomenological environment.

The main virtue of film sound is to grant information not thoroughly conveyed by the images alone. The movie screen shows a man sitting alone in a room, dejected. We hear a baby cry and see the man turn his head. The acoustic index makes us infer that the child is in a nearby room. Adding the two data together, we wonder what the man's relationship is to the baby. The cry of the baby may help us interpret the man's dejection. Additional visual data could lead us to believe that he is unemployed and rearing this child alone. Street noises now ring out offscreen. They suggest that the apartment housing this man and baby are located in a brash metropolis. We hear an explosion offscreen. Was it from outside the window or from within the apartment? Each sound ties consciousness to a space our eye cannot perceive.

That is sound's cognitive advantage over the image, as Leopardi had suggested, transporting a sign from elsewhere, perforating or distending the space we fill. Audiovisual art applies that principle, making screen art also an art of the offscreen.[12] The sounds of film are binding. Diegetic film sound gives acoustic depth to the events that we see, projecting the screen's impression of reality more fully. The first sound film in Italy, *La canzone dell'amore* (1930), highlighted not, as we might expect, the speaking of humans, but the clatter of knives and forks during dinner. Extradiegetic sound, which is not internal to the screen's acoustic horizon (not "hearable," as it were, by the characters in the film), adds a commentative function to the image, cuing the audience to respond in a certain way to the action in question (violins during kisses, for example). A film's extradiegetic sound is mainly made up by the musical score, bonding screen drama to human affects. The crying of the unseen baby in the previous example is different; it is diegetic, but offscreen, sound. Both we and the man in the frame hear the cry, but its source lies outside our purview. The sound ties the scene that we see to one that we don't, in a case of acousmatics.

There are also nonsynchronized sounds in film. One is a sonic flashback, superimposing a sound heard earlier on the present image before us, bridging present to past. Voice-overs "translate" the screen drama for an interpreting mind, illuminating the significance of an action, or narrating what we see happening, and setting us at an interpretive distance. Internal diegetic sound enables the audience to hear what should only be heard by characters in the film. The easily aroused Eugenia in *Till Marriage Do Us Part* (dir. Luigi Comencini, 1974) has a heartbeat that is amplified through the speakers in the theater.

Then there is the sound bridge proper, where a motif in the soundtrack plays over two different scenes, establishing a link between them. There the acoustics of a scene earlier or later than the one we are watching bleeds in from an adjacent space to which it properly (diegetically) belongs. Usually it serves to soften the space-time transition between scenes. Sometimes, as in *Seduced and Abandoned* (dir. Pietro Germi, 1964), it does the opposite, inciting a double reading. Two characters kiss, and organ music swells up. The sound initially appears to be extradiegetic, giving us the impression of wedding music overlain on the embrace. However, the music continues to play in the next scene and forces us to reach a different conclusion. The film has now cut to a close-up of a priest reprimanding the same girl in a church confessional. We now understand that the music belongs diegetically here—in the punishing place of moral accounting, signifying not marriage at all but Catholic guilt. Though we do not hear the girl's confession, we deduce it from the words of the outraged priest: "You wretch! You gave in! Did you feel no guilt?!" She answers, "Yes, father, I did. Immediately afterwards," and the priest: "Too late, you shameless girl!" Agnese's words confirm what the sound bridge has already demonstrated: operating in the present is one thing, but attaining a perspective on it is quite another.

Voices from the Bridge

Real, material bridges can heighten intellectual perception in similar ways. They are resonant structures, amplifying normally inaudible vibrations, like the small bridge of a stringed instrument. Great material bridges produce resounding reverberations.

The Old Bridge (Alte Brücke) of Heidelberg described in a poem by Friedrich Hölderlin generates sonorous, light movement through the air like the resonant flight of a bird:

> Wie der Vogel des Walds über die Gipfel fliegt,
> Schwingt sich über den Strom, wo er vorbei dir glänzt,
> Leicht und kräftig die Brücke,
> Die von Wagen und Menschen tönt.[13]
>
> As the forest bird crosses the peaks in flight,
> The bridge oscillates over the river
> shimmering past you, airy and strong,
> Ringing with vehicles and people.

The verb *schwingt sich* (swings over, oscillates) precedes its subject, the bridge, but follows the bird, which inclines us to see the bird as performing that action. That simple technique bridges the two fields of action. After its birdlike motion, the second action of the bridge is more typical of a musical instrument: *tönt*. The bridge rings out, hums, or resounds. That ringing is an acoustic performance created by the passage of people and wagons over the vibrating structure; on another level, however, the ringing appears to be "the bridge's own voice," sounding beneath "the percussion of the carriages and people."[14] Either way, the sonorous effect of what for Hölderlin was the "new bridge" of Heidelberg (1788; his poem is from between 1798 and 1800) is produced by the way its materials span the air. Its conduit of bodies resounds with something transcending its materiality.

Another poet more explicitly connects the structure of a bridge with music, and particularly with a song, He also sees the song as creating bonds between liminal, nameless selves. The poem is "Nostalgia" (1916) by Giuseppe Ungaretti:

Quando
la notte è a svanire
poco prima di primavera
e di rado
qualcuno passa

Su Parigi s'addensa
un oscuro colore
di pianto

In un canto
di ponte
contemplo
l'illimitato silenzio
di una ragazza
tenue

Le nostre malattie
si fondono

E come portati via si rimane[15]

When
night is fading
a bit before spring
and hardly
anyone passes

Over Paris
an obscure color
of weeping
condenses

In the song
of a bridge
I contemplate
the limitless silence
of a slender
girl

Our ailments
fuse

And we remain as though carried away

This poem evokes mysterious fusions and dissolutions of people, impressions, and places. It concretizes "an obscure color of weeping," making it condense over the city of Paris. It sees the night as being on the point of vanishing (*è a svanire*). These transformations come to rest in the song of a bridge (*un canto di ponte*; the word *canto* can also mean "corner") in which the speaker contemplates "the limitless silence" of a slim or tenuous (*tenua*) girl. The architectonic structure of this nameless bridge is what enables the poet to hear the unlimited, subjective silence of its song.

Ungaretti frames the already liminal space of this bridge—between two banks of a river—in a doubly liminal time, just before dawn and just before spring. The bridge is thus a chronotopical border, both temporal and spatial in nature. At this particular place and time there occurs a reverberation, relating the space-moment to a vast home, or the wish for one (*nostalgia* evokes homecoming, *nostos*, accompanied by pain, *algos*). The space-time in which the sky of Paris is pervaded by mourning evokes something that remains silent and cannot even be properly seen; even the speechless girl is not clearly "there" on the bridge. She is merely brought to mind, or "contemplated." The bridge-song brings her into being. A scene evokes a mood, this yields a sound, and in this sound the speaker hears silence.

The setting of the bridge explains the importance of the song and the sensation that it carries the two subjects away. A bridge carries people away from the sounds of the street to a space over water. The fluid element itself carries sounds farther than solid matter. A bridge heightens acoustics, made doubly keen by the subjective receptivity of a person's presence on a bridge, where another self seems to reach out and grip the first. The boundaries of the hearing subject become as porous as the boundaries between the senses, where the sound of weeping assumes color and selves make contact. The contact is so strong that the "ailments" of the two persons (*le nostre malattie*) run together (*si fondono*). The fusion is implicitly affected by the liquefying effect of the waters beneath the bridge. Joining as it does two banks of a river, this bridge creates a comparable confluence of subjects.

The most striking element of the poem involves the result of that confluence: *E come portati via / si rimane*: we remain as though carried away. In Italian the pronoun *si* designates an impersonal subject. What "remains" is neither "we" nor "I," but a general, unlocalizable "one." And this unidentifiable subject remains *as though carried away*. Or rather, it remains as the *two* are carried away (*portati via*, indicating a plural). The two, who are carried away, with their ailments fused, remain a unity, possessing both the fixity of a bridge and the transience of the flowing waters beneath it.

This conclusive image transcends boundaries between spatial and temporal being, between perduring and parting presence. It turns this spot on the bridge into the site of a seemingly unnatural, existential paradox: a place of firm footing established over an element in ceaseless motion, of stability in a scenario of change. Bridges always allow us to "remain" as though carried away. They unite two finitudes (banks of the river) by traversing an aqueous infinity. To stand or walk over that water is to pass from one finite condition to another *through* the infinite.

Ungaretti's "Nostalgia" elaborates implications of Guillaume Apollinaire's "Le Pont Mirabeau," discussed earlier in these pages. There we find the same paradox of subjective perdurance on a bridge above interminably changing waters: *Les jours sont vont je demeure*: "the days go by but still I stay." Nietzsche's poem "Venice," discussed later in this book, also features a song calling to a hearer in his solitary position on a bridge. Indeed, the song perforates his subjective borders. "From afar there came a song . . . My soul sang to itself in reply a gondola song." Nietzsche's song wells up synesthetically as a "golden drop"; Ungaretti's *pianto* assumes dark hues in the sky. The resounding bridges produce connections not sensed in the city proper, with its constant palaver. The rarefied calls perceived by the lone figures ring out tones that are both inner and outer, of a family with the call of conscience that the narrator of Albert Camus's *The Fall* hears when a woman he passes on a bridge jumps off and he fails to respond. He too achieves a realization: "on the bridges of Paris, I, too, learned that I was afraid of freedom."[16]

Bridge Music

Hart Crane's poetic suite *The Bridge* (1930) magnifies the voices of the bridge into a colossal Aeolian harp. Named after the god of the wind, this harp contains a sounding board with strings stretched across two bridges, its strings vibrating in different tones in response to the wind. Romantic poets like Coleridge and Shelley had identified poetry with this Aeolian harp, set into motion by the in-blowing, or in-spiration, of surrounding life. For Crane, New York's Brooklyn Bridge is precisely that harp, suspended by cables quivering in response to the motion occurring on them:

> O harp and altar of the fury fused
> (How could mere toil align thy choiring strings!)
> Terrific threshold of the prophet's pledge
> Prayer of pariah, and the lover's cry,—[17]

As we shall see in "Word Bridges," Crane generates a thousand-line lyric poem from what he hears reverberate by means of this sounding bridge.

For the centennial celebration of the same bridge, sound artist Bill Fontana recorded the effects that the Brooklyn Bridge registered of the wind and other contact phenomena. He placed microphones below the structure's roadway to capture the oscillating tones produced by cars speeding along the studded grids. Then he transmitted the sounds to speakers concealed behind struts on the facade of One World Trade Center nearly a mile away. The result was *Oscillating Steel Grids along the Brooklyn Bridge* (1983), eerily filling the plaza below Manhattan's Twin Towers with the bridge's displaced drone. The sounds produced something like chords in a redoubled and changing soundscape, where "normal changes of the day, such as traffic (less traffic meant faster cars producing higher pitched tones) and weather (thunderstorms occurring simultaneously at the bridge and the plaza created an interesting acoustical delay)" could be heard along with "the special sounds of the Brooklyn Bridge centenary (the parade, boat whistles, and fireworks)."[18]

Four years later, on the fifty-year anniversary of the Golden Gate Bridge, Fontana tied the sounds of the Californian bridge to those of an insular wildlife refuge offshore for migrating sea birds and marine mammals. The sound artist titled this live duet *Sound Sculptures through the Golden Gate Bridge* (1987).[19] The presuppositions of the earlier *Oscillating Steel* here became explicit: Bridges are not only *producers* of these sounds and their recordings; they are also their conceptual objective. While the earlier piece transported urban sounds from one location in the city to another, the San Francisco recording fused altogether different acoustic environments. Indeed, the places were separated by thirty-two miles, one with a population "of more than 500,000 birds and three thousand marine mammals," the other a complex material bridge, punctuated by insistent sounds of foghorns.[20]

To expand the bridging effect of the doubled soundscape, Fontana made it a component of his transatlantic *Cologne San Francisco Sound Bridge* (1987). This carried environmental sounds between San Francisco and Cologne via satellite. The simultaneous broadcast, American Public Radio reported, was the "first intercontinental live sound bridge between Europe and North America, the first time in the history of radio that two continents have been united through the transmission of acoustic sound sculptures."[21]

Sound bridges of this sort contain a purpose as old as John Cage. "Wherever we are, what we hear is mostly noise," the composer remarked in the same year the Golden Gate Bridge was finished (1937). "When we ignore it, it disturbs us. When we listen to it, we find it fascinating."[22] Fontana intended as well as to undo city dwellers' compulsion to lower the volume that surrounds them. Sound art reframes what they discount as noise in order to make them listen more carefully to what reaches their ears, creating thereby "a sound bridge to an enhanced experience of city life."[23] Ears linked to environments become venues to extensive awareness. In 2006 Fontana increased the volume on the virtually imperceptible "musicality of sounds" emitted by the dynamic motions along London's Millennium Footbridge, and transmitted the bridge murmurs to the Tate Modern museum and a station in the London Underground. *Harmonic Bridge* (2006) created access to the offscreen sounds of an acoustically active, engineered human space, the reverberations of a "sonic world inaudible and hidden to the natural ear."

Both types of bridge-sound—many publicly audible, others virtually imperceptible—have been explored by others on Fontana's example. In 1994 Jodi Rose began to record sounds of dozens of bridges between the Mekong Delta and Sydney's Glebe Island Bridge, describing these *Singing Bridges* as a sonic sculpture produced by "playing the cables of stay-cabled and suspension bridges as musical instruments . . . [listening] to the secret voice of bridges as the inaudible vibrations in the cables are translated into sound."[24] For Rose there are spiritual and animistic implications in this bridge-resonance, with contact microphones liberating the inner voices of the cables and pylons of bridges as though they were media of semantic passage, drawing messenger angels to places of human interaction. Indeed, Rose invokes Michel Serres's study of angels to explain this effect, a work the philosopher eventually supplemented by his own collection of poetic meditations on bridges.[25] Rose invokes John Cage as well, or, more precisely, an idea that Cage inherited from Otto Fischinger: "Everything in the world has its own spirit, and this spirit becomes audible by setting it into vibration."[26] A sounding board of transcendence, Rose's bridge, to say it with the title of one of her recordings, is a "transporter of infinity."

Another noteworthy bridge-sound engineer is Michael Gambacurta, who, in collaboration with Matthias S. Krüger and Yuki Higashino, recorded a performance on the Kaiserlei Bridge over the Main which he issued on an audio CD called *Autophones: Hearing with the Ears of the Bridge* (2008). Where others see only a bridge, Gambacurta discovers an *autophone*: "a musical instrument whose own substance produces sound with a vibrant tone . . . a soundboard tuned by traffic, wind and weather—an endless concert, endless variations of a theme."[27]

What interests ambient sound artists are the transductive effects of bridges on sound and the symbolism contained within that sound. (The word “transductive” is inspired by Jean Piaget, who spoke of the transductive reasoning of children; unlike adults, children are able to see connections between unrelated occurrences, using neither inductive nor deductive means to do so, he claimed.) The transductive capacity of bridges arises from the structural fibers of which they are built, especially sensitive to circumambient reverberations. Bridges, extended horizontally over considerable distance, make contact with a wide range of space. They are exposed, outward-turning structures. Their composite, slender components ring out to movements over, under, and around them. Slung between two points, bridges create conduit both to and fro, like sound itself, bringing evidence of elsewhere. Bearing witness to the transcendence of boundaries, they give an image of cerebral triumph and spiritual concord, lending themselves to metaphysical yearnings and wished-for unions.

The animistic undercurrent of bridge-sound is wrapped up with all these properties. “Hearing with the ears of the bridge,” Gambacurta’s sound installations produce a kind of cosmic canal between substantially different spaces, letting vibrations of one interact with those of the other.[28] The tones emitted are recurring and looping, not linear or progressive, conveying a theme of unity in difference. The idea of “sound sculptures” attached to the works of Fontana and Rose also aims at the synesthesia, or joining of different sensory perceptions, articulated by Ungaretti’s poem.

Playing into the hands of a musician, a bridge allows listening to turn into active performance: the clanging of bridge railings, scratching one’s nails along twined steel cables, stomping one’s feet, and the like. *Bridge Music* by Joseph Bertolozzi (Delos, 2009) uses a trained percussionist’s mallets to evince sounds from the Mid-Hudson Bridge which he assembles into a traditional musical structure, creating studies in theme and variation. His objectives are as ideal as those of his fellow sound artists, leading him to imagine an ensemble of musicians spread over the three-thousand-foot span of the Mid-Hudson Bridge and performing these pieces live, projected toward audiences in parks on different sides of the river. The bridge becomes the stage of a theater composed of two riverbanks, producing spatiotheoretical binding.

These are material bridges creating music; but music itself can forge bridges. A documentary filmed at the geographical divide between Europe and Asia, *Crossing the Bridge: The Sound of Istanbul* (dir. Fatih Akin, 2005), presents music as a space where cultural differences meet. The real but also symbolic locus of this juncture is the Bosphorus Bridge that spans two continents, once the longest suspension bridge outside of the United States. The film tracks Alexander Hacke, the bass player of the German experimental group Einstürzende Neubauten, as he crosses that bridge, journeying from Europe to the portal of Asia to explore what musical results that geopolitical meeting has yielded. There he discovers fusions of Eastern and Western forms: hard rock, gypsy combo, classical arabesque, hip hop, grunge, Mevlevi devotional music, electronic rock, folk, jazz, and the blues.

As we observe the club and street performers of Istanbul in this documentary, we can easily understand why no art resounds more easily than music on shores far from its origin. Schopenhauer offered some reasons for this in his *The World as Will and Representation,* in reflecting on the imponderable, universal appeal that is carried by strong musical melodies.[29] To be sure, the cultural and political supports for the global movement of music have given it a mainly west-to-east direction, carrying classical and popular genres (rock, jazz, blues) from America and Europe to Asia and Africa. Just as the European form of the novel undergoes extraordinary transformations in other continents, the same holds for Western musical forms on the other side of Akin's Bosphorus Bridge. But reverse influences also prevail, and the film is not short on examples, like that of Canadian singer Brenna MacCrimmon, who unearthed Turkish ballads from the 1950s and 1960s in Bulgaria and sang them to both Turkish and Western European ears in an impeccable native accent. The world music phenomenon has been rebalancing the flow-of-goods direction for several decades, even if still usually under Western management.

Appropriations of musical art are facilitated by bridge-places and cultures that are sympathetic to neighboring influences. When working as a disc jockey in Istanbul, says a character in Akin's *Crossing the Bridge,*

> you pay attention to what happens in the South, the East, the West, America, everywhere. But over there [in mainland Europe] people are usually more limited. In America the record store is around the corner, the radio station is local and the DJs have a limited musical cosmos. But when you live here your ears are open to everything, even if you don't want them to be.[30]

The record store, alas, is no longer around the corner in America; certainly there are more per capita in Istanbul today. Yet the DJ's point is that openness resides in that soil of history and culture we call geography (a terrain explored later in "Sea Bridges and Selves"). Before migrating west, the Turks lived at the remote foot of the Altai Mountains near the current border between Mongolia, China, Russia, and Kazakhstan. After bringing their nomadic ways to rest in Anatolia they themselves changed in innumerable ways. The new setting, witness to high-density crossings between Europe and Asia for centuries, gave Turkish nomadism a formidable external scenario. Even if they wanted to plug their ears to sounds wafting into their waterways from every direction, the DJ suggests, they would not succeed. Music seeps into this location at the straits between Asia and Europe in rare and extraordinary ways, as do other influences in the mixed culture and mores of Aegean Turkey.

The Musical Bridge-Passage

So far we have been discussing the external spans of sound and music: their phenomenological, architectonic, and cultural conduits, and the way these affect the ears. But the spanning effects of music are also internal; they are embedded in formal features of compositions. One of those features is known as a "bridge passage." It is a section of a song that acts as a fulcrum across which the main threads of the song are strung, carrying listeners from one musical locus to another. Subordinate to those stable points of support, the primary function of that transitional passage we call a bridge is "to connect two passages of greater weight or importance in the work as a whole."[31]

The conventions of sonata form admit such a bridge. A sonata's exposition, or first movement, often presents two themes and modulates between them. The modulating bridge allows the exposition to make a rhythmic or harmonic turn from first to second theme. Bridges can also transition between larger main sections of the composition. Popular American and European music of the twentieth century uses bridge passages more consistently than a sonata. Here the bridge presents a critical minimovement in its own right; it turns away from a repetition of patterns (the main theme) that could otherwise become monotonous. As established by the music industry of New York City between 1880 and 1950, the bridge usually consists in a section of eight bars, or measures, in a thirty-two-bar song organization. The standard scheme of these Tin Pan Alley songs sets forth two eight-bar sections with identical musical form (AA) followed by a new configuration of an eight-measure bridge (B). The middle eight bars or measures provide musical contrast and then return to A for a final eight measures, creating the pattern of AABA. While James Brown rarely uses an AABA form, this is what he means when he cries, "Take 'em to the bridge!" in "Get Up (I Feel Like Being a) Sex Machine" (1970). Given the way a bridge connects A sections, jazz musicians occasionally call it a "channel."

Considering that this bridge leads away but also *back* to A, it is not transitional in the way that it would be if it led to something totally new (say, a different musical verse C). Rather, it is a divagation within a recurring pattern, carrying an independent interest of its own. Not landing us on a new musical shore, it first leads elsewhere, but turns back to where we started, enjoining us to resume the journey. The popular bridge-passage invites listeners to tarry on the intermediary element.

When the invitation proves especially appealing, the bridge can develop into a chorus, which itself repeats. The vocal refrain of a chorus—that catchy point in a song where listeners are most tempted to sing along—is more definitive and autonomous than a bridge. When the B section of the verse-bridge structure becomes increasingly striking, as for instance in the 1960s, the AABA form makes way for a repeating overall pattern of verse-chorus (AAB). The verse had been the focal point of AABA, while now the verse-chorus structure of AAB makes the chorus just as important, giving listeners a greater proportion of B. At this point the B is what the verse leads to and prepares for.

The most important distinction between a bridge and a chorus may be precisely that repetitive nature of the chorus, while the bridge typically only occurs once. In his comments to the catalog of Beatles songs, John Lennon refers to the term "chorus" only once, even though this is what several B sections of Beatles songs, with their recurring vocal refrains, strictly are.[32] Lennon avoids making a distinction between bridge and chorus by speaking of the "middle eight," which would suggest that some composers consider the distinction between bridge and chorus fairly immaterial. What is *not* immaterial is the recursive function of that middle eight, operating a musical shift and then turning listeners back to the main verse.

What may still appear unusual is the use of the word "bridge" to designate an element that both departs from and returns to its origin. Why did musicians call the B a bridge instead of a road? Is it because a road leads to a destination out of sight while a bridge connects two visible embankments? Taking us elsewhere, it also provides a means of return. It is a recursive structure. If we consider the arch of a material bridge, for example, we understand it as a geometric counterpart to the concavity at the bottom of the riverbed. The opposite curve of a bridge mirrors and links the rising riverbanks, looking back to where they begin (fig. 3.1). We can therefore amend the canonical definition of Leon Battista Alberti according to which a bridge is essentially only a part of a road, overcoming natural barriers.[33] The bridge is also a link that enables a structure to circle back on itself. It completes a ring.

Figure 3.1. John Sell Cotman, *Greta Bridge, County Durham* (1805).
British Museum

The Blues Turnaround

By extending these recursive implications of the musical bridge, we find it operating in ways so obvious as to be overlooked. Traditional musicology identifies no bridge at all in the blues, for example. What it does attribute to a standard blues song is a *turnaround* at the end of the chord progression. But this serves a comparable function. A twelve-bar blues turns around at the completion of one chord cycle to give way to another. If we designate the tonic base of the song I, the blues progression moves from there to subdominant IV, then back to I, then to dominant V, then back again to a final resolution in I:

BARS	1	2	3	4	5	6	7	8	9	10	11	12
CHORDS	I	I	I	I	IV	IV	I	I	V	IV	I	I

The conclusive V-IV-I segment creates the blues bridge, or turnaround. Blues instrumentalists reserve the word turnaround for their own embellishments at bar 12, usually on guitar, but those arpeggiated moves are themselves continuations or responses to the transitional V-IV-I, where the broader turnaround begins. That conclusive, cadential return of V-IV-I is a deepened variation on the song's first excursion IV away from I—an added venture to a farther shore (V) followed by a return to I.

This turnaround, or blues bridge, assures the stability of the twelve-bar progression. It creates a reversion to I after a tantalizing step away (first IV, then V), leading up to a final pull home. The turnaround operates in the manner of a harmonic refrain: a "refraining" from desire or temptation. The desire is to go, but the bridge that points away also pulls back. After one twelve-bar pattern has been completed, any number of additional sets can be added to develop the lyrical theme. Each twelve-bar unit is concluded by the return via V-IV-I, allowing for progress within repetition.

This is where the turnaround makes semantic difference. It generates the potentials of the blues lyric. Those lyrics exploit and reinforce the turnaround effect. During the verse they voice and repeat one single statement, and then follow this by a second. We can call these 1.1.2. The statements give a conceptual reason to the completed and resolved twelve-bar cycle: The first statement expresses a crisis, the second brings closure. The way both fit the harmonic structure of the twelve bars is key to the turnaround effect that they have.

The first statement is sung over the first four bars and recurs over the *different* harmonic structure of bars 5–8. That gives it emphasis and new color. The second statement (in the third line) responds to the reiterated crisis—which could also be called an appeal or call—in bars 9–12. All lines rhyme, at least approximately:

> 1: You've got to help me, darling, I can't make it all by myself.
> I I I I
>
> 1: You've got to help me, darling, I can't make it all by myself.
> IV IV I I
>
> 2: If you don't help me darling, I'll have to find somebody else.
> V IV I I
>
> ("HELP ME," BY SONNY BOY WILLIAMSON II, WILLIE DIXON, AND RALPH BASS, 1962)

The mininarrative of a twelve-bar song like this is temporarily concluded, the story ended—but it gains new chapters with each resumption of the cycle. The final turnaround, the bridge to the beginning, concludes the first chapter but enables a second.

Blues history accounts for the "call and response" of 1.1.2 by reference to the singing and surreptitious communication of African American slaves on cotton fields. In that setting a singer forced to communicate stealthily under the censorship of guards would deliver a call which a chorus of voices would repeat or vary, acknowledging receipt in the process and occasionally providing an answer. As the form of the blues song proper develops, the opening call tends to launch an autobiographical anecdote. It grips the audience's attention by presenting a dramatic situation. Here are the beginnings of five songs, showing how the announcement calls for resolution:

> I feel so lonesome, you hear me when I moan . . .
>
> It's my own fault, darling, treat me the way you wanna do . . .
>
> Got my mojo workin', but it just won't work on you . . .
>
> When the sun rose this morning, I didn't have my baby by my side . . .
>
> Give me one reason to stay here, and I'll turn right back around . . .[34]

In this conflicted and critical situation, the foregrounded "I" of the singer either addresses a "you" or bemoans a "she" or "he." Reasserting this articulated stress, the performer makes it echo solidly in the ears of the audience. In fact, a slow blues number gives listeners a full fifteen to twenty seconds to ponder a single idea. Once the idea has stuck it receives its response or twist, achieving a microplot. Laid over the musical turnaround of measures 9–12, that turn or twist provides a skeletal narrative that resonates easily in the mind of any adult in the world:

> I'd rather see my coffin comin' right through my front door,
> I'd rather see my coffin comin' right through my front door,
> Than to hear you say, you don't want me no more.

(RORY GALLAGHER, "LEAVIN' BLUES," 1969, BUT AFTER DAVY GRAHAM [1965] AND LEADBELLY [1941])

> I ain't goin' down, dirt road by myself.
> Babe, I ain't goin' down this old dirt road by myself.
> If I don't carry you, baby, I' goin' to carry me someone else.

(HOWLIN' WOLF [CHESTER BURNETT], "AIN'T GOIN' DOWN THAT DIRT ROAD," 1968)

If the initial call of the lyric casts a line out into the water, its response reels in a fish. Other responses on the part of guitar, piano, or harmonica enhance the development, occurring between the vocal call-and-response (generally at bars 3–4, 7–8, and 11–12). Three or more units of this 1.1.2 cycle expand on the opening narrative position until the song is brought to its conclusion, as in Howlin' Wolf's "You Gonna Wreck My Life" (1959): "How many times you gonna treat me like you do? / How many more times you gonna treat me like you do? / You took all of my money and all of my love too. // Now I'm old and gray, got no place to go / Now I'm old and gray, got no place to go / You got yourself a youngster [young stud?] and you can't stand me no more. // I'm going to the stairs, I'm gonna beg ya for my clothes / I'm going to the stairs, I'm gonna beg ya for my clothes / For where I go, nobody knows."

Each additional 1.1.2 unit complicates or extends the narrative resolution of the first, giving a blues song the potential to develop unending variation in repetition. What makes the repetition tolerable—indeed interesting and aesthetically cohesive—is the fact that two *semantic* positions (1.1.2.) are interlocked with three *harmonic* ones (I-I-I-I | IV-IV-I-I | V-IV-I-I). Just as the first announcement is repeated, the music moves from its tonal base I to IV. Still the musical divagation remains anchored to its origin by the repetition of the lyrical theme. In the third harmonic block, the chords venture even further away from the base (to V) as the lyrics provide an awaited solution. But here too the recurring end rhyme offsets the distance, stressing the tie between V and the resolving measures of I. The simple verbal pattern strengthens the recursive bridge.

This recursive bridge solidifies the performance and cultural appropriation of the blues around the world. Ninety percent of twelve-bar-blues songs repeat both the same I-IV-V progression and the two-statement base. In fact, the only notable differences between one song and another involve the *performance*: the look, sound, and sexual gender of the singer; the song's instrumentation, improvisations, and solos; its tempo and vocal timbres. Trapped within a virtually immobile harmonic paradigm (which, of course, can also be articulated in six, eight, or another number of bars, but still preserving this three-chord/two-line pattern), the objective of a blues song comes down to the following stable elements: (1) the self-exposition of an emotional subject, often developing dialogically (which means beginning in one mood and concluding in another), (2) the bond established between singer and audience, and (3) the insistent message about a weight that needs lifting.

This is what allows the blues form to captivate thousands of listeners in an immense range of very different societies that have heard the same tale repeated a hundred times. The stable strategies of the blues forge social, cultural, and thematic bridges with each new performance, calling and responding across a divide.

An Emotional Turnaround

Singing and hearing the blues takes us across those bridges. The songs, originally voiced by the oppressed black race in white America, do not make philosophical claims. They portray simple and typical plights. They tell tales that are concrete and anecdotal—about being down on one's luck, not having a penny, living on the road, erotic betrayal, being unjustly imprisoned. Both bluntly personal and socially generic, this music sings of pain and distress with no permanent resolution, of problems with which one can only learn to cope. The irresolvability of these collective dilemmas is the justification for the recursive melodies of the blues.

Yet the blues would not have achieved worldwide appeal if all it did was sound a repetitive dirge. No matter how individualized the experiences related in a song, what is decisive is that they are voiced by a member of the same listening community or at least a community that is seen as shared. The effect is an emotional turnaround on both sides. This is how the blues transformed the function of two vocal processings of deep African American burdens—one on the fields of slave labor and the other in the consolatory arms of Church gospels. Sung after backbreaking work, in evening gatherings to drink and dance, the songs—however despondent their premise—could only prove heartening. Their uplifting effect activates the ancient principle of tragic aesthetics, where the ability to reflect on one's condition—framing it and calling it into intellectual awareness—puts one in a position to control it. "When I'm down, I drive the hearse," sing Porcupine Tree (*The Incident*, 2009) in a different context: One lightens one's load through an act of psychological mirroring and projection of oneself into worse conditions. The *representation* of damaging experience is key, calling out and asserting the problem that needs addressing, inciting the subject to resist or take action. The transposition of experience into mind affirms the value and power of the "I" that bears the burden.

Formulated as "this is my own unique case," the blues song also inevitably externalizes feelings shared by its audience. Whether in desolate rural countrysides or urban clubs, the disconsolate "I" of a blues performance is read as a "we," drawing performers and audience together, binding a solitary mind to a collective one. Innerness pulled into public space has a cathartic, consolatory effect (bringing solace together, producing it by means of one another). In the early performative contexts of the blues, interaction and improvisation would have played a key role in the therapy. A single listening humorist is all that it took to make light of the singer's grief. It is easy to imagine that the bridges at the end of the tercets (the responses to the calls) were originally supplied by a different voice in the audience, casting the grief into new perspective:

> I'm gon' get up in the morning, believe I'll dust my broom.
> I'm gon' get up in the morning, believe I'll dust my broom.
> Girlfriend the black man you been lovin', girlfriend, can get my room.
>
> (ROBERT JOHNSON, "I BELIEVE I'LL DUST MY BROOM," 1936)

> You know you shook me, shook me all night long.
> You know you shook me, shook me all night long.
> Oh, you kept on shakin' me, darling, you messed up my happy home.
>
> (WILLIE DIXON AND J. B. LENOIR, "YOU SHOOK ME," 1962)

The blues performance creates a dialogue between a musical voice and a social voice, a reciprocal, antiphonal exchange. Self-criticism, irony, and gestures of bravura frequently enter the lyrics, singers boasting of being none the worse for their misfortunes. Tales of abandonment and betrayal in love simultaneously allude to sexual prowess and plans for vengeance. Puns and linguistic mischief produce emotional transference, bridging the gap between dejection and joy. Psychological shifts at the ends of verses draw singer and audience to eye-opening conclusions. The singer's state of mind crosses over to the space of the audience, the audience answers, and both receive mutual support.

Blues in Transit

The blues exchange occurred not just from individual to community but from gender to gender, from race to race, and from culture to culture. The transmission was vastly multiplied by vinyl recordings. They liberated human voices from corporeal persons and live, interactive events. An originally exogenous and socially circumscribed music—practiced by groups living outside their place of origin (Africa), vocalizing to one another the effects of that outsideness—suddenly reached thousands of like-minded subjects and groups. It gained international appeal, undergoing several migrations on the way.

The first migration, as already suggested, lay in the move from the field hollers of American slaves to the blues music of their freed descendants. The second occurred in communication between men and women, through the sexual substance of the lyrics and the dynamics of the musical performance. The third crossing took place from black to white performers, who had already appropriated many features of the blues in the 1930s and adapted them for a mass audience by 1960. This also meant a transfer from one community to another, in two-way direction. The fourth migration crossed the Atlantic. A fifth brought the music back home to America in British attire. All were linked by a subtle art of processing grief.

The first popularization of the blues was brought about by the vinyl recordings of women singers in the 1920s. Although men were the primary performers in the Mississippi Delta, urban audiences favored the renditions of women. Jelly Roll Morton claims that the first blues he ever heard was sung by a prostitute called Mamie Desdunes around 1900 in New Orleans. She prepared the way for Mamie Smith, Ma Rainey, Bessie Smith, Ethel Waters, Victoria Spivey, and many others. This female blues specialized in bawdy love appeals to men, often suggesting that they, the women, were fully entitled to their own sexual satisfaction. Was this a license accorded to the seemingly gentler gender or was it grafted onto it by male desire, catering (frequently in the words of male composers) to what men wanted to hear? African American bluesmen had to be more circumspect with their lust if they wanted to dodge the risk of violent reprisals by male rivals—like Robert Johnson, poisoned, legend tells us, by the husband of one of his lovers. The female blues was encouraged to explore pointed, innuendo-filled sensual lyrics, amplified over time by the likes of Alberta Hunter, Koko Taylor, Etta James, and Bonnie Raitt. As early as the 1930s the popular recordings by urban blueswomen began to leave a mark on the delivery styles of rural male blues performers in the Delta.[35]

Between 1920 and 1940, then, the blues was a two-way affair, from one gender to the other and back again. Men and women interacted within the performances and the lyrics of the songs as well as recordings. Just as the moods of singer and audience were jointly affected, so too were the gendered renditions of the blues, migrating from small live groups to solitary phonograph listening, and from country to city, where the conventions of the genre continued to develop.

The most radical crossing of musical territory was racial and transcontinental. Through records the blues bridge spanned the ocean, moving from American blacks to British whites, and laying another way home for the music to both races in America. How did a form so geoculturally autochthonous find such resonance across the Atlantic? With what cultural right did white Britons, who were so different from Amiri Baraka's "blues people," appropriate a form rooted in racial, social, and economic inequity? They did so by assuming the right to listen, following in the wake of a behind-the-scenes, white-led blues excavation that gained traction in the early 1960s.[36]

It was not the first time. Black-to-white transfer had already occurred in country music of the 1930s and rock and roll of the 1950s, where it moved from the likes of Chuck Berry to Bill Haley and Elvis Presley and then on to soul. But there was a difference. Rock and roll was not as dissonant and dissident to the white community as the blues, not half as alien, burdened, and ridden with tension. Rock and roll music was backed by solid commercial support, catering to the dance-oriented energies of a sensual, self-affirming youth. Its rhythms and lyrics were upbeat and good-humored; those of the blues were doleful and steeped in ethnic idiolect. In the early 1960s there was hardly an American white audience at all for Muddy Waters, Howlin' Wolf, Sonny Boy Williamson, and John Lee Hooker. They had all been recorded on "race records," marketed directly to African Americans.

The story of how Britain "got the blues" has been told many times over.[37] It begins with the airing of the race records over American military radio in Europe and by black GIs disembarking in the British Isles after World War II. That develops into an enthusiastic embrace refashioning the blues in a form that makes it more palatable to Americans in a shape no longer indigenous. When blues records reached Europe and the British Isles they were heard with much less semiotic interference than at home; they did not resonate with the bitter tensions evident to Americans both black and white. Oceanic distance between emitter and receiver allowed the foreignness of the work to register in all its fascination. To European ears, the blues had the exotic appeal of an immigrant never before seen.

Invited to appear on the American television show *Shindig* in 1965, the Rolling Stones agreed only on the condition that the blues master Howlin' Wolf, whose songs they covered, would be invited to perform alongside them. Now barely two months had passed since Bloody Sunday on Edmund Pettus Bridge (March 7, 1965), when hundreds of African Americans came under attack in the company of Martin Luther King Jr. on their march from Selma to Montgomery. Averse to the Stones' request, the producers of the white-audience *Shindig* did finally yield. By doing so they helped build another bridge—a small but significant symbolic step along a much larger trajectory envisioned by the Reverend King, revalidating a major part of America's culture.

"The strange thing was, we had gone to what I considered to be the home of the blues, but they'd never heard of most of them, and I couldn't believe it—'Big Bill who?' . . . We were recycling American music and they were calling it the English sound."[38] These words of Alvin Lee, guitarist of Ten Years After, recall the band's first U.S. tour in 1968. Big Bill Broonzy was just one of a dozen bluesmen—with Albert, B. B., and Freddie King, Magic Sam, Otis Rush, J. B. Lenoir, Willie Dixon, Otis Spann, Buddy Guy, and Junior Wells, to say nothing of their predecessors—who were now coming into white American sight. The mediating effects of the Animals and the Yardbirds, Manfred Mann and Them, the Spencer Davis Group and Ten Years After, along with British recording labels like Mike Vernon's Blue Horizon, directed attention to the black American foundations of these transatlantic recordings.

Admittedly, the blues masters did not prove as appealing in America as they did to connoisseurs in Europe. The sonic versions of the British were preferred by far, embodied as they were in socially progressive and more conventionally sexy young men. There the blues shed most of its racial briars. The new performers did not ignore those briars, however; they transposed them into other communities of feeling. The British, less defended against the racial and sociological otherness of the blues singers, read their own crises and postwar sufferings into the song templates. "Now I didn't feel I had any identity," says Eric Clapton, "and the first time I heard blues music, it was like the crying of a soul to me. I immediately identified with it. It was the first time I'd heard anything akin to how I was feeling, which was an inner poverty. It stirred me quite blindly. I wasn't sure just why I wanted to play it, but I felt completely in tune."[39] The recasting of the soul-crying into British blues-rock proved bewitching on account of a combination of important cosmetic changes, different conditions of performance, a downplaying of race, and the aestheticizing of the blues experience within an international culture of charismatic sexuality. The blues that had come to Britain were loose forms, not precisely codified or centrally managed. They ranged from one-man acoustic performances to urban, jazz-inflected renditions and electric combos in Chicago. With variants in eight, six, and sixteen bars, the I-IV-V songs were improvised with idiosyncrasies by musicians recorded on the cheap. In England a different and polished product arose from better economic and more expansive social conditions. It reworked the rough-hewn blues in sophisticated recording studios, chiseled by sometimes virtuoso instrumentalists and performed in swinging youth clubs. This all took shape in a culture of fusion; it culminated in that incarnation of the continental blues-crossing called Jimi Hendrix, his image and style preened in London between 1966 and

1968. His critical companions included Cream and Peter Green's Fleetwood Mac, Savoy Brown and Chicken Shack, Rory Gallagher's Taste and ultimately Led Zeppelin, with its often uncredited borrowings. Earlier even than this, a bridgehead for the blues had been laid on the British Isles by John Mayall, Alex Korner, and Cyril Davis, who added their own originals to standards.

In the meantime psychedelic, hippie, and hybrid musicians were also reproposing the blues in the United States, most notably the Paul Butterfield Blues Band (1965–66), which played with Muddy Waters, Otis Rush, and other blues masters in Chicago. By 1967 basic features of blues music had become embedded in The Doors, Big Brother and the Holding Company, and white interpreters like Canned Heat and Johnny Winter. Home and abroad, cultural transfusions had put an end to the music's insularity.

The material bridge to limitless listeners was built by the recording industry, converting a performative event into fixed, disembodied renditions dispatched into acoustic migration. One example points to how intricate the ethnocultural relations of the process could be. Europeans would never have had an occasion to be inspired by the black artists of Chicago were it not for two white Jewish brothers who thought that the city's street and club performers, including Wolf, Muddy Waters, and many others, were important enough to record. Penniless sons of Polish refugees, Leonard and Phil Chess created vinyl pressings of their products on a label they called Chess Records. Beyond modest commercial intentions, the Chess brothers were decisively moved by the spirit emanating from this music. Poland had its own strains of folk dirge, not to mention its own share of poverty and itinerant bards. The brothers saw common ground in the blues they recorded for others to hear. So did Alan Lomax, the ethnomusicologist and reader of Nietzsche, as well as the German promoters of the American Folk Blues Festivals in Europe in the 1960s, many of them filmed. Technology built a blues-bridge to Europe, where it struck the aforementioned chords and inspired emulation. "Your music," says the front man of an Irish band playing African American music in the novel *The Commitments* by Roddy Doyle (1987), "should be abou' where you're from an' the sort o' people yeh come from. . . .—The Irish are the n——ers of Europe, lads. . . . An' Dubliners are the n——ers of Ireland. . . . An' the northside Dubliners are the n——ers o' Dublin.—Say it loud, I'm black an' I'm proud."[40]

In the same spirit a Jewish lad from the East End of London gravitated to the blues and became one of its most distinguished performers. Peter Green, born Greenbaum in 1946, the author of "Black Magic Woman," lifted himself out of the meat-packing business to apprentice with John Mayall and then form Fleetwood Mac in 1967. Three years later, just when they were on the verge of superstar status, he quit the band, considering their amassment of profits and thefts from the American bluesmen obscene. A deep feeling of personal oppression had led him to the blues to begin with and later, after leaving Fleetwood Mac, to living in a cardboard box on the street. His fellow band member Danny Kirwan also became homeless. Interviewed in a shelter, Kirwan invoked the old legend of the blues being the work of the devil and claiming one's soul at a crossroads. Whenever a white man sings the blues, Kirwan claimed, he is full aware that "he might do himself damage."[41] The truth may be closer to the opposite. The damage, irrespective of race and color, comes first. It can lead to the bridge of the blues, and the bridge can help mend it.

CHAPTER 4

Bridge Brothers and Foes

Les Frères Pontifes

The earlier chapter "The Great Bridge-Building of God" examined portals to a spiritual domain, or human structures of transcendence. Real, material bridges often call for movement in the opposite direction, from the heavens down to the earth. Innumerable bridges in history have required the assistance of immortal spirits to be assured of solid foundations. From the depths of Christian medieval history comes a stirring story about the constructive devotion of a group of friars—the *frères pontifes* or bridge-building brothers—to projects they saw coming from the Father Almighty. Tellers and retellers of the tale have depicted them as a small confraternity that eased the travels of pilgrims by creating passageways to Rome and other sacred sites over streams and roaring rivers. In 1818 the Abbé Grégoire explains the mission of these pontiff brothers as follows:

> To lodge travellers, to care for them if ill, to facilitate their way across rivers, to escort them and lend them a strong hand against the aggression of brigands, who often formed themselves into bands in those times of anarchy, to construct bridges, ferries, dykes, roads, such were the continual occupations of the bridge-building brothers, who contributed in this way to develop several branches of industry and were in several ways restorers of architecture and commerce.[1]

The story of these bridge-building brothers originates in 1177, when a twelve-year-old sheepherder receives a vision enjoining him to build a bridge across the great Rhone River at Avignon. Bénézet by name, the boy descends the mountain and relays his charge to the inhabitants of the city. Immediately he meets with ridicule. But divine inspiration is not so easily dispelled. Bénézet proves the credibility of his charge by hurling into the river a boulder that takes thirty men to lift. As angels guard his flock, he receives secular permission to build a stone bridge at Avignon, nearly a kilometer long, singlehandedly. (The four standing arches and piles of the 1177–84 bridge rest on the foundations of a preexisting Roman bridge; this may help explain the rapidity with which this oldest medieval bridge in France was built.)

Other miracles occur over the course of Bénézet's brief life. The deaf regain their hearing and the blind their sight. Sponsors of the faith thus flock to fund the operations of the bridge of Bénézet. Soon a Bridge-Building Brotherhood—the *frères pontifes*, or *fratres pontifices* –is formed and it repeats his enterprise over other rivers in France and Italy. The boy Bénézet, the legendary founder of the brotherhood, dies at age nineteen, is interred in a chapel on the bridge itself, and canonized. Every pope who has crossed the Avignon Bridge over the last eight hundred years has stopped at his chapel to give alms and pray. Within a century and a half after its construction, or between 1309 and 1377, the papacy itself was transferred to the city. Seven consecutive French popes took residence in Avignon (plus two antipopes between 1378 and 1403).

While an early record of the prodigious feats of St. Bénézet lies in a thirteenth-century parchment, the bulk of the details are supplied by a seventeenth-century biography by the Jesuit Théophile Raynaud. More ample documentation exists for the *frères pontifes*, including several scholarly studies in the nineteenth century. A papal bull of 1245 notes that Bénézet's confraternity began and nearly completed another bridge across the Rhone River at Lyons (but the seal of Pope Innocent IV on the bull as well as the date "are evidently forgeries," asserts Nikolaus Paulus).[2] Bénézet and his companions were also credited with the construction of the third great bridge across the Rhone, the Pont-Saint-Esprit, and their order is said to have spread throughout Spain, Scotland, and other countries. The members of their community, writes the nineteenth-century scholar Georg Ratzinger, "pledged themselves with a vow to protect merchants and travelers from being plundered, to take them across the rivers free of charge, to build hospices for the sick and poor travelers on the river banks and in remote regions, and to construct bridges and roads."[3] The Bridge Brothers of Avignon appear also to have evolved into (or joined) the Italian Brothers of St. James of Altopascio in Tuscany, remembered for an extraordinary hospital and their care for the sick.

Not all the legends about the activities of the Bridge Brothers of Avignon bear scrupulous historiographical analysis. The appellation *frères pontifes*, or *fratres pontifices*, was applied to different associations of people "that the same need called into being at different places at the same time."[4] The very oldest such society in France predated Bénézet by a century. They were the Brothers of Bonpas, who may have bridged the river Durance in 1084. Originally the bridge-building societies may not even have been religious orders, at least if by religious orders we understand groups vowed to chastity, poverty, and obedience (although it is also true, as James Brodman notes, that norms for religious orders were not articulated before the thirteenth century).[5] Even so the Avignon association did live together as a community of mixed brothers and sisters. Documents from 1196 and 1208 mention their refectory and dormitory, their chapel and cemetery, the habit they wore, and the fact that the head of the confraternity was named a "prior." Confraternities like the one at Avignon did not call themselves *fratres pontifices*, but merely "Brothers of the Bridge at Avignon, of the Bridge at Lyons, and so forth. The name 'fratres pontifices' is first found among later authors."[6] Their main function may not have been to build bridges per se, but to collect alms for their building and upkeep, for ferries across the Rhone, and later for the management of hospices.

Still the ties between these confraternities and the Roman Church were automatic, for in the European Middle Ages "the building of a bridge was valued next to the building of a church." The church sanctioned the construction of bridges as "a most meritorious work" and "papal and episcopal indulgences were granted therefor" by the middle of the twelfth century.[7] Theologians justified these indulgences, or reductions of penance for sinners, on the same principle that justified feeding the hungry, giving drink to the thirsty, clothing the naked, and harboring the stranger. The actions were rewarded for the sheer good they did one's neighbor. They were prized for the favor they bestowed on their benefactors as well as the church, manifested by the prayers of succored neighbors and their reciprocated good works.

The bridges that were financed with alms lay along pilgrimage routes to Rome, where the brothers of the bridge sustained their service by managing *xenodòchi*, or hospices, for travelers at river fords. On this there is solid consensus, as there is on the indispensable backing of the church for the founding and safeguarding of such hospitals, where friars or monks provided free food and shelter for journeymen and pilgrims.[8]

The Devil's Bridge

There is also consensus—or there was in the European Middle Ages—that it was hardly possible to construct bridges like these without spiritual sanction. The nature of the structures invited continual disaster. A mere misstep on a bridge by a worker or passerby would spell instant death. Poor engineering, poor maintenance, and the wearing of time would make bridges collapse. They could be suddenly washed away by floods both before and after they were built. Only wizards were thought capable of making bridges stand; human ingenuity alone was not enough. It was wisest to begin by propitiating supernatural opposition to the construction of a bridge, whether expressed by demons of the river or the devil himself, who exacted tolls for its successful completion. The collusion between bridge-building and great powers of light or darkness is evidenced by stories told the world over about sacrificial victims immured in the foundations of bridges as well as by the pancultural name "Devil's Bridge" given to every manner of perilous overpass.

As they opened artificial passageways, bridges made natural defenses vulnerable. Fortified chatelets and towers were built at their entrances. At their foot lay talismanic, protective icons of Januses and herms, guarding against the unauthorized crossover of spirits from one side to the other. It was as though demonic forces were involved not only in bridging what nature had chosen to separate but in enabling the comings and goings on these structures. The idea that a bridge contravenes a natural interdiction against walking over a body of water from one bank to another informs folktales, legends, poems, and reputedly even some of the architectonics of bridges like the zigzag designs of China (fig. 4.1). Oral traditions, often dismissed as nonsense by Chinese scholars, have explained that these crooked bridges are designed

Figure 4.1. 24 Bridge, Slender West Lake, Yangzhou, China.
zhangyuqiu / Shutterstock.com

to confound evil spirits, forcing them to bang up against the angled parapets as they struggle mindlessly to move forward in a straight line. Perhaps the interpretation is foisted on China and Japan by the traditions in the British Isles, where bridges were often said to bewilder spirits and witches and came accompanied in the popular imagination by colorful narratives about the hazards the spirits posed to unwary wayfarers. Tam o'Shanter's narrow escape on horseback from witches over the Brig o'Doon was attributed to the conviction that evil spirits were thought unable to follow their victims past the middle of a running stream. The most famous telling of the tale is by Robert Burns in his poem "Tam o'Shanter" of 1791.

Given the unnatural peril entailed in breaching an aqueous division between lands, river communities almost always opposed projects to replace ferry crossings with bridges. The novel *The Three-Arched Bridge* (1978) by Ismail Kadare delivers a rich description of this radical ordeal. As one might expect, the most vociferous objection to the construction of the fourteenth-century bridge that Kadare describes comes from ferrymen with vested interests. An even deeper level of resistance is lodged in local superstition. In medieval villages like the one in this novel, the grave danger of a bridge lies in the desecrating nature of the new technology itself, stirring a rebellion in the "Wicked Waters River" (Ujana e Keqe) that it crosses. In this respect Kadare's story is archetypical. Even when medieval bridges have the backing of a holy man or saint like Bénézet, they still must vanquish the forces of darkness to achieve their purpose.

Kadare situates the Albanian bridge project in the Muslim culture of southeastern Europe and envelops it in an atmosphere of august, arcane undertakings. Its architects seem quasi-demonic beings whose mental processes are beyond the comprehension of everyday people, proceeding with their task almost in a state of trance. (Ivo Andrić gives a similarly compelling picture of the master builder not in his great novel about Višegrad, but in his story of 1925, *The Bridge on the Žepa.*) The construction of Kadare's three-arched bridge, a fictitious exemplar of many Ottoman bridges in Albania (none of which predates the seventeenth century, however; an eighteenth-century one can be seen in fig. 4.2), begins when a stranger appears out of nowhere at the banks of the river, disappears into a hut, and then "emerged on the third day" as though from a tomb. He had a "tousled, tightly curled mop of red hair, and pockmarked cheeks," with eyes that "somehow seem not to allow you to look straight into them. A sick gleam that appeared as soon as you caught his eye would totally confuse you."[9]

A single local gravitates toward the master builder once the

Figure 4.2. Mesi Bridge (1768), spanning the Kir River in Albania.
ShkelzenRexha / Wikimedia Commons

construction is under way: the idiot Gjelosh, making incomprehensible signs with his hands while the shadows of his limbs perform an improvised dance over the spine of the devilish bridge. The old woman Ajkuna calls it "Beelzebub's backbone" and prophesies nothing but ill for the bridge. Its sponsors are no more reassuring than its architect. After "buying up the great western highway that had once been called the Via Egnatia," they journey without rest for more than three months and appear before the villagers speaking a Babelic combination of tongues brought over from the same lands they had purchased. They make mathematical calculations in eleven languages. The raft that the bridge is intended to replace has demonic associations as well. It is moored beside "crosses on the bank for every person drowned" and is steered by a "hunchbacked ferryman."[10]

This feeling of menace and unfathomable intent is inextricable from the Faustian impulse driving the construction of the bridge and the bargain that must be struck with the devil to bring it about. The paradigmatic European narrative, familiar to most of Kadare's readers, tells of the devil being incensed by bridge construction and destroying its progress by night until the builders promise the fiend something—at least the soul of the first creature to cross. Sometimes the dilemma of this sacrifice is resolved by a trick. The devil expects a human to cross, while the townsfolk devise to have the first creature be a chicken or a dog, goading it over by throwing onto the bridge a loaf of bread. James Joyce tells of the use of a cat for the bargain at Beaugency Bridge.[11] In the best of cases this ends the traumatic pact. But the legend survives.

Figure 4.3. Ponte della Maddalena, or the Devil's Bridge, across the Serchio River near Borgo a Mozzano, Italy. Probably commissioned by the Countess Matilda of Tuscany between 1080 and 1100, it was renovated in the early fourteenth century.
Chiara Boracchi / Pexels

Bridges that are narrow and arched like a donkey's spine, or cling to peaks in the mountains, suspended over vertiginous spaces, are still called the Devil's Bridge. Dozens dot Europe from the Alps south—over the Natisone in Cividale, the Stura in Lanzo, and the Serchio near Borgo a Mozzano (fig. 4.3). They include the Saracen Bridge near Marineo, the Devil's Bridge over the Reuss, the covered bridge over the Ticino in Pavia, and many more.

Demonic pontification rarely ends happily for humans. The devil often gets what he wants. One way he exacts his toll is by getting the villagers to perform the ritual of walling a live person into bridge masonry. This immurement typically favors a child or woman. Beyond propitiating the demon, the practice would also have appeared to grant an animating and protective power of life to the structure. A symbolic birth, claims Mircea Eliade, is thereby "brought about by an immolation."[12] The strongest union between natural fertility and artificial construction would be produced by using a young mother as sacrificial victim.

In a recurring version of the South European bridge-building story, the mother pleads to be allowed to stick one of her breasts out from a wall in the bridge to continue suckling her newborn child. Kadare takes inspiration for his variant on the topos from the tale of the immured mother in his native Albanian legend of Rozafa Castle. There the immured woman wants not only to keep her right breast exposed to feed her infant, but also "her right eye to see him, her right hand to caress him and her right foot to rock her son's cradle."[13] Ivo Andrić had given a similar version of the story in *The Bridge over the Drina*. Following the mysterious destruction each and every night of what the masons of the Ottoman bridge had erected during the day,

> "something" had whispered from the waters and counselled Rade the Mason to find two infant children, twins, brother and sister, named Stoja and Ostoja, and wall them into the central pier of the bridge. . . . The children were walled into the pier, for it could not be otherwise, but Rade, they say, had pity on them and left openings in the pier through which the unhappy mother could feed her sacrificed children. Those are the finely carved blind windows, narrow as loopholes, in which the wild doves now nest. In memory of that, the mother's milk has flowed from those walls for hundreds of years. That is the thin white stream which, at certain times of year, flows from that faultless masonry and leaves an indelible mark on the stone. . . . Men scrape those milky traces off the piers and sell them as medicinal powder to women who have no milk after giving birth.[14]

In "Ballad of the Bridge at Arta," of which variants exist throughout the Balkans, the sacrifice calls not for just any woman or bride, but for the master builder's own wife (fig. 4.4). The song makes no mystery of the fact that this ritual of immuring the architect's wife intends to balance, respond to, and compensate the man's technical ingenuity by way of the woman and her forces of nature; but more study of the ghastly relationship of the two genders of production is required.[15] While being walled up, the young wife issues a passionate curse on the bridge and those who use it: "As my heart is shaking, so may the bridge shake; / and as my hair is falling out, so may those passing over fall off." In most variants of this ballad the wife's curse is ultimately recanted or neutralized, haunting future imaginations but not taking effect, though she still loses her life. The devil and his bridge-builders prove victorious.

The Walled-up Albanian

Few archaic bridges were immune to mortal tolls, no more than the construction of contemporary bridges. But ritual sacrifices in medieval bridge-building aimed proactively to satisfy or provide metaphysical justification for deaths still to come. A simple shift in perspective was all it took to make the bridge's motivating spirit appear to be God rather than Satan—or vice versa, which is the twist given political inflection

Figure 4.4. Bridge of Arta, Greece (Ottoman, early seventeenth century). Frédéric Boissonnas (1913)

in Kadare's *Three-Arched Bridge*. His bridge, like the two about which Andrić writes before him, is the work of the Ottomans. And that makes it an instrument, as Kadare sees it, in a diabolical conquest of south-central Europe.[16]

Reared as he was in the Marxist-Leninist People's Republic of Albania—a country touted by its dictator Enver Hoxha to be the "world's first atheist state"—Kadare is perfectly explicit in his hostility. Although Andrić's earlier *Bridge over the Drina* is more appreciative of these Balkan bridges, its description of Ottomans impaling a Serb alive on the Višegrad bridge inspired compatriots in Bosnia-Herzegovina to accuse him of demonizing the Muslim bridge-builders and their regional descendants (supporting their accusation with evidence from his academic dissertation, *The Development of Spiritual Life in Bosnia under the Influence of Turkish Rule*, 1924).

The Catholic monk Gjon, Kadare's narrator, often suggests that this fourteenth-century bridge in Albania did nothing but precipitate the doom-bringing occupation of the Ottomans. A bridge that others might view as a means of integration portended a frightful erasure of Albanian autonomy, letting world-leveling imperial forces prevail against natural and cultural defenses. The initiative for the construction extended beyond the profiteering motives of the infidels. It was supported by sinister forces of global capital, mobilized by a plan to rationally manage the earth's raw materials. Facilitating the Ottoman domination of south-central Europe, the bridge was created following the orders of a faceless rich Western businessman. He surfaced roads, sold tar to the Ottomans to help them shore up their naval military ports, and owned several banks.[17] This bridge was projected, commissioned, and financed by the budding medieval force of European capital. Perplexed by the technology brought into play, the monk Gjon could not fathom that this bridge was linked to "a new order that would carry the world many centuries forward." That new order, the master architect explains, involves

> the opening of new banks in Durrës, growing numbers of Jewish and Italian intermediaries dealing in twenty-seven different kinds of coin, and the almost universal acceptance of the Venetian ducat as a form of international currency. There was also the increasingly heavy traffic of merchant caravans, the organization of trade fairs, and especially (Oh Lord! How he emphasized that word "especially"), especially the construction of roads and stone bridges. And all this movement, he said, was a sign simultaneously of life and death, of the birth of a new world and the death of the old. (101)

Even as it shows the birth of capitalism out of the spirit of medieval European mercantilism, the three-arched bridge of 1377 reflects the sufferings of Kadare's contemporary Albania. To vanquish natural and communal resistance, the Ottoman bridge had to wall up an Albanian man within it. Quashed between the forces of a Muslim East and a capitalist West, the victim represents a tiny principality overrun by overwhelmingly advantaged world powers. The walled-up Albanian is even Christological. Faced with the power of these massive political forces, the reigning count of the Albanian territory withdrew to one side and did "nothing but wash his hands like Pontius Pilate" (122). Thus the bridge-builders plaster the Albanian man into the bridge center in such a way as to let the public behold his naked torso and open eyes. By doing so, they also deny him transition to the afterlife. The very *unburiedness* of the man, exclaims the monk in horror, "was something that violated everything we knew about the orders between life and death. The man remained poised between the two like a bridge, without moving in one direction or the other" (128).

The strange fusion of Christological and anti-imperial politics in this book thus returns us to earlier themes. In Roman times the absence of a bridge between death and life—the "irremeable" Styx River coursing between them, and preventing such a bridge—beckoned, or so it seemed to Hermann Broch, to the need for a radical or "crucial" (cross-like) Christian turn. The turn was signaled by Virgil, the pre-Christian guide of Dante. Broch's prescient Roman in *The Death of Virgil* could not abide the idea that death amounted only to a cessation of breath. It bordered a borderless afterlife—what the philosopher Anaximander called the *apeiron* and others cataloged as a primal chaos outside the known world of forms. The mistake of pragmatic, materialist pagans apparently lay in positing two categorically opposed ontologies of life and death between which *no bridge whatsoever was possible*. By failing to come to terms with *how to achieve* a life after death, they opened a chasm in which to reflect on death itself as a bridge—as a gateway to something more absolute.

Near the end of his chronicle Kadare's monk draws his three-arched bridge into the ambit of this larger perspective. He ties the construction of the bridge to a transcendent inspiration: "And suddenly it flashed into my mind," he reflects, after having vilified the structure throughout the novel, "that nothing other than a rainbow must have been the first sketch for a bridge, and the sky had for a long time been planting this primordial form in people's minds" (151). Actual, material, historical forms of that ideal, primordial bridge are rather immersed in violence, immurement, and political injustice. "A rainbow, the bridge's model and perhaps its inspiration, is something that . . . nobody yet knows how to build, and still less to chain in fetters; but is it not also something frightening, fragile, and incomprehensible to people?" (157). The monk's fear and lack of assurance suggests that the great bridge-building of God, which binds all differences together, is not to be achieved on earth. The novel appears marked by a premonition that these ethnic and cultural hostilities of 1377, between Ottomans and Albanians, would never properly be settled but rather would break out again—as they did in neighboring Kosovo, little more than a decade after Kadare's novel was published.

At the time of Kadare's writing in the 1970s, Albania was bordered by Yugoslavian Kosovo, an autonomous province inhabited predominantly by ethnic Albanians of Muslim confession. At the time of Kadare's novel, in the fourteenth century, Kosovo was instead the political and cultural hub of the Serbian kingdom. Half a millennium later, in the nineteenth century, things had changed again, with Kosovo spearheading the movement of Albanian national awakening. On the cusp of the twenty-first century, ethnic and ideological conflicts over the identity of the region exploded. Between February 1998 and June 1999, after the other Yugoslavian wars of Slovenia, Croatia, and Bosnia-Herzegovina had abated, Serb nationalists turned their attention to the autonomous province of Kosovo. A million inhabitants fled their homes.

Considering once again the date when the action of Kadare's novel takes place—1377—the mathematical sum adds up. The three-arched bridge was built twelve years before the ruling kingdom of Serbia suffered a crushing and definitive defeat at the hands of the Ottoman Turks (in the Battle of Kosovo of 1389). Serbia-Kosovo was overrun by Muslims in 1389, and Serbian nationalists took reparatory action six hundred years later, in 1998. After NATO bombs arrested the Serbian offensive, Kosovo was divided between two ethnically cleansed components—Albanian Kosovo on the one side and Serb North Kosovo on the other. Populations were driven at gunpoint from one side of the Ibar River to the other, the two sides then fortified by heavily armed sentinels to prevent incursions by the unwanted ethnic group. To this day the autonomous political units continue to face off on either side of the bridge in the border town of Kosovska Mitrovica.[18]

The paradigm for the Slavic bridge as flashpoint had been presented a few years earlier in Stari Most, the Old Bridge in Bosnia and Herzegovina, demolished during the Yugoslavian wars for no other reason, apparently, than its conciliatory symbolic value. It was located 200 kilometers from Andrić's bridge at Višegrad and was commissioned by Suleiman the Magnificent, designed by a student of the incomparable Ottoman architect Sinan called Hajruddin in 1566. Mostar, where it stood, was "a fully multi-ethnic, multi-confessional city" in which, apologists for unity write, approximately one-third of marriages were mixed and ethnic ghettos were unknown.[19] Here it was that the "cultural war crime" occurred that blasted the graceful bridge of Hajruddin to pieces.

First, as Serbian artillery and rocket-launched assaults besieged the town between April and June 1992, Croats and Bosniaks of Mostar banded together in defense. Then once the Serbs were repelled, Croat forces unexpectedly turned on their Muslim comrades—"rounding them up at gunpoint in the middle of the night, assembling them in detention camps," starving them, and killing two thousand between May 1993 and February 1994.[20] On November 9, 1993, Croat artillery fire targeted the old Ottoman bridge at Mostar. The demolition of this bridge carried no military objective at all. It simply crossed a line of division running between the Bosnian Christians and Muslims of the city, the Neretva River. The bridge of Stari Most was "a cultural symbol that did not fit with the narrative of Serbian or Croatian nationalists."[21]

History without Ears: The Bridge over the Drina

Kadare's concession that the rainbow might be the primordial model for human bridges pays tribute to that predecessor novel which is Andrić's

Bridge over the Drina. There is as much historical and human bereavement in Andrić's narrative as in Kadare's, indeed even more, but more faith in the bridge. In Bosnia, too, the river crossed by Andrić's bridge marks a frontier between the Ottoman and the Christian territories; but there is more hope invested in what this bridge can do.

The bridge over the Drina witnesses more strife than integrity over the four centuries that it spans. Yet it owes more to the rainbow-logic than Kadare's nefarious structure over "wicked waters." Andrić attributes its building to a spiritual need festering in its commissioner, the Ottoman ruler. The eleven-arched bridge still standing in the Bosnian town of Višegrad was devised not by a Turk but by a grand vezir. He was Sokollu Mehmed Paša, a Christian Serb, torn from his Slavic parents at the age of ten and forced to convert to Islam and to become an Ottoman Janissary. Eventually this Bajica Sokolović, as he may have originally been named, grew up to become the de facto ruler of the Turkish Empire between 1565 and 1579.

When the Grand Vezir Sokollu Mehmed ordered work to begin on the bridge in 1571, the political stakes were as high as ever for Ottoman foreign policy. The Turks had driven out the Venetians from their strategic outpost at Cyprus the very same year, a situation Shakespeare soon referenced in *Othello*. The Ottoman conquest provoked a massive Christian reaction: the Holy League, the formation of an anti-Turkish federation combining the armed forces of the Vatican, Spain, Naples, Sicily, the Republic of Venice, Genoa, Tuscany, and the Maltese Knights. On October 7, 1571, the league attacked and defeated the Turkish fleet at the Battle of Lepanto (Miguel de Cervantes being shot three times). Despite the great strain in Mediterranean relations at this time, Andrić does not factor in a political cause for the origin of the bridge, and properly so, for it was buried in Ottoman hinterlands. Rather, he assesses its social and personal, its everyday and long-term effects, alongside public works like fountains, mosques, and schools for which the Ottomans were praised.

In Andrić's telling, the reason the grand vezir built this transcultural bridge was essentially to repair a rift at the core of his being. Abducted and ferried across the Drina River as a boy on a cold November day, within a long file of guarded children helplessly pursued by their desperate mothers, the dark-skinned adolescent felt "a sharp stabbing pain" within him. Over the years the pain did not subside. On the contrary, it kept recurring and

> from time to time seemed suddenly to cut his chest in two and hurt terribly, which was always associated with the memory of that place

> where the road broke off, where desolation and despair were extinguished and remained on the stony banks of the river, across which the passage was so difficult, so expensive and so unsafe. It was here, at this particularly painful spot in that hilly and poverty-stricken district, in which misfortune was open and evident, that man was halted by powers stronger than he and, ashamed of his powerlessness, was forced to recognize more clearly his own misery and that of others, his own backwardness and that of others.[22]

Bajica Sokolović's traumatic experience of the ferry across the forbidding Drina River revealed the misery of the human condition to the grown Sokollu Mehmed—its helplessness, disunity, desolation, and despair. As he aged, the eradicated convert to Islam acquired a power that he lacked at the bank of the river. Yet the sting of separation kept returning and cut ever more deeply. The massive, long bridge over the Drina was its reparatory outcome.

Sokollu Mehmed believed that the black knifelike sensation might be abolished

> if he could do away with that ferry on the distant Drina, around which so much misery and inconvenience gathered and increased incessantly, and bridge the steep banks and the evil water between them, join the two ends of the road which was broken by the Drina and thus link safely and for ever Bosnia and the East, the place of his origin and the places of his life. Thus it was he who first, in a single moment behind closed eyelids, saw the firm graceful silhouette of the great stone bridge which was to be built there. (26)

Mehmed's bridge (fig. 4.5) offers the promise of mending a soulscape, and the "evil water" between its banks, overcoming its divisions, separations, and limitations.

Once the bridge was completed each inhabitant of Višegrad sensed the transcendent effect of its structure:

> Even the least of the townsmen felt as if his powers were suddenly multiplied, as if some wonderful, superhuman exploit was brought within the measure of his powers and within the limits of everyday life, as if besides the well-known elements of earth, water and sky, one more were open to him, as if by some beneficent effort each one of them could suddenly realize one of his dearest desires, that ancient dream of man—to go over the water and to be master of space. (66)

Figure 4.5. Bridge over the Drina (Mehmed Paša Sokolović Bridge, 1577), Višegrad, Bosnia and Herzegovina.
Vladimir Mijailović / Wikimedia Commons

This was the spiritual objective of the bridge over the Drina: to create new possibilities for human existence, perhaps even leading that existence to step beyond its limitations. There is tragic irony in the fact that, despite the intentions of the grand vezir, this bridge between Muslim and Christian worlds, instead of creating political unity, only marked conflict after conflict up to, and beyond, the time of the novel's composition. Not only were the bitter hostilities between Turks and Serbs from the fourteenth through the seventeenth centuries renewed in the nineteenth; they were accompanied by others between Turks and Austro-Hungarians, and then by wars between Serbs and Austro-Hungarians to either side of the Great War of 1914–18. Later, and to the surprise of Europe, came attacks of Serb nationalists on their Muslim compatriots in Bosnia in the 1990s. For nearly four hundred years the bridge of Andrić's novel remained more steadfast and reliable in purpose than the history that it witnessed, like being beneath the tremors of time.[23]

The supreme protagonist of Andrić's historical novel does not only outlive the communities that use it; it operates as a silent and transcendent judge of their actions. That is why the end of each of the twenty-four chapters of *The Bridge over the Drina* steps back from the mentality of the time it depicts, refocusing its attention on the material, geographical, and ontological solidity of the bridge, dazzlingly unchanged in its substance, offering a grand framing structure for history, erected by "great and wise men of exalted soul" for essentially nothing other than "the love of God." This is the ultimate perspective that is taken by Andrić's book, put into words by the Muslim sage Alihodja. It is he who delivers the novel's parable about why bridges, modeled on angels' wings, were built at all:

> When Allah the Merciful and Compassionate first created this world, the earth was smooth and even as a finely engraved plate. That displeased the devil who envied man this gift of God. And while the earth was still just as it had come from God's hands, damp and soft as unbaked clay, he stole up and scratched the face of God's earth with his nails as much and as deeply as he could. Therefore, the story says, deep rivers and ravines were formed which divided one district from another and kept men apart, preventing them from travelling on that earth that God had given them as a garden for their food and their support. And Allah felt pity when he saw what the Accursed One had done, but was not able to return to the task which the devil had spoiled with his nails, so he sent his angels to help men and make things easier for them. When the angels saw how unfortunate men could not pass those abysses and ravines to finish the work they had to do, but tormented themselves and looked in vain and shouted from one side to the other, they spread their wings above those places and men were able to cross. So men learned from the angels of God how to build bridges, and therefore, after fountains, the greatest blessing is to build a bridge and the greatest sin to interfere with it, for every bridge, from a tree trunk crossing a mountain stream to this great erection of Mehmed Pasha, has its guardian angel who cares for it and maintains it as long as God has ordained that it should stand.[24]

Yet the sage Alihodja is too optimistic: He becomes the novel's last victim on a bridge used by men for their narrow purposes. The significance of his parable about the function of bridges is tempered by his historical fate: During a political conflict, an anti-Muslim foe seizes Alihodja and nails him to the bridge by the ear. He is punished for being an idealist, just like the Apostle of Una Troy's novel discussed in my eighth chapter of this book. The bridge lauded by Alihodja turns into an instrument of torture. History and angel-bridges share little in common. Later conflicts in Bosnia would also ignore the soul-mending intentions of the Višegrad Bridge, despite the hopes the novel expresses at its conclusion. The work ends celebrating nascent Yugoslav self-consciousness in the first decades of the twentieth century, promising a resolution of the region's clashes between East and West, Muslim and Christian, Serb and

Croat—clashes that returned after the late-century dissolution of the Yugoslav Republic.

Finally, Andrić foresees the complicity of technology and industrial economy in antiangelic allegiance. By the time he is writing, that allegiance rendered the bridge-work of angels and humans obsolete through the construction of a 160-kilometer-long railroad adjacent to the Sokolović Bridge, "on which were about 100 bridges and viaducts and about 130 tunnels," where the substantial connections of Andrić's bridge were contrasted with the merely "functional-structural" ones of modernity.[25] What significance now attaches to the bridge of Andrić? The name Višegrad now evokes no more than xenophobic dissenters within the European Union called the Visegrád Four, a splinter group of former Soviet Union satellite states, named after not Andrić's town at all, but after a homonymous one in Hungary.

Even Balkan readers of Andrić's novel are prone to misreading its intentions, some finding within it a nationalist ideology that the writer expressed as a Yugoslavian statesman, one incapable of encompassing "the totality of contending ideologies in the Balkans."[26] The ultimate failure of Andrić's hopes became clear when the Socialist Federal Republic of Yugoslavia, founded in 1945 (the same year that the novel was published), experienced its breakup, and the ten-day war between Serbs and Slovenians (June–July 1991) was followed by the war between Serbs and Croats. Then what happened? A clandestine alliance between those groups in the Karadordevo meeting of March, 1991, led Serb and Croat nationalists to spill the blood of their Bosniak compatriots and carve up the republic of Bosnia-Herzegovina. At this point Andrić himself became a flashpoint in a war his novel could not have condoned, when massacres more gruesome than any described in the 350 years spanned by his novel occurred in his hometown of Višegrad. Perpetrators of the attacks on Bosnian Muslims in Višegrad justified the killings as retribution for something very clear: the vandalization in the town of a statue of Andrić, the Christian and Serbian bard of the bridge, a vandalization purportedly sparked by anti-Muslim sentiments attributed to the novel and more explicitly to Andrić's doctoral dissertation. To hear the other side, however, these works by Andrić, "who wrote some of the most lyrical passages about a multi-ethnic Bosnia, were edited by the Bosnian Serbs and selectively quoted to support ethnic cleansing."[27]

After two decades of war-trial testimony and collective archival study about the events in Bosnia, it is hard to find a historian moved by this rationalization—the vandalization of a statue—for the decimation of all but a handful of Višegrad's Muslims in 1992. Many were burned alive. Others were drowned in the Drina, shot in the air while being thrown off the great Višegrad bridge. Because they connect, bridges become props and public theaters of attack, observes war journalist Christopher Hedges.[28] To any group aiming to oppress its enemies, the ostensible bridge-building of God appears only to be the bridge-building of the devil. Operating without ears for future or past, history turns into a destroyer.

CHAPTER 5

Word Bridges

A Bridge of Dance and Song

We have Avignon's St. Bénézet to thank for associating bridges with singing and dancing. Or rather, it is a song *about* his bridge, "Sur le pont d'Avignon," that presents singing and dancing as bridge-building acts, linking human hands and voices in a communal chorus. The singing and dancing on his bridge came years after Bénézet, when the Avignonese appropriated the location for festivities. The first version of the song was composed in the sixteenth century and was called "Sus le pont d'Avignon": not on, but beneath, the Avignon Bridge. Less than five meters in width, Bénézet's bridge provides little space for dancing in the round. Joseph Roth indeed reports his amazement to see dancing depicted on it in an old engraving.[1] Greater breadth for revelry lies on the Barthelasse Island beneath the bridge, which still today is a site for fairs and folk dancing. Since its inauguration in 1184, the Avignon Bridge has provided shelter for revelers from the sun and rain, creating the pleasure of dancing beneath the bridge's protection.

The version of the song that French schoolchildren learn by heart dates from the nineteenth century and begins as follows, generating as many stanzas as one likes by substituting soldiers, musicians, gardeners, and other townsfolk for the "gentlemen" and "gentlewomen" first mentioned:

> Sur le pont d'Avignon
> L'on y danse, l'on y danse
> Sur le pont d'Avignon
> L'on y danse tout en rond
> Les beaux messieurs font comme ça
> Et puis encore comme ça.

Sur le pont d'Avignon
L'on y danse, l'on y danse
Sur le pont d'Avignon
L'on y danse tout en rond
Les belles dames font comme ça
Et puis encore comme ça.

On the bridge of Avignon
We all dance there, we all dance there
On the bridge of Avignon
We all dance there in a ring
The handsome gentlemen do like this
And then like that.

On the bridge of Avignon
We all dance there, we all dance there
On the bridge of Avignon
We all dance there in a ring
The beautiful ladies do like this
And then like that.

This song about dancing *produces* the dancing of which it sings, ringing people together into a circle without beginning or end. Linguistic arts of other types create a similar effect, some singing about the broader effects of song, some celebrating poetry within poetry, but all joining dimensions of human experience that would otherwise remain mute or disconnected.

The Smallest Cleft is the Hardest to Bridge

Nietzsche would have known "Sur le pont d'Avignon" as well as any schoolchild of his time. Some decades after the song's composition, he himself fuses bridge, song, and dance into a series of metaphors about the nature of language. They occur in a chapter of the third part of *Thus Spoke Zarathustra* called "The Convalescent," where the despondent philosopher stands on the verge of abandoning his mission of sharing his intellectual discoveries. What has brought him so low is the thought that everything that has happened so far in the world might recur *forever* in the forms it has taken, and in meaningless disconnection.

Having lain catatonic for a week, Zarathustra is slowly nursed back to good cheer through the mellifluous prattle of his animal companions. "Step out of your cave," they urge him,

> the world awaits you like a garden. The wind is playing with heavy fragrances that want to get to you, and all the brooks would run after you. All things have been longing for you, while you have remained alone for seven days. Step out of your cave! All things would be your physicians.[2]

Appreciating his animals' affection, Zarathustra is nonetheless skeptical about their harmonious visions of nature at play. He answers, no doubt with a smile on his face,

> O my animals, chatter on like this and let me listen. It is so refreshing for me to hear you chattering: where there is chattering, there the world lies before me like a garden. How lovely it is that there are words and sounds! Are not words and sounds rainbows and illusive bridges between things which are eternally apart? [*Regenbogen und Schein-Brücken zwischen Ewig-Geschiedenem?*]

In Zarathustra's view, things at bottom are endlessly at variance with one another, a condition not acknowledged by the intimate relationships into which sounds and words bring them. He explains:

> Precisely between what is most similar, illusion lies most beautifully; for the smallest cleft is the hardest to bridge. . . . But all sounds make us forget this; how lovely it is that we forget. Have not names and sounds been given to things that man might find things refreshing? Speaking is a beautiful folly: with that man dances over all things. How lovely is all talking, and all the deception of sounds! With sounds our love dances on many-hued rainbows.

These "many-hued rainbows" are all the more beautiful when they join things *that seem alike,* allowing minds to brush over small differences. In the suasive flow of sounds and words one fails to register clefts. How lovely, Zarathustra reflects, that we are able to forget the nonequivalence of things and imagine them working together. Mellifluous speech and song produce dancing among things brought together in continuity, in vibrantly colored links. The operation is sentimental and aesthetic rather than cognitively sound.

As he muses over the illusions tendered by his animal friends, Zarathustra gradually opens himself up to the concord of which they speak. "Where there is chattering, there the world lies before me like a garden," he echoes. Despite his intellectual misgivings about the truth value of these statements, Zarathustra lets his animals gain the upper hand in this chat. By its end the philosopher-prophet concedes that in order to convalesce he too must dance, sing, and rejoice about the turning over and over of the world, without rhyme or reason—the eternal recurrence of meaningless events which he has found so intellectually intolerable, which has broken his will to act.

His animals reject his dismissal of words as imaginary bridges: "To those who think as we do," they say, the world is not made up of infinite and insuperable solitudes. On the contrary,

> all things themselves are dancing; they come and offer their hands and laugh and flee—and come back. Everything goes, everything comes back; eternally rolls the wheel of being. . . . Everything breaks, everything is joined anew; eternally the same house of being is built.

Now, who would have thought this is where Heidegger took his idea of language as the house of being?[3] That entire house is built, or fabricated, from the speaking, singing, and dancing of language, joining what is eternally apart.

Zarathustra allows himself to be persuaded. He rises to the challenge of life affirmation, celebrating the creation/destruction of all things in perpetuity, turning and dancing on being's rolling wheel. Thanks to the speech of his animals Zarathustra recovers from his inability to find meaning in things. He begins to imagine the senseless recurrence of all being coming together. Zarathustra's *author*, on the other hand, struggles with the illusory effects of language his whole life long. The brilliance and pathos of his writing lie precisely in the balance that it achieves between a corrosive skepticism toward the unsatisfactory means of knowledge and an unflagging commitment to its philosophical ends. Perceptions and words are the means, reliable and verifiable truth its ends.

Hardly had Nietzsche finished his first book, *The Birth of Tragedy* (1872), than he postulated that language could neither seize nor communicate the continuities it seeks to establish: "Every concept originates through our equating what is unequal." Conceptual simplicity makes us see shapes on dissimilar trees as formal variations of one and the same phenomenon, "leaf." It is the power not only of concepts, but of creative "metaphors, metonyms, and anthropomorphisms," that allows us to do this.[4] Even at the very end of his career Nietzsche harbors an arsenal of doubts about the linguistic resources on which his mission of philosophy draws. *Dionysus Dithyrambs*, the final book he prepared for publication, opens with the self-accusatory poem, "Only A Fool! Only A Poet!" It suggests that each one of the philosopher's words—again associated with rainbows—is just the howl of a clown. As throughout the second half of *Zarathustra*, where the palinodic poem first appeared, the language used to pursue truth is a bridge of illusions and lies, a platform for intellectual revelry.

"Der *Wahrheit* Freier—du?" [The suitor of *truth*—you?"] the poem asks of its speaker, and answers:

> Nur Narr! Nur Dichter!
> Nur Buntes redend,
> aus Narrenlarven bunt herausredend,
> herumsteigend auf lügnerischen Wortbrücken,
> auf Lügen-Regenbogen
> zwischen falschen Himmeln
> herumschweifend, herumschleichend—
> *nur* Narr! *nur* Dichter! . . .[5]
>
> No! Only a fool! Only a poet!
> Only speaking in a motley way,
> only crying colorfully out of fools-masks
> climbing around on mendacious word-bridges,
> on misleading rainbows,
> between false heavens,
> roaming, stalking—
> *only* a fool! *only* a poet!

This motley fool is the same person placed on a bridge between animal and overman at the opening of *Zarathustra*. Now he is characterized as a thinker who knowingly lies, prowling along deceitful word bridges spanning false heavens and false earths. An earlier aphorism of Nietzsche had attempted to distinguish poets from more pedestrian *thinkers*: "The poet presents his thoughts festively, on the carriage of rhythm: usually because they are incapable of walking."[6] Anticipating the cavorting on multicolored rainbows of *Zarathustra*, these surfaces rolled over on poetic rides of rhyme would better be gauged by a surveyor's measured tread. But Nietzsche's later thinking does not discover a nonpoetic way to tread the ground.

Passages like these may be overly dismissive of poets. They do not develop the implications embedded in Nietzsche's own theory of words as bridges. For what is most interesting about language is *not* that its signs fail to seize the true nature of things, but that it articulates whatever nature we are *able* to understand—in and by means of its linking signs. This is what the ancient Greeks meant by *poiesis*—the creative making or fabrication of language. Not quite so ethereal a rainbow or bridge, creative language is the very ground of conceptual perception, prestructuring all significance that we discover in and by means of mentally apprehended things. Nietzsche acknowledges the paradoxical value of this rhetorical venue of poetry in a draft of notes for the same text in *Dionysus Dithyrambs*:

> Der Dichter, der lügen kann
> wissentlich, willentlich,
> der kann allein Wahrheit reden.[7]
>
> The poet, who can
> knowingly, willingly, lie,
> he alone can speak the truth.

Thus we must be suspicious of Nietzsche's thoughts on language as mere semblance and intellectual approximation. We, like his animals, must reevaluate the positive achievements of its semantic bridging.

Metaphoricity

The idea that linguistic knowledge is "over here" and the reality to which it refers over there, in some independent or prelinguistic condition, has been debunked since at least Wittgenstein's *Philosophical Investigations* (1953). That is an Adamic notion of language which sees us naming this or that thing "dog," "house," or "tree" and then stringing such concepts together to reflect a complex state of affairs that we already perceive. Though the word "dog" does refer to the quadruped, and the word "I" refers to the person uttering a sentence, both words receive actual meaning from the speech acts in which they occur. The result is a kind of conceptual scaffolding allowing for communicative passage from word to word—words that otherwise say little on their own.

Paul Valéry felt the effects of this unusual situation in each line of poetry that he wrote. The "strange condition of our verbal material," he notes, is this:

> Each and every word that enables us to leap so rapidly across the chasm of thought, and to follow the prompting of an idea that constructs its own expression, appears to me like one of those light planks which one throws across a ditch or a mountain crevasse and which will bear a man crossing it rapidly. But he must pass without weighing on it, without stopping—above all, he must not take

> it into his head to dance on the slender plank to test its resistance! ... Otherwise the fragile bridge tips or breaks immediately, and all is hurled into the depths.[8]

The difference between dancing on this bridge and traversing it swiftly is the difference between poetic and prosaic compositions. Prose gets its meaning across quickly and as efficiently as possible. Poetry gains intellectual rewards through risk. It makes an issue of the very "steps" that the mind takes, as Valéry here argues. It weighs upon words so heavily that the passage of thinking is obstructed, or at least slowed down. The outcome no longer makes easy, unequivocal sense.

Inspired no doubt by the essay of Valéry, Italo Calvino emphasizes another feature of this language-bridge. Many signs do not make reference to material things at all. More abstract in direction, they connect "visible trace with the invisible thing, the absent thing, the thing that is desired or feared, like a frail emergency bridge flung over an abyss."[9] Calvino is thus as preoccupied as Nietzsche by the great distance between a word and its referent: Language tries to name a reality over across an abyss, or unreachably deep down below. The frail bridge of language's platform makes it impossible to get to the bottom of the very words that we care about most, and that make most intellectual difference. Valéry gave "Life" and "Time" as examples, capitalizing them. Others that belong with them are "Love" and "Justice," "Truth" and "Rights."

Language, like music, links other things as well, like minds. It brings intelligences into contact, like Iris, the rainbow, and Hermes—both messengers of the gods—whose utterances must be decoded. The gaps between words themselves are accompanied by others: between the intentions of a mind and its expression, between an expression and its interpretation. We therefore have links between words and words (grammar), between words and their ultimate meanings (the concerns of poetry and philosophy), between minds and minds (in the communicative situation of speech acts). All of these relationships are implicit in Karl Jaspers's retort to Heidegger, discussed elsewhere in these pages, that language is less a house than a bridge of being.

All these aspects of language are, in a broad sense of the word, *metaphorical*. The word is compounded from the Greek *meta* + *pherein* and conveys the idea of carrying over, transporting, transferring. A leap takes place from word to word, and from sentence to sentence, and even earlier from feeling or thought to its proper articulation, and even before that from a person speaking to another listening. All are implicit in Hans Georg Gadamer's characterization of language as a "medium where I and world meet." There the world and I "manifest [our] original belonging together."[10] In language they reveal their copresence and first let themselves be distinguished, like the banks of a river. If hermeneutics, or the science of understanding, has a "main problem," as Paul Ricoeur claims, it lies in understanding the contours of this interactive space—the encounters, convergences, and interfusions on which meanings rely.[11]

Through that original, metaphorical encounter we come to entertain the notion of metaphor as a particular linguistic act, or more specifically the transference of the (literal and established) meaning of one word into the domain of another. This narrow understanding of metaphor sees it as a figure of speech "in which a term or phrase is applied to something to which it is not literally applicable in order to suggest a resemblance, as in *A mighty fortress is our God*."[12] This figure of speech would constitute an *exceptional* word-bridge—stretching a commonly accepted meaning to a place it doesn't "properly" belong. Yet the question that this limited understanding of metaphor begs is where "literal" or "proper" uses lie. Cognitive linguistics abundantly demonstrates that metaphorical bridges inform hundreds of everyday turns of phrase that we generally think are literal, like "I am filled with emotion" (where a person is conceived as a container and feelings as fluids).[13] The idea that there is a proper use of words—where "licking one's wounds" is properly applied to a cat—and then a metaphorical one—where suffering humans are spoken of through feline analogy—fails to take account of how many aspects of our thinking are structured metaphorically to begin with. At its deepest level metaphor is a conceptual rather than simply verbal linkage; it arises from a "sphere of shared attention" out of which speakers produce "sets of systematic correspondences, or mappings, between two domains of experience."[14] In the intersubjective space of these shared physical and cultural contexts, actions and phenomena are interrelated from the start. The idea of metaphor as a particular turn of phrase that embellishes a proposition we first think of literally, is a prosaic rather than a poetic conception of the language-bridge.

A broader understanding of metaphor casts into doubt even the distinction between thing and word, or *res* and *verbum*, that underpins Western science and reason—disciplines that "more or less began with the insight that a word is *only* a name," or a mere representation of being.[15] In earlier ways of thinking, thing and word were not different ontological realities. But then there came a point where "true being" was imagined to be something existing prior to words, which words then matched as best they could. Even Nietzsche occasionally gives in to that rational conception. His idea of words as bridge-structures constructed between things assumes that phenomena in their essence (as intuited or perceived) precede or are independent of their linguistic formulations. Gadamer's hermeneutical position instead stipulates that experience is intrinsically and primordially linguistic.

He therefore concludes that "the living metaphoricity of language" is the very thing "on which all natural concept formation depends."[16] Metaphoricity is a condition in which experiencing, feeling, and thinking register one thing inevitably in terms of another. It thus marks "the beginning of language," says Jacques Derrida. The quest for a final or proper meaning of our terms, leading us to cast aside one figurative pronouncement for another, is "the very movement of language" itself.[17] The movement determines the shape of thinking, which determines the shape of history. The narrow stylistic conception of metaphor is "only the rhetorical form of this universal—both linguistic and logical—generative principle."[18]

Thus it is that words generate new and different senses of the real. We say "something comes into language" in order to indicate a new understanding of being, accessing new regions of thought and action. Surely that is why Aristotle's *Poetics* claimed that the coining of metaphors was the most important poetic function of all. Without metaphors there would be no bridge to cross "from the minor truth of the seen to the major truth of the unseen," to say it with Ernest Fenollosa.[19]

Two for One

To understand this extended metaphoricity it helps to revisit the more narrow stylistic conception of metaphor. A traditional handbook of rhetoric might analyze the statement, *A mighty fortress is our God*, by identifying *God* as the primary subject and *fortress* as secondary—a predicate modifying the first. The interpreter would then "translate" the predicate into its most essential connotation ("protection") to come up with a sensible understanding of the claim. Once the substitution was completed, the initial discontinuity between the terms would be neutralized, leaving us to understand the crystalline paraphrase, "God protects us from our enemies." One could also give it a more complex variation: "Strong as a fortress, God cannot be successfully attacked by those who do not believe in Him."

The problem with this idea of a translational process lies in the options it still leaves open. For how can we tell which literal paraphrase is best suited to the figurative original? There is no rulebook to consult for substitutions. Moreover the 1 + 1 of the statement's two elements (*God* and *fortress*) do not yield an equation. The compounded elements remain two (and more than two, considering that each term harbors more than one connotation). Bridging the terms *God* and *fortress* only expands the options, turning the joined 1 + 1 into something more like 2 + 2 or 3 + 3. The point that this manual would miss is that odd semantic combinations oblige us to *rethink* the connotations of their component parts, expanding and developing the associational logic of communicative form.

When the classic theorist of metaphor I. A. Richards proposed that the two parts of a metaphor be called *tenor* and *vehicle,* he wanted to dispel the idea that the "rhetorical" second term was a form shaping a primary content. He wanted to put both terms on a par and he traced his argument to an intuition by Dr. Samuel Johnson: A metaphorical utterance is always richer than one that tries to say things simply insofar as it "gives you two ideas for one." It displays the affinity and alliance of "co-present thoughts."[20] Metaphorically tied, concepts interact, resulting in an "intercourse of *thoughts,* a transaction between contexts," contexts that are at once material, cultural, conceptual, and ontological. Each transports its own field of significance to the union (94). In the case of the word *fortress* the context is military defense, in the case of *God* theology. A statement combining them produces a tense union of domains instead of a translational equivalence substituting one synonym for another along a vertical, paradigmatic lexical axis. The criterion for a metaphor is therefore whether it "gives us two ideas for one; whether . . . it presents both a tenor and a vehicle which co-operate in an inclusive manner" (119).

"What should such fellows as I do crawling between earth and heaven?" cries Shakespeare's Hamlet, positing a resemblance between humans and something they consider beneath them (worms). Some literary metaphors span even greater conceptual distances, from the conceits of metaphysical English poets to the surreal aesthetics of paradox. "To compare two objects as far distant as possible one from the other," suggests André Breton, "or, by any other method, to confront them in a brusque and striking manner, remains the highest task to which poetry can ever aspire."[21] The French surrealist takes it for granted that any old fool can draw analogies easy to comprehend (and post-Bretonian fools thrive on a converse assumption, believing that transgressing convention is *all* that a poet need do, overlooking the fact that phrases like *black snow* and *stony breasts* are as formulaic as the ready-made combinations they replace). In any event, the greater the conceptual distance between words that are joined, the more difficult it is to process their union.

Conspicuously innovative formulations stretch discontinuities already bridged by semantic junctions. Related figures of speech accomplish a comparable purpose: irony (saying one thing but meaning another), personification (speaking of a thing in terms of a person), synecdoche (using a part to signify a whole), metonymy, zeugma, hyperbole, and so on. The list grows when we move from these figures of speech that change the conventional meanings of words ("tropes") to those changing their syntactic *orders* ("schemes"). Schemes, playing with the grammar of word composition, eventually burgeon into those elaborate compositions we call poems, stories, plays, and novels. They are extended and complex metaphors.

Each possesses a field of reference (what it is about) and a field of reception (the mind or world of the reader), so that "when we interpret it, when we uncover its 'unity,'" notes David Lodge, "we make it into a total metaphor: the text is the vehicle, the world is its tenor."[22] Literary reading examines and interprets the transits produced by the formulations of creative writing. It looks for where they take us.

A parable is one narrative development of a metaphor: a curious, uncommented tale relating one domain of reference to another that remains inexplicit. Some parables, like those of Jesus about the kingdom of God, create considerable disparity between the first domain and the second. If their "tenor" is quite extraordinary, their "vehicle" is utterly banal. In the New Testament accounts of this kingdom of God, notes Ricoeur, we find

> no gods, no demons, no angels, no miracles, no time before time, as in the creation stories, not even founding events as in the Exodus account. Nothing like that, but precisely people like us: Palestinian landlords traveling and renting their fields, stewards and workers, sowers and fishers, fathers and sons; in a word, ordinary people doing ordinary things: selling and buying, letting down a net into the sea, and so on. Here resides the initial paradox: on the one hand, these stories are—as a critic said—narratives of normalcy—but on the other hand, it is the Kingdom of God that is said to be like this. The paradox is that the extraordinary is like the ordinary.[23]

Peter Sloterdijk reprises the theme: "In the kingdom of God, what appears in being as a discontinuity is pure continuity."[24] Martin Buber had reached the same spot many decades earlier, noting that a parable typically bridges a gap between what *is* and what *ought to be* (or historical fact and moral justice). A parable presents "the insertion of the absolute into the world of events"; it ties an abstract far bank (of a river) to the near one, taking us there to bring us back. The converse strategy marks the metaphoricity of myth: "the insertion of the world of things into the absolute."[25]

The likeness/difference inscribed in a parable aims to remain irreducible. Whoever tries to translate a parable into a literal, explicit moral teaching does so only at the cost of alleviating the *strain* between the two realms of which the parable speaks. Parables take the form that they do in order *not* to be reduced to a teaching. That is why the Gospels say nothing about the kingdom of Heaven "except that it is *like* . . ."; they do not say *what* the kingdom of God is, but only "what it *looks like*."[26] The Scriptures even defend their textual decision not to posit unequivocal teachings:

> All these things spake Jesus unto the multitude in parables; and without a parable spake he not to them: That it might be fulfilled which was spoken by the prophet, saying, I will open my mouth in parables; I will utter things which have been kept secret from the foundation of the world.
>
> (MATTHEW 13:34–35)

In parable, then, we have a language which, "from the beginning to the end, *thinks through* the metaphor and never *beyond*," forcing us to seize meaning figuratively.[27] One parable (*Gleichnis*) of Franz Kafka is in fact titled "The Bridge." It depicts a bridge as person and a person as bridge, not allowing the two-in-one to be reduced either to a characteristic they share or to a new synthesis beyond the two. Just as the metaphorical functions of language extend beyond the specific trope called "metaphor," so the terse parabolic utterances of the Gospels issue into related paradoxical strategies like the antithetical formula ("Whoever seeks to gain his life loses it") and hyperbolic commands ("Love thine enemies"). Their purpose is "to jolt the hearer from the project of making his life something continuous."[28] They disorient our ways in order to provide new direction. That is their conceptual ethos.

Wallace Stevens and the Motive for Metaphor

We are approaching the "motive" for metaphor—the reason for this cognitive bridge that can be crossed in either direction, that possesses a reciprocal, reversible structure. "I start with a head and wind up with an egg," remarks Picasso about his method of painting. "Or even if I start with an egg and wind up with a head, I'm always on the way between

Plate 1. Wassily Kandinsky, *Composition IV (Battle)* (1911). Oil on canvas, 159.5 × 200.5 cm. Kunstsammlufigarng Nordrhein-Westfalen, Düsseldorf, Germany

Plate 2. A procession of Shinto priests crosses a ceremonial bridge to the Kamigamo shrine in Kyoto, Japan.
AP Photo / Junji Kurokawa

Plate 3. Edvard Munch, *Friedrich Nietzsche* (1906). Oil on canvas, 201 × 160 cm.
Thielska Galleriet, Stockholm

the two." His figurative freedom is released by the relativity of the referential vectors: "What interests me is to set up what you might call the *rapports de grand écart*—the most unexpected relationship possible between the things."[29] Even if this bidirectional movement does not do away with a semantics of resemblance (for a head and an egg *do* look alike), it recoils from a semantics of identity. It does not say that the head *is* an egg. It creates more interest in the relationship between head and egg than in the distinguishing characteristics of each. While not all art elaborates relationships of such great divergence as those of Picasso or the surrealists, it all works on intersections and consociations. It brings the presuppositions of signification into question, investigating sites of extension and interconnection.

Wallace Stevens testifies to the process in a poem aptly titled "The Motive of Metaphor." Even as he activates the language of metaphor, he accounts for its virtues and raison d'être.

THE MOTIVE FOR METAPHOR

You like it under the trees in autumn,
Because everything is half dead.
The wind moves like a cripple among the leaves
And repeats words without meaning.

In the same way, you were happy in spring,
With the half colors of quarter-things,
The slightly brighter sky, the melting clouds,
The single bird, the obscure moon—

The obscure moon lighting an obscure world
Of things that would never be quite expressed,
Where you yourself were never quite yourself
And did not want nor have to be,

Desiring the exhilarations of changes:
The motive for metaphor, shrinking from
The weight of primary noon,
The A B C of being,

The ruddy temper, the hammer
Of red and blue, the hard sound—
Steel against intimation—the sharp flesh,
The vital, arrogant, fatal, dominant X.[30]

Stevens contrasts a list of things the "you" likes—vague, intermediate features of autumn and spring—to conditions peremptorily marked by an "arrogant, fatal, dominant X." That dominant X plummets into the poem with the "weight of primary noon," announcing its force of solid, unequivocal identity. Metaphor, a coalescence of related-but-different things, lies more at home with the half-states of the poem's first three stanzas: trees in autumn, where "everything is half dead," the limping movement of the wind, "the half colors of quarter-things" in spring, with its melting clouds and obscure moon, the "obscure world / Of things that would never be quite expressed." The half-states belong to spaces and times where "you yourself were never quite yourself / And did not want nor have to be"—where you existed, one would like to paraphrase, without compulsion.

The motive or purpose of metaphor serves this ambiguity of conditions where phenomena are growing or getting crippled, showing brightening skies and quarter-grown things in half colors. Peremptory, definitive language fails in the face of these transitional seasons. The autumn wind "repeats words without meaning"; spring reveals matters "that would never be quite expressed." The semi-illuminated being of these times leads the mind to register no X, but rather something between X and Y.

The motive as goal of metaphorical language can then be deduced from the final six lines, where the poem stresses what metaphor shies away from: the blacksmith's hammer, the alphabet of correct linguistic usage ("the A B C of being"), the "hard sound," "sharp flesh," and the final, "vital, arrogant, fatal, dominant X." The poem progressively leads us to understand that the linguistic objective is recognition and celebration of, not being, but not-definitively-characterizable becoming. Metaphor loosens empirical fixity, validating ontological passage. Rejecting intransigent identity-discourse, it endorses connection between phenomena that cannot be kept firmly or essentially separate. It recoils from sequential, differentiated, hammer-like ipseities.

Exemplifying the ambivalence it defends as theme, the poem is metaphorical even at the level of scheme, or in the way it arranges those qualities to which it gives words. It links them so compactly together that they cannot be brought into any definitive syntagmatic relation—whether synonymic or antonymic, causal or subordinate, complementary or mutually exclusive. Our interpretation of the poetic utterance remains suspended within and between the phrases that Stevens strings together. In simple terms, he only *bridges* the notions and phenomena of the last two stanzas, bringing them into uncharacterized, unspecified alliance. Everything that follows the colon (:) after "exhilarations of changes" could just as easily be oppositional as appositional to the "changes" before the colon (different from them or examples of them). The poem dissuades the reader from making a choice.[31]

As juncture, the colon does not call for decision. It is the purest, most uncommentative bridge there is in punctuation (a practice perhaps best deployed by the poetry of A. R. Ammons). The colon says neither A = B, nor A is dissimilar to B; it just stipulates a connection between them. Other types of punctuation—commas, periods, and semicolons—can accomplish virtually equivalent effects, instilling mutuality or parity among the terms they join. The signature dashes of Emily Dickinson, for example, often work that way, instilling a space between syntactically related elements, and thus keeping them joined in distance:

> Behind me—dips Eternity—
> Before me—Immortality—
> Myself—the Term between—[32]

"Connections between unconnected things are the unreal reality of Poetry": that is the lesson that Susan Howe reaches in interpreting this poet.[33]

When translating Dickinson into German, Paul Celan must have felt there was enough discontinuity in her poems to forgo the majority of her dashes. Yet in his own practice he was no less compelled to create turning, bridged combinations. His last five collections of poems are called *Breathturn, Threadsuns, Lightduress, Snowpart,* and *Timestead* (*Atemwende* [1967], *Fadensonnen* [1968], *Lichtzwang* [1970], *Schneepart* [1971], and *Zeitgehöft* [1976]). The only thing missing from these unusual compounds is a hyphen distinguishing their parts, but that only unifies the notions better. (And hyphens between nouns do not *perform* conceptual bridging as much as dashes and colons, which mark syntactical space between pieces of an unfolding, extended thought.) The master builder of the dash is Nietzsche, using it to cleave thought-separations, to signal unrecognized ties, to produce surprising, paradoxical deviations. "A people is nature's detour to arrive at six or seven great men—and then to get around them."[34] His decisive afterthoughts are the prerogative of a thinker bent on prancing and leaping among rainbow-thoughts. His dashes possess a Janus-faced nature, at once "pushing the argument forward by providing it with a sudden twist," and pulling the reader "back to what he or she has just read, to reconsider and reinterpret it in light of new data."[35] At the end of a seemingly completed thought, a Nietzschean dash can announce that this reflection remains essentially unfinished, marking the margin of something unsaid. "Everything I have written up to now," writes Nietzsche to his sister in 1885, "is foreground; for me it all starts with the dash."[36] His term for dash is *Gedankenstrich*, "thought-stroke," connoting suspension as well as extension. The thought-strokes of dashes connect with an "other." At the time when he writes this letter, Nietzsche has begun giving *Gedankenstrich* just as much pride of place in his method of philosophizing as "thought" (*Gedank*) and "question" (*Frage*). Book and section titles drafted for the book he was then working on, *Beyond Good and Evil*, include *Thoughts and Dashes of a Good European*; *Questions and Dashes*; *Preliminary Thoughts and Dashes of Friedrich Nietzsche*; and *Dashes of a Psychologist*.[37]

The bridging operations of these elements of syntax (we have mentioned the colon, the semicolon, the dash) do not actually build; they clasp together. Getting from one component to the other is a task left to the reader. Comprehension in the very largest sense requires more extensive steps along a more complex bridge. We tread its planks whenever we listen to someone speak or make sense of the things around us. Modern and experimental poetry like that of Stevens activates greater insecurity and mobility of linguistic understanding than usual, presenting "meeting points at which regions of experience which can never combine in sensation or intuition come together."[38] Its semantic couplings—produced not only by metaphor, metonymy, and synecdoche, but also alliteration, rhymes, antithesis, anaphora, assonance, litotes, pun, oxymoron, and synesthesia—create sympathies/antipathies of both sound and sense that affirm and safeguard the distance between sign and meaning. Poetry, in other words, builds bridges in order to keep us on them, suggesting that meanings are not already "out there" in the manner of individual, self-standing buildings.

Hart Crane's Unfractioned Idiom

Wallace Stevens takes one step along these bridges, Hart Crane quite another. And it would be difficult to conclude a study of metaphorical language without considering the vast, ambitious composition he himself chose to call *The Bridge*. The way it links history, urban description, and geographic legend on a long journey of intellectual bridging seems often to appear more like a maze. Crane marshals all manners of analogy, semantic affinities, myth, and conceptual crossovers to pursue two complementary objectives: a poem about metaphoricity as the master operation of human comprehension, and a picture of the evolution of America from Columbus up to and beyond the construction of the

Brooklyn Bridge, a heterogeneous panorama that the poet mines for symptoms of cosmic process.

Ultimately *The Bridge* does less justice to the second topic, the cultural complexity of America, than the first, the intellectual challenges that understanding *of* it poses. From the very start the metaphorical results of the poem show rapturous reach, radiating out from the central locale of the Brooklyn Bridge over the course of a single fluctuant day. From the tumultuous metropolitan encounter of land and sea that we call New York City, innumerable word bridges follow the geocultural features of eastern America to places where their substance and connotations are connected to others. *The Bridge* thus attempts to tie together Europe, America, and Asia despite their considerable divergences; prophecy, legend, and erotic desire; rational comprehension and Dionysian revelry; music and religion; the flight of gulls and human leaps to death. The entirety of *The Bridge* is cast over the piers of the opening and closing poems addressing the Brooklyn Bridge, between which Crane builds plank after plank of verbal connection. More than a few are tenuous, ultimately raising the question of how solid poetic bridges can be. The first to doubt the credibility of some of Crane's refashionings of cultural reality were his friends Alan Tate and Ivor Winters, whose reactions have been echoed or contested by Harold Bloom, John T. Irwin, R. W. B. Lewis, Brian Reed, and Alan Trachtenberg. When poetry strains as hard as this does against everyday forms of conceptual linkage, it becomes difficult to estimate just where its words will land.

Startling achievements can be illustrated by two poems in the section of *The Bridge* called *Powhatan's Daughter*. "The Harbor Dawn" and "Van Winkle" are perfused by sights and sounds, memories and dreams, voices and legends, and by the place of a "you beside me" (the poet's awakening companion) at daybreak in wintry Brooklyn. The narrator draws this companion's attention to a "tide of voices" and "fog-insulated" noises which "meet you listening midway in your dream." Semiconsciously, the sleeper only half hears these sounds. Then the acoustic phenomena begin to register as tactile, building on the physical and emotional contact between the two lovers. Their "soft sleeves of sound" accompany other sensations "echoing alley-upward." Then the poet conflates the place of the bedroom with the world outside the window, where resonances fill "the pillowed bay" like "signals dispersed in veils." The synesthetic realignment of the senses becomes antiphonal, the tangible arms of the lovers themselves acquiring voice: "Your cool arms murmurously about me lay."[39]

Flakes of snow start sticking to buildings. Their contact looks (or feels) like tiny hands, mirroring other ties between impressions and bodies, while touching links hearing and doing:

> While myriad snowy hands are clustering at the panes—
>
> *your hands within my hands are deeds;*
> *my tongue upon your throat—singing*
>
> *arms close . . .*
>
> (*THE BRIDGE*, "THE HARBOR DAWN," LINES 17–21)

This awakening awareness had begun "immemorially" (line 19), not fully impressed on the recording mind. Yet recollection, sight, and projection into the future emerge along with it. When struck by the sun, the once Odysseus-blinded, one-eyed "Cyclopean towers across Manhattan waters" (skyscrapers) reveal reflective "bright window-eyes aglitter" (lines 32–33 and 19). Separating inner from outer space, these windows that are eyes also become active seers.

The next poem, "Van Winkle," examines the legendary figure who fell into a slumber in the secluded glen of Sleepy Hollow. When he awoke twenty years later, Rip Van Winkle found himself straddling two eras. Spatially, the "Macadam" highway at the outset of the poem does the same, crossing the expanse of the American continent from Long Island to the straits of the Golden Gate:

> Macadam, gun-grey as the tunny's belt,
> Leaps from Far Rockaway to Golden Gate:
> Listen! the miles a hurdy-gurdy grinds—
> Down gold arpeggios mile on mile unwinds.
>
> (*THE BRIDGE*, "VAN WINKLE," LINES 1–4)

The musical instrument of the hurdy-gurdy grinds out miles rather than notes, unwinding "gold arpeggios" across the highway. This road = a bridge = Rip Van Winkle, who inhabits a time and a space in which he "was not here / nor there" (lines 26–27). According to the same principle, "memory . . . strikes a rhyme" between current happenings and those of "times earlier." Even now, in the present of the poem, "It is the same hour though a later day" (lines 5, 6, 28).

And so the rhetorical connectivity of *The Bridge* proceeds, setting up correlations between distant events and sensations unfolding in the present, often so audaciously as to befuddle interpreters. To those who had already found the conceptual leaps of Crane's *For the Marriage of Faustus and Helen* arduous four years earlier, the poet explains that his associational meanings give voice to a sunken and irrational level of the understanding:

> The entire construction of the poem is raised on the organic principle of a "logic of metaphor," which antedates our so-called pure logic, and which is the genetic basis of all speech, hence consciousness and thought-extension.[40]

Such thought-extension carries the motion of *The Bridge* forward, between the inaugural and final poems apotheosizing the great figure of this material and symbolic logic that is addressed as a biblical "Thee." The "choiring strings" of the Brooklyn Bridge suggest both "harp and altar." Presenting a "Tall Vision-of-the-Voyage," it marks a "Terrific threshold of the prophet's pledge, / Prayer of pariah, and the lover's cry" ("To Brooklyn Bridge," lines 13, 29–30, 31–32; "Atlantis," line 42). Prophet, pariah, and lover are emblems for the poet himself, cruising, at the poem's beginning, to make erotic contact beneath the bridge, below the erect towers soaring above.

Crane's extensive poetic ambition helps explain why he invests so deeply in this idealized theme of the bridge. It is a symbolic facilitator of cultural union between Europe and the Americas and then onto the imagined lands of Cathay/Asia. The bridge lifts them all up into a comprehensive span of mind and history. Indeed, the poem implies that global unity itself is consubstantial with Faustian objectives of human understanding. That may be why *The Bridge* concludes its evocation of the great structure in New York with the words "O Thou steeled Cognizance" ("Atlantis," line 57). This cognizance, comprehension, or intelligence is capable of theoretically binding into one all conceivable events in nature and history. The historical materialization of thought would be the ultimate bridge that assimilates lands of both past and future into the transcendent embrace of poetic structure. The articulations of this Cognizance aim at an "Unfractioned idiom" ("To Brooklyn Bridge," line 34): a language overcoming the scissions of reason no less than of culture, articulating a primordial apperception that resolves even the poet's conflicted motivations and self-understandings along the way.[41] If his ethical singularities fuel a drive for universal acceptance, his cultivation of prelogical metaphor operates as the engine for that communion. Love, in which everything can be united, is another word for the Unfractioned idiom, overleaping spiritual divides.

Yet on the surface the divides remain irreducible. They are devil's clefts on the earth that bridges were devised to repair. Why otherwise would Crane head up his poem with an epigraph underscoring the *origin and motivation* of his all-unifying metaphorical composition?

> From going to and fro in the earth,
> And from walking up and down in it.
> —The Book of Job
>
> (*THE BRIDGE*, TITLE PAGE)

These words are uttered by Satan, who in that Book of Job explains to the Lord why he appears in the condition he is in. The great sower of discord has been wandering back and forth across the planet, hither and thither, with neither firm purpose nor direction. Is this Crane's way of suggesting that *The Bridge* itself arises from the insuperable ground of divisions it is designed to repair? If so, then all eleven hundred lines of the poem pursue the same project with which this chapter began, and toward which Nietzsche's Zarathustra was so skeptical: to make language join what is eternally apart.

No literary project can accomplish such a lofty goal, especially if it aspires to grasp historical material through an optics of metaphor. For the more one phenomenon is assimilated to another, the more it loses its specificity, its nature *de*natured through transformations, semantic abstraction, and the multiple associations of the relations into which it is bundled. Rhapsodic contacts eloquently convey the ecstatic experience of a lyrical "I" at the foot of the Brooklyn Bridge, but they do not easily integrate the fractious dynamics of cultural history. Even the "Cathay" that Crane's Columbus believed he had reached is not actually the historical and geospecific Asia. Even in the economy of his poem, as the poet himself conceded, this signifier Cathay "is ultimately transmuted into a symbol of consciousness, knowledge, spiritual unity."[42] The cognitive fusion of Crane's Unfractioned idiom is also con-fusion, leaving us in the throes of the very dilemma that the poetics of metaphor was designed to resolve: how to respect the eternal apartness of things while making them dance together. Aiming as it does at an ideal and infinite unity, *The Bridge* pushes interminably from one shore of cognition toward another that is ultimately, and by definition, impossible to reach. The poem presents a great symbol for the human creation of symbols, "a metaphor for the world-making power of metaphor itself."[43] Whether in the poetics of Crane or that of surrealism, with its far-flung analogies, as well as in the practice of certain trope-spinning philosophers, bewitched by their own language, as Ludwig Wittgenstein might have put it, the figurative stretch is what needs to come into question. The distance between starting point and destination must be acknowledged, enhanced by awareness of the span. This will convey how a seemingly single situation, affirmation, or understanding (a "half" state of Stevens) is completed by another quite often out of sight. In this way differences can be confirmed while made to dance together.

CHAPTER 6

The Bridge as Gallows

Sun and Angels

A bridge considered by many to be the most beautiful in Rome once led to the tomb of the great Emperor Hadrian. It was built for no other reason than to create a thoroughfare to the resting place of the ruler, which would continue to serve as a mausoleum for other Roman emperors right up to Caracalla. That is the huge drumlike building now called Castel Sant'Angelo, constructed four years after the Aelian Bridge, or Ponte Elio in Italian, in 139 CE. The city of Rome lay across the river on the left bank of the Tiber, where the bridge began. The geographic symbolism of this tomb on the far side of human habitation suggested a crossing of the Styx to Hadrian's permanent abode in the great beyond (fig. 6.1).

This Aelian Bridge was not merely a bridge between life and death but a connector of two categorically different orders of being. Hadrian was deified by the Roman senate after his death; the bridge and mausoleum were his preparation for that condition. The name Aelius, by which Hadrian, born Publius Aelius Hadrianus, preferred to be called, derives from the word for the Greek god of the sun, *Helios*. Hadrian's Bridge of the Sun was to act as a massive golden gate—a conduit from the mortal to the divine state.[1]

After Rome was Christianized, the Aelian Bridge became a pathway to an even more important resting place than Hadrian's, although one equally attached to eternity. That was the tomb of St. Peter, Christ's vicar on earth, buried a few hundred meters beyond the mausoleum beneath the heart and most sacred basilica of Christendom. The Aelian Bridge thus eventually came to be called Ponte San Pietro, the Bridge of St. Peter, and more definitively, for reasons we shall see shortly, Ponte Sant'Angelo, or Bridge of the Holy Angel. It now directed mortals to *two* of the most important tombs in universal history, one secular, one

Figure 6.1. Hadrian's Mausoleum and the Aelian Bridge, Rome.
Courtesy of Alain Janssoone

sacred. The emperor's symbolic passage over the Styx created a road to salvation, meting out death to death itself, undoing the mortality of souls who had sufficient devotion to tread the apostle's path. It became an entry point to the citadel of the Holy See and the key to all processions to and from the Basilica of St. Peter. By the time Gian Lorenzo Bernini designed the bridge's famous angels in the seventeenth century, the structure had become a step on the city's Via Crucis, which re-created the drama of Christ's Passion. The procession is often relived by the faithful in a ritual of expiation, activating the *humilitas* and *contritio cordis* that are needed to gain admittance to the paradise on the far side of life. Bernini adorned the bridge's sculptures with icons of the Stations of the Cross—nails, thorns, and the superscription INRI. He also designed the open-armed *piazza* in front of the sacred basilica, the bridge's new destination, which gave form to the immense embrace of Heaven awaiting each faithful traveler who crossed over the bridge and followed the *via salvationis* along the narrow street of the Borgo Nuovo.[2]

Before Bernini and his pupils glorified that way with statues of angels, the bridge passage famously displayed other bodies. They belonged to the executed enemies of the church. In the sixteenth century, Roman locals, sardonic as always about the ways of authority, used to say that there were more heads on this bridge than melons in the market (fig. 6.2).[3] The site in Rome where the impaled heads were severed from

Figure 6.2. Pope Sixtus V (1585–90) crosses Ponte Sant'Angelo among heads of convicts impaled on two rows of pikes.

their bodies was "the place of justice"—*il luogo della giustizia*—at the foot of the bridge. The most beautiful of all decapitated Romans is still said to haunt that spot head in hand.[4] This site for Rome's rituals of punishment and communal expiation was also due to Ponte Sant'Angelo's vicinity to the *prisone del papa*, the papal prison of Tor di Nona. But rituals are not governed by practical concerns; they enact symbolic lessons. This Bridge of the Holy Angel was not only a marker of death; it gave death its rationale.

As Rome came to be ruled by the Vatican, the mausoleum of Hadrian became the fortified bunker of popes, from which they defended themselves against their enemies. They even devised a secret corridor that led straight from the holy basilica to the mausoleum. And in that bastion they were virtually impregnable. After the invading forces of the Ostrogoth Totila laid siege to Rome in 547, writes historian Cesare D'Onofrio, making no beans about his republican sympathies, the mausoleum acted over and over as "a terrible arm turned *against the city*." From then on the popes used the Castel Sant'Angelo to "hold the city hostage, along with its headstrong Romans, who never cease[d] aspiring to give a secular structure to their society."[5]

The square at the foot of the bridge, where most executed bodies were displayed, was originally conceived to commemorate something quite different: a mass tragedy of religious pilgrims. It occurred in a rare Jubilee Year (1450), when Catholics throughout Europe expiated their sins by coming to the eternal city. It was a disaster that had been averted by great throngs of people one hundred and fifty years earlier, when

Figure 6.3. One of the earliest sketches of Hadrian's Mausoleum and Ponte Sant'Angelo, by Giuliano da Sangallo (late fifteenth century).

Dante himself crossed the same bridge in the Holy Year 1300, and wrote about it in that simile we examined in chapter 1. On December 19, 1450, as they returned from celebrations at the basilica, the pilgrims ran into a bottleneck on the bridge that was the only return route from the Vatican to the city (fig. 6.3). The jubilee crowd was "so vast and tightly packed" that "in the words of a contemporary chronicler, grains of millet scattered over it would not have reached the ground."[6] On the bridge lined with shops, an uncontrollable mule caused lethal havoc. Carrying two women, this mule of Cardinal Pietro Barbo (later Pope Paul II), beaten and prodded on, backed up and bucked against the flow of traffic, creating a stampede that broke the bridge's parapets (recalling an idiom we have no use for today: [*battre quelqu'un*] *comme asne a pont*, "[to beat someone] like a donkey at a bridge"). Donkeys, mules, and cattle are notoriously afraid of crossing bridges, especially those with platforms of wood, like this one, showing water between the planks.[7] They suffer from gephyrophobia. Leon Battista Alberti, who was present at the misfortune on the Jubilee of 1450, estimates that more than three hundred dead bodies were fished out of the Tiber following this catastrophe.

To expiate the tragedy, the pope of the time, Nicholas V, rebuilt the Bridge of St. Peter and cleared a commemorative space on the left bank of the river. On each side of this new Piazza di Ponte he erected octagonal chapels, one dedicated to Mary Magdalene and the other to the Holy Innocents. These chapels fulfilled their religious functions without incident until another pope was besieged in the castle-mausoleum during the Sack of Rome in 1527. The German mercenaries of the besieging Spanish Emperor Charles V—Landsknechts specializing in firepower—took shelter behind and within the holy chapels, from which they bombarded Pope Clement VII's castle. The perverse service thus rendered by the chapels, compounded by the damage they suffered, was reason enough to tear them down. In 1534 they were replaced with the statues we see there five hundred years later of Saints Peter and Paul.

While the two chapels commemorated those killed by no fault of their own, their removal made institutional executions easier. And they continued apace, weighing so heavily on Romans that they inspired another bridge saying, *er boja nun passa ponte* (the executioner doesn't cross the bridge). The notion is that this agent of the powers of the river's right bank—the side of St. Peter's—would be taking his own life into his hands if he crossed over to the left side, where relatives and friends of the executed lived.[8] When the executions were moved to the Piazza del Ponte to be rendered more public, there developed a related expression announcing the advent of more beheadings: *Mastro Titta passa ponte!* (Titta is crossing the bridge). Mastro Titta was the most notorious of Rome's executioners and the author of grisly memoirs detailing more than five hundred killings. His moniker "Mastro Titta" was a bastardization of *maestro della giustizia*, master of justice. The memoirs of this Giovanni Battista Bugatti are published as *Mastro Titta, il Boia di Roma: Memorie di un carnefice scritte da lui stesso*.

Since its inception, then, the holy bridge leading to the castle and dungeon of the mausoleum has been overdetermined by death. Death even plays into the bridge's new name: Ponte Sant'Angelo: the Bridge of the Holy Angel. The reference is to the great Plague of Justinian at the end of the sixth century, a pandemic that claimed about 100 million lives in Europe and all but decimated the population of Rome.[9] Finally, in the year 590, miraculous respite came. It was announced by way of a vision to Pope Gregory of Heaven's most prestigious representative, the Archangel Michael, standing atop Hadrian's mausoleum and sheathing his blood-drenched sword (fig. 6.4). The apparition and gesture of the angel signaled that Rome's suffering had come to an end. From that point on Hadrian's mausoleum assumed the name of the Castle of the Holy Angel (*castellum sancti angeli*). Given the violence it had witnessed since 547, in the cataclysmic siege of Totila, the fortress had become the city's focal point of a struggle between death and life, and it was appropriate that the Archangel Michael appeared precisely there, atop the city's great sepulcher.

Michael, the supreme enemy of Satan and his rebel angels, was known as the Angel of Death (like Azrael and Azrail in Judaic and Islamic traditions) because it was his job to swoop down to shield a dying person from the clutches of the demon and give that gasping soul

Figure 6.4. Archangel Michael at the top of the castle, Hadrian's Mausoleum.
Yana Zapa / Shutterstock.com

one final opportunity to redeem itself. (An Islamic *hadith* recounts a symbolic variant, positioning the scene of dying on a bridge: Archangel Gabriel stands at the foot of a bridge leading souls to the afterlife, and Michael in the middle. Here Michael, the psychopomp, or conveyer of souls, interrogates them about the lives they have led and directs them to their appropriate destinations—some toward Heaven, the others toward Hell.)[10]

There is some coherence, then, to the fact that the people the church believed to be contaminating the holy city of Rome met their end precisely at the bridge overseen by the Archangel Michael, beneath the tomb of the divine emperor, transmuted into a sacred castle. Public executions in the city continued well through the nineteenth century, when heads of republican Romans fighting for independence from the Vatican were hung alongside the twelve angels sculpted by Bernini's school.

Old Men from the Bridge

Notwithstanding this coalition between death and the Bridge of Angels, historians of ancient Rome associate death more readily with another bridge in the city: the Pons Sublicius. The bridge predates Hadrian and few traces remain. The maintenance of this most ancient bridge in the city was the sacred responsibility of the priests called *pontifices*. Each year on the Ides of May, or thereabouts, recounts Ovid, the College of Pontiffs oversaw a sacred ritual on this Pons Sublicius, or Sublician Bridge. The head priest led highly guarded Vestal Virgins in a solemn procession through the city to the bridge, and from there the Virgins threw straw effigies of old men, bound hand and foot, into the Tiber. Many historians believe that this event was a symbolic reenactment of real drownings of the elderly from the bridge, a ritual whose origins lay so far back in Rome's history that Ovid himself had a bit of trouble understanding it. Repulsed by the very notion that a society bearing such respect for elders could have cast feeble men off the Pons Sublicius, the poet offers another explanation for this springtime renewal.

He notes that the twenty-seven effigies of men (*Argei*) were collected at city chapels dedicated to the graves of Hercules's Greek companions, called *Sacella Argeorum*. This leads him to hypothesize that the figurines represent not true Romans once thrown into the river, but legendary Argive chieftains who accompanied their leader to Italy on his historic journey. The Argives, Ovid recalls, requested that after death their corpses be thrown into the river to float back to the Greek homeland that their souls so deeply missed.

Despite Ovid's account, the identification of the effigies with historical Romans cast to their deaths has proved more intriguing. It is also in keeping with the river-propitiating rites exacted by bridge-builders across Europe. If this was the case, and actual victims were tossed to their deaths in ancient Rome, it may have been because they were no longer fit for military service, or were over the age of sixty, or were deemed in some other way to be no longer of use to the city. While there is no historical evidence for such a practice, an ancient proverbial expression, *sexagenarios de ponte*—"old men from the bridge!"—was well known in Ovid's time and could well refer back to ceremonial human sacrifices to the god Tiber.

That is the view of Ovid's contemporary Dionysius of Halicarnassus,[11] of James G. Frazer, of the cultural anthropologist Anita Seppilli, and many others. "Indeed, so rooted in the Roman mind was the association of sexagenarians with a bridge and watery death," observes Frazer, "that an appropriate and expressive word was coined to describe them—they were called Depontans (*depontani*), which means 'Down from the bridge with them!'" Plutarch believed that an ancient tradition of sacrificing real men off the Pons Sublicius had been a fact and speculates that marriages were forbidden in Rome during this month of May—when the rites of purification occurred—precisely for this reason.[12]

In time analogous killings of Christians became common upstream. The religious deviants were hurled into the river from the Ponte Aurelio, their desecrated bodies unable to be retrieved unless they washed up on the Tiber Island. Other Christians were made to climb the *scale Gemonie*, or Stairs of Mourning, at the Capitoline Hill and strangled, cast down to the forum and allowed to rot. Then they were thrown into the Tiber, making their burial and public commemoration impossible.[13]

If socially purgative, collective homicides on behalf of the health of Rome did once occur at the Pons Sublicius, they could have given way to the symbolic killings of Ovid's time, figured in the effigies of bound men. Certainly the idea of doing in elders from a bridge was familiar enough to ancient Romans to elicit spontaneous laughter from the court when Cicero exclaimed during a civil lawsuit, "Sexagenarians from the bridge!"[14] The love poet Catullus also invokes the bridge-fortifying sacrifice of sexagenarians to construct an extended metaphor. His poem #17 begins with a picture of a rickety, patched-up bridge in Verona that is too weak to support all the revelers intending to use it for the upcoming festival. The mischievous poet proposes a remedy. He scapegoats an old "jackass" who has no clue about the amorous desires of his sanguine young bride and recommends casting him into the waters, a gesture, Catullus claims, that will rejuvenate both man and bridge.

Whatever lies at the origin of the effigies cast from the Sublicius, it is clear that their plunge aims at a fluvial, purgatorial renewal of life. Just as the Ponte Sant'Angelo provides a thoroughfare to a tomb overseen by the transfigurative effects of the Angel of Death, so the execution of sacred victims at the Sublician Bridge rids the social body of impure souls, appeasing bloodthirsty gods in the process. The culture of bridges owes tribute to the waters whose currents it breaches.

Gods of the river had numerous ways of exacting their toll. Before bridges over the Tiber became plentiful, Romans ferried themselves over in small boats operating at all times of day for minimal fees. The use of these *barchette* came repeatedly to be outlawed, and not merely because greedy ferrymen stuffed their vessels so much that they capsized. Sixteenth-century Romans engineered rather sinister crossings by way of these ferries. On a pitch-black night, a boat operator, or more likely someone impersonating him, would be stirred from his rest on the riverbank to transport an unwary victim to unsuspected death. Crimes of this sort, reports Sergio Delli,

> typically committed for political reasons or for private revenge, were not infrequent, and nearly every day the Tiber would cough up corpses of those who had been cudgeled or driven through by swords or beaten with pistols. The method was always the same: the unfortunate person was drawn into a snare—possibly in the hope of a furtive sexual encounter on the other side of the river—and in the middle of the waters a good thrust of the dagger fixed the wretch forever.[15]

Enough of these murders occurred in the rough city to mete out prison sentences in 1556 for the mere use of these barks.

Death by water has the advantage of achieving formal closure. It casts life back to the element from which it came, and by which it can again be carried away. It closes a circle, enacted by river-bound journeys to death in a canoe or bassinet, or a vessel steered by Charon. The Argives' wish to make a fluid return to Greece confirms an extended cultural mythology by which the deceased are swallowed in transporting waters. The mythology may even be operative in the minds of those jumping to their death from a bridge and in the selection of that scene for the execution of wartime foes.

Death's Noose on Life

When ethnic, religious, and military enemies are hung or impaled at liminal, high-traffic places and protests are staged at bridges, as at the Edmund Pettus Bridge on the Bloody Sunday of March 7, 1965, they give ostentatious evidence of a community's power over life. The corpses of American mercenaries in Iraq provided such evidence at a bridge over the Euphrates in Fallujah on March 31, 2004, and city bridges were killing centers during the Yugoslavian Wars of 1992–95.[16] A remarkable literary treatment of the practice lies in the scrupulously detailed description of a rebel impaled on the Mehmed Paša Sokolović Bridge near the outset of Andrić's *Bridge over the Drina*. A prior story about a wartime hanging investigates instead the uncanny inner freedom achieved by a condemned man at this critical juncture.

What is most striking about the story called "An Occurrence at Owl Creek Bridge," written in 1890 by the war journalist Ambrose Bierce, is not the event that it relates—the death of a Confederate activist in the American Civil War—but the difficulty readers have in distinguishing between what did in fact happen and what was merely imagined, seeming to issue from a space beyond life's pale. The ambiguity of the occurrence at Owl Creek Bridge in Alabama makes only one thing sure: each bridge is potentially a gallows and each gallows a bridge.

The opening facts are clear as the light of day. A Southerner called Peyton Farquhar is arrested by Union soldiers for plotting to destroy the bridge over which the army's supply trains run. The opening description of him fixed to the end of a noose is clinically crude and raw:

> A man stood upon a railroad bridge in northern Alabama, looking down into the swift water twenty feet below. The man's hands were behind his back, the wrists bound with a cord. A rope closely encircled his neck. It was attached to a stout cross-timber above his head and the slack fell to the level of his knees. Some loose boards laid upon the ties supporting the rails of the railway supplied a footing for him and his executioners—two private soldiers of the Federal army, directed by a sergeant who in civil life may have been a deputy sheriff. . . . The preparations being complete, the two private soldiers stepped aside and each drew away the plank upon which he had been standing. . . . These movements left the condemned man and the sergeant standing on the two ends of the same plank, which spanned three of the cross-ties of the bridge. The end upon which the civilian stood almost, but not quite, reached a fourth. This plank had been held in place by the weight of the captain; it was now held by that of the sergeant. At a signal from the former the latter would step aside, the plank would tilt and the condemned man go down between two ties. The arrangement commended itself to his judgement as simple and effective.[17]

In the story's next action the sergeant steps off the plank, and the narrator reports that Farquhar "fell straight downward through the bridge" (12). And here the prose glides off into something very different. The noose snaps, Farquhar tumbles into the stream and swims clear of the bullets ringing out in the water all around him. The description of his "preternaturally keen and alert" (13) perceptions in the river is every bit as detailed as the preparations for his hanging—except that Farquhar's fine observations are filled with wonder, passion, and life-and-death sensitivity:

> He felt the ripples upon his face and heard their separate sounds as they struck. He looked at the forest on the bank of the stream, saw the individual trees, the leaves and the veining of each leaf—he saw the very insects upon them: the locusts, the brilliant bodied flies, the gray spiders stretching their webs from twig to twig. He noted the prismatic colors in all the dewdrops upon a million blades of grass. The humming of the gnats that danced above the eddies of the stream,

> the beating of the dragon flies' wings, the strokes of the water spiders' legs, like oars which had lifted their boat—all these made audible music. A fish slid along beneath his eyes and he heard the rush of its body parting the water. (13)

Farquhar now dodges bullets and cannon fire to reach the river bank and makes a breakneck flight through the forest. He makes an all but impossible return to the front lawn of his house, where to his relief his wife steps down from the veranda to meet him. A narrative disjunction now pushes readers from this second phase of the story into a third. It is related in the present tense, as we continue to experience the events through his eyes:

> At the bottom of the steps she stands waiting, with a smile of ineffable joy, an attitude of matchless grace and dignity. Ah, how beautiful she is! He springs forwards with extended arms. As he is about to clasp her he feels a stunning blow upon the back of the neck; a blinding white light blazes all about him with a sound like the shock of a cannon—then all is darkness and silence!
>
> Peyton Farquhar was dead; his body, with a broken neck, swung gently from side to side beneath the timbers of the Owl Creek bridge. (16)

The unexpected ending of this story jolts us out of the present into the past of Farquhar's death. Everything that has occurred between the tightening of the noose and Farquhar embracing his wife now appears to have been merely imagined in the space of seconds. The interval between the objective, empirical facts and the subjective fantasy is bridged by stylistic transformation. The matter-of-fact hanging preparations had proceeded with metrical precision and martial order. The emotions, desires, and sensations crowding into the three yards of tightening rope convey instead a sensation of immeasurable extension and time. The horizontal planks making up the surface of the bridge—representing life's progressive, step-by-step order—are transected by the vertical plunge to death, interrupting the rectilinear trajectory with an edifying, swirling fantasy sequence. The passion of the fall gives the imagined events a pulsating rhythm and lyricism altogether lacking in what happens on either side of the tightening of the noose.

If the story initially focuses on the components of a horizontal crossing (one wooden railway tie after another, from this side of a river to the other), its real interest lies in the *vertical* crossing. Death crosses the plane of life as human imagination contravenes the order of facts. This is the crux of the tale, converting the means of conveyance which is a bridge into a gallows.

A superb cinematic adaptation of Bierce's story in 1962 called *La rivère de hibou,* directed by Robert Enrico (winning the Best Short Subject Film Award at the Festival de Cannes and an Oscar for Live Action Short Film the following year) adds much visual poetry and narrative shock to the story's verbal source. One can only quibble with this detail: The film does not make Farquhar fall *through* the ties of the bridge: The plank on which he stands juts out from the bridge's side. Bierce's hanged man instead falls *into* the space separating one foothold of the bridge deck from the next. The written story associates Farquhar's death and imaginative process with an interstice within a reiterative structure—the joined planks of a bridge, metaphorical not merely of teleological progression and narrative continuation, but of consecutive steps on life's way. If Farquhar's hanging on a bridge "reinforces the idea that he is transfixed between the shore of life and death,"[18] it does not identify death with the far end of that shore. Death lies between the footholds of life itself.

This is the true "occurrence" at Owl Creek Bridge—the fall between footholds, unleashing an irrepressible attempt to *alter* Farquhar's destination, to dictate the nature of the step that lies ahead, the remainder of a life he cannot control. Does this occurrence take place at Owl Creek Bridge because the owl is a bird that sees through darkness, a "keeper of souls transitioning from one plane of existence to another?"[19] Bierce's story breaches the space between those planes, like Broch's novel *The Death of Virgil,* discussed in chapter 1. The incident reported by Bierce illustrates the trauma that occurs when the purposive motion of life is suddenly crossed by death—indeed, when death is shown to be the *only true end* within this round of objectives and ends, which can be interrupted at any given time. The story shows how the bridge from A to B and C is built over an empty, underlying, vertical space, over the repressed and constitutive fact of death. Farquhar's swaying at the end of a noose offers a cruel denouement to his wishful thoughts of evading his end.

His passage from one plane of existence to another is predicated on his inability to make forward progress through life. His bridge subverts another received notion of a bridge as a point of heroic transition. For example, in the Middle Ages symbolic bridges test the valor of knights and carry them to a higher level of being. The more forbidding the bridge-tests, the more glorious the ability to traverse them. In one of Lancelot's adventures his beloved Guinevere has been abducted by the anti-knight Méléagant and is held captive in a castle beyond a river.

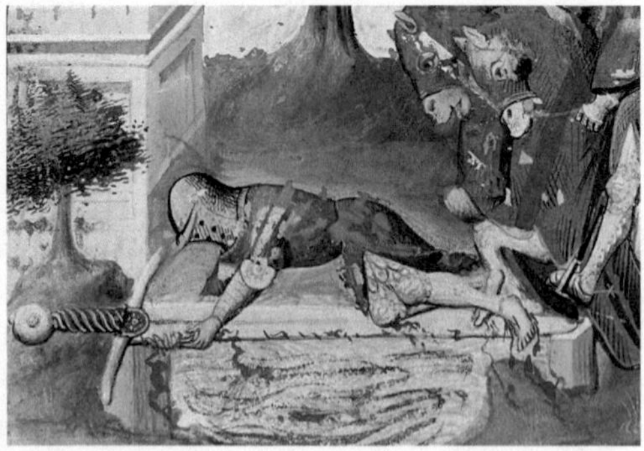

Figure 6.5. (*Left*) Lancelot crossing the Sword Bridge. Detail of an illustration of the *Lancelot-Grail* (1230–35) from a 1344 manuscript from the Hainaut Province, Belgium.
Bibliothèque nationale de France, Français 122 fol. 1

Figure 6.6. (*Right*) Lancelot crossing the Sword Bridge. From an early fifteenth-century illustrated manuscript of the *Lancelot-Grail*, Paris.
Bibliothèque nationale de France, Français 119 fol. 321v

Lancelot cannot even defy his opponent unless he first crosses over. There are only two daunting routes to the castle: one underwater and the other a razor-sharp sword bridge. Our hero leaves the easier option to Gawain his friend and tackles the passage across the sword. The price Lancelot will pay for challenging the formidable Méléagant is registered by deep lacerations on his hands, feet, and knees (figs. 6.5 and 6.6). The bridge in stories like this symbolizes a rite of passage attained through virtually superhuman self-overcoming. It designates a place for courage and "assays to obtain a supplement of being," and often through the intercession of providence.[20] It is in contrast to such scenarios that Farquhar meets his end. He embraces his beloved wife precisely by being denied an opportunity of passage. He falls to his death through the life-deck to which he is tied, on a structure he intended to burn. He has burned his bridges.

The execution of the Confederate cuts away at another symbolic meaning of the bridge: its equivalence with a penis. In Freudian psychology the extended penis itself is a life-giving bridge, linking two human beings to create a third.[21] Here the bridge-penis of Farquhar undergoes castration, a life-sapping cut, fortifying his desire to embrace his wife. Between one step and another impossible to take, there issues forth a power he cannot defeat. It undoes the life-battle with death through copulation. Death breaks the copulative bond, symbolized already by the bridge.

The life-and-death situation at and on this bridge also conjures an image of the umbilical cord. The placental exchange from mother to fetus along this primordially productive bridge "creates the first medial 'bond' between these dyadic partners," notes Peter Sloterdijk. The umbilical cord ties them in "a trinitary unity from the start; the third element turns two into one." The two ends of this single connection, mother and child, "are, in their mode of being, only ever poles of a dynamic in-between."[22] By being cut, the umbilical cord creates the very possibility of penis and sexual intercourse, preparing a way for the fecundating transfer of semen to egg. (Yet clearly we are involved in a circle: without cord no penis, and without penis no fetus or cord.) The relevance of this story of the umbilical cord to the story of Ambrose Bierce is analogical. That cord is figuratively attached to Farquhar's neck. If it breaks, Farquhar can live. If it holds, he cannot be released into life. Here too we have a circle. The life that he projects in fantasy so long as the cord pulls taut, while he exists between life and death, consists in unity, not separation, with the woman he loves. If the noose fails to break, Farquhar-infant cannot achieve a separate existence; nor can he return to the woman from whom he has been separated.

To add another layer of significance to the story, its political context reaffirms a belonging-separation scenario. As an American secessionist, Farquhar rejects the broader, ideal nation, the Union, from which the Confederates seek to withdraw. The emblem of that Union is the bridge, shuttling supplies from one end to the other. Farquhar asserts secessionist fervor in attempting to burn this bridge. He individuates himself through a rebellion that the Union will not tolerate. He has one great and single moment of bliss—exactly between his two choices, in believing that he is replacing one union with another, the communal, political union with an intensely personal one: an amorous-maternal idyll annihilating strife altogether. Both the crisis of birth (the breaking of the umbilical cord) and the castrating death experience (the abolition of copulation) activate a life of fantasy (where he imagines what life does not allow). The conduct of life is granted by death.

Jungian interpretations of bridge narratives offer one additional insight, and particularly to the story's stylistic shift from objective, prosaic reporting to the fabulous adventures of the escaping hero. In Jungian analytical psychology, folk tales about bridges are often associated with a turn from one level of knowledge to another.[23] They signal access to the space of the unconscious, allowing the subject to tap into archetypal spiritual resources to make a significant existential transition. In Farquhar's vertical plunge, that other space comes to the forefront of consciousness, allowing intense needs to be acknowledged. Farquhar descends into his psychic depths thanks to a disruption of the logically sequential grammar of his wakeful narrative. That is the practical order in which he normally operates, where everything seems to be matter of fact. The imaginative intuition unfolds instead *from within*. Did Ambrose Bierce want to make it perfectly clear that the final tightening noose gave the lie to Farquhar's imaginary, unconscious story? No, for nothing in the story suggests that Farquhar *did not believe* that in dying he came home to clasp his wife.

Kafka's Bridges to Nowhere

The possibility of death accompanies each truly critical decision. Even the behavior of Farquhar himself has something suicidal about it. The suicide, at one level, is a person who rejects transitional options: the premium of ethical change, the progression invoked by every symbolic bridge. Suicide is an ostensible confession of life's failure, declining ameliorative rites of passage. It is a rite of counterpassage, transiting *away* from acts of transit.

Franz Kafka stages homicide-suicides at bridge junctures in a number of stories. In "The Judgment" (1912), family tensions culminate in an explosive argument between Georg and his father, who blasts his son with these final words: "I sentence you now to death by drowning!" Georg voluntarily acts out the judgment, and one cannot tell whether in acceptance or in a spirit of parody. He flees the apartment and hurries down the staircase to throw himself into the river. "Out of the front door he bolted, across the roadway, driven toward the water." He then clutches the railing of the city bridge

> as a starving man clutches for food. He swung himself over, like the accomplished gymnast he had been in his youth, to his parents' pride. With weakening grip he was still holding on when he spied between the railings an approaching bus that would easily cover the sound of his fall, called out in a faint voice: "Dear parents, I have always loved you," and let himself drop.
>
> At this moment an almost endless line of traffic streamed over the bridge.[24]

As Georg holds onto its railing, the bridge initially provides support. Then he looks *through* the interstices of the railing, like Farquhar through the wooden ties of his bridge, noticing the busy traffic passing over. He clings and looks for a moment at the life of others, making his fall coincide with—and be masked by—the vehicular mobility of the platform.

The ending of Kafka's *The Trial* (1914–15) is just as ambiguous, stressing the passivity no less than the agency of its protagonist. Joseph K., too, has been condemned to death, though it is no clearer here *why* he must die than it was with Georg. His death is also tied to the juncture of a bridge. There K. tarries with two strangely accommodating captors:

> In complete harmony all three now made their way across a bridge in the moonlight, the two men readily yielded to K.'s slightest movement, and when he turned slightly toward the parapet they turned, too, in a solid front. The water, glittering and trembling in the moonlight, divided on either side of a small island, on which the foliage of trees and bushes rose in thick masses, as if bunched together. Beneath the trees ran gravel paths, now invisible, with convenient benches on which K. had stretched himself at ease many a summer. "I didn't mean to stop," he said to his companions, shamed by their obliging compliance.[25]

While K. recalls relaxing on that island beneath the bridge in the past, one wonders what relationship that island may have with archetypal islands of the dead in the midst of the oceans. K.'s fixation on it at the moment preceding his death, on the bridge in the moonlight, is tied to reluctance to move forward in life's progression ("I didn't mean to stop"). Once he and his companions do cross the bridge and reach bedrock at the quarry, they twist a knife into his heart. Was it homicide or suicide? In his last moments of consciousness K. "perceived clearly that he was supposed to seize the knife himself, as it traveled from hand to hand above him, and plunge it into his own breast."[26] Kafka's short parable called "The Bridge" (1917), examined further on in these pages, also reinforces the structure's association with death both inevitable and willed, personifying the bridge as a man who dies by turning around to see what is crossing over. Its perplexing moral declares that a bridge cannot cease to be a bridge without falling.[27]

Suicide Bridges

While Romans may or may not have cast sexagenarians from the Sublician Bridge, and certainly did expose corpses of others on the Ponte Sant'Angelo, another bridge in ancient Rome was favored for leaping to death: the Pons Fabricius. On this score we have the testimony of Horace, who beseeches a desperate friend not to be as foolhardy as he himself was when his investments went bad and he nearly jumped off the Fabrician Bridge.[28] Built in 62 BCE, it still connects Rome's island to the Tiber River's left bank. The right bank is attached to the Tiber Island via the Pons Cestius, built a few decades later. Both bridges figure into the old name of the island: *Insula inter duos pontos* (the island between two bridges), the interstitial position of which is made structurally relevant in the film *L'avventura* by Michelangelo Antonioni (1960), where a meticulously staged early scene shows both flanking waterways through the windows of an apartment on the island. Beneath the Pons Fabricius the fluvial currents accelerate as they stretch around the island and shallow out over sharp rocks at the south side of bridge. Horace was not the only one who referred to ancient Romans jumping to their death at this river-divided site of the city. Fellow poet Juvenal recommends to a friend (strangely called "Postumus") that he should sooner throw himself off another bridge at the end of the island than commit the folly of marriage. That bridge, the Pons Aemilius, now stands broken in the river and has taken on the name of the Ponte Rotto:

> Postumus, you were sane once. Are you really taking a wife?
> Which Tisiphone is it, with her snakes, driving you mad?
> You surely don't have to endure it, with so much rope about,
> Those vertiginous windows open, the Aemilian bridge at hand?[29]

Present-day Romans more often drive to the towering Ponte di Ariccia, seventy-two meters high and now equipped with protective metal netting. Others choose the viaduct on the freeway from Rome to Aquila or the suicide span (Ponte delle Torri) at Spoleto, celebrated by Goethe.[30] Northern Italy has the Ponte Fossano, the final stop for the son of business magnate Gianni Agnelli. Many cities have their suicide bridges. The most notorious is the Golden Gate, but there are three more in southern California: the Arroyo Seco (or Colorado Street) Bridge in Pasadena (also outfitted with steel guard rails, the one where Chaplin shot *The Kid*), the Coronado Bridge in San Diego, and the Cold Spring Canyon Bridge in Santa Barbara. In Scotland, from the Overtoun Bridge, dogs inexplicably jump to their deaths, in an act so mysterious as to have inspired a small industry of mystical studies.

There are also suicide bridges in reputedly suicide cities. Not Rome, but its rival for tourists, Florence, is one of them. "Florence has always been a popular destination for suicides," declares the opening line of a memoir, with sensational nonchalance.[31] Clinical psychologist Dr. Graziella Magherini accounts for the deeply disquieting effect of the Renaissance city in terms of the Stendhal syndrome, a destabilizing and often overwhelming effect provoked by the city's great works of art. The condition takes its name from the French novelist's account of how he became breathlessly incapacitated by Florence's artistic splendors during his visit in 1817. Magherini provides clinical evidence for the syndrome by analyzing otherwise inexplicable symptoms manifested by foreigners hospitalized for mental breakdown in her home city, several saved as they jumped or attempted to jump from bridges.[32] While the root of their traumas is perfectly independent of the city's beauty and bridges, one can easily understand how these sights could aggravate the symptoms. Ponte Vecchio, Ponte Santa Trinita, and the city's visual splendors are emblems of cultural and spiritual transcendence. Triggering critical reactions in subjects, the artistic works function like mirrors, reflecting attention back onto the viewers, drawing existential frustrations to the surface of consciousness and pulling senses of underachievement into relief. Extraordinary beauty impugns all that is mediocre, unhappy, and squalid. I dare say that were it not for the uplifting effect of Italians in general, anyone who feels bad will feel worse in Florence. Sublime experience exacerbates the unhappiness of the unhappy. Those tourists who have committed suicide in the city of Brunelleschi probably felt even more estranged there, in those dazzling surroundings, than in the country they left behind. Perhaps they had already embarked on their Italian journey to remove themselves from their own community; increased alienation may have stretched that removal to its ultimate consequence.

No speculation can plumb the psychological depths of a person who leaps off a bridge. Each case remains opaque, closed to the understanding of the outside world. As for *why* people choose to end things from a bridge rather than elsewhere, speculation is just as limited. Jumping from a bridge possesses some convenience, if one can use a glib term of that sort in this context; it requires no special equipment or advance preparation, possesses little risk of failure, and so on. Some writers on bridge jumpers have concluded that they are likely to be impulsive suicides, who would not have leapt if they had taken more time to consider their decision. A survivor of a leap from the Golden Gate Bridge, Kevin Hines, has campaigned for suicide-prevention measures precisely by emphasizing this point. Counterlogical as it seems, he argues that the decision to kill oneself amounts only to a temporary way of thinking; suicide is "a permanent solution to a temporary problem."[33]

Some bridges host death more than once a month. The best known are listed in table 1. A bridge rarely included in these statistics, so as not to dissuade tourism, is the Rainbow Bridge at Niagara Falls, where, between 1856 and 1995, the last date that figures were compiled, there were 2,780 documented jumps into the falls from that bridge as well as the nearby sites of Whirlpool Bridge, Prospect Point, the rapids at Devil's Hole, and spots around Goat Island and Three Sisters Islands.[34]

Table 1. Bridge Deaths by Suicide

Year Built	Bridge	Deaths by Suicide*
1864	Clifton Suspension Bridge in Bristol, UK	1000
1886	Netty Jetty Bridge in Karachi	1050
1897	Hornsey Lane Bridge (Archway Bridge) in London	2000
1918	Bloor St. Bridge (Prince Edward Viaduct) in Toronto	500
1930	Jacques Cartier Bridge in Montréal	400
1932	Aurora Bridge (George Washington Memorial Bridge) in Seattle	230
1937	Golden Gate Bridge in San Francisco	1700
1942	Segovia Viaduct in Madrid	520
1957	Wuhan Yangtze River Bridge in China	1500
1968	Nanjing Yangtze River Bridge in China	2300
1969	San Diego-Coronado Bridge in California	400
1973	First Bosphorus Bridge in Istanbul	400
1973	Nusle Bridge (Nuselsky Most) in Prague	350
1978	West Gate Bridge in Melbourne	700
1981	Humber Bridge in Kingston upon Hull, UK	240
1987	Sunshine Skyway Bridge in Florida	200

* These conservative estimates must be assessed relative to the age of the bridge.

Leaps from these bridges are often evaluated in reference to the accessibility of the sites, the low parapets on the bridges, the higher density of traffic there than elsewhere, presenting more opportunities for fatality, and so on. The effectiveness of retrofitting bridges like these with suicide-prevention devices has also been debated, some arguing that such strategies would only drive suicidal subjects elsewhere. If statistics themselves are any measure, however, jumping from bridges does not seem to be particularly inspired by the "facility" of the practice. Less than 3% of all suicides worldwide appear to happen this way. On the other hand, nearly 40% of all suicides in Marin County, California, between 1998 and 2009 occurred as jumps off the Golden Gate Bridge, suggesting the galvanizing effect of the *notoriety* of particular sites.[35] The fatal jump may take more resolve than pulling a trigger or swallowing pills after all.

Accounts of surviving jumpers from the Golden Gate Bridge are abetted by the chilling evidence of Eric Steel's film called *Bridge* (2006). Documenting twenty-three suicides over the course of one year, the film makes it clear that many returned to the Golden Gate several times before mustering up the necessary conviction or courage. Steel's film raises the question of another factor potentially at play in jumping off a bridge. Some "choose it because they know they'll be seen, and I think that this act of witness, of bearing witness, is part of the desire."[36] In this interview Steel addresses the issue of why he embarked on his project at all. He posits tacit sympathy between the recording of his camera and the *publicity* of the jumpers' final gesture, conducted before strangers. The casual remark by Alexander Theroux to the effect that on the Golden Gate Bridge "virtually every person jumps, not from the bay side, but from the side facing land, and people" suggests that distraught jumpers aim to settle accounts with the community by whom they've been wronged, delivering themselves up as a public sacrifice.[37] The problem with this reasoning is that the pedestrian walkway of the Golden Gate Bridge—where the parapet is waist-high, and from which it is easiest to jump—*already* faces the city and the bay. As one humorist replies to the Theroux statement, "No one with his heart set seriously on a high dive into the frigid waters of San Francisco Bay would be so foolhardy as to risk a dash across six lanes of high-speed traffic."[38] Still, the idea of facing one's tormentors at the desperate hour makes for a good story.

Beyond these statistics and issues of pragmatics lie archaic and ritual associations with death by water. On the one hand, envelopment in water estranges a body drawing lymph from the earth and the air. On the other, water is the encompassing fluid from which that bodily life begins, making it appropriate to return it to that element by which it is reabsorbed and made to disappear. The irrecoverability of a corpse lost to the Tiber, which was so dreaded by the persecuted Christians of Rome, dissolves a person into anonymity, undoing its brief experiment in individuality.

For all those seeking witnesses to their pain, there are probably just as many others wishing to slip away unseen. The poet Paul Celan was one. Jumping (as we assume) into the Seine off the Pont Mirabeau on a night in 1970, he sought neither onlookers nor wanted his body to be recovered. Another poet, Weldon Kees, apparently also delivered himself invisibly into the waters. His car was found abandoned near the Golden Gate Bridge in 1995 with its key in the ignition. Hart Crane leapt off a ship into the Gulf of Mexico in 1932 and was not recovered either. Giving adamantine verbal expression to strong, individual subjectivity, these poets apparently did not hold their bodily selves in the same high esteem. The poetic enterprise requires firm commitment to self-transcendence. One wonders whether, in ending their lives, Celan, Crane, and Kees felt they had failed even in that, believing that the pages they wrote fell short of an envisioned shore—toward which their writings tended like a bridge, perhaps even like a platform of self-undoing. "Here lies One whose Name was writ in Water" reads the epitaph of

John Keats (he not a suicide). The words express tension between permanent, verbal, individual inscription and the effacing effects of the water. Conclusive being beckons to inconclusive selves from within those waters. "We have an interval," writes Walter Pater, "and then our place knows us no more."[39]

Fluvial Regeneration

The ritual of death by water is as old as the Hyperboreans. That mythical but superbly happy community of creatures reputedly had the power "to be immortal, as they have no infirmities or labours or wars or quarrels or famines or vices or faults." Yet "in spite of this they all die: for after a thousand years of life or thereabouts, weary of the earth, they leap of their own accord from a certain cliff into the sea, where they drown."[40] The passage is by Leopardi, and one of his sources was Pliny the Elder, who imagines that the Hyperboreans, by jumping into the sea, achieved a most blissful burial: "Discord is there ignored, and so is disease. People there do not die but from the satiety of living. After a festive banquet, full of the joys of old age, the one who wants to die jumps into the seas from a lofty rock. Such is for them the happiest way to die."[41]

There were also legendary lovers of Leucadia who chose the same route, jumping off tall cliffs from the cape of the island into the Ionian Sea. The poet Sappho is said to have been one of them. Those not killed by the leap found their despair instantly transformed into a love of life.[42] The myths of both Hyperboreans and Leucadians allude to the sacred allure of the fluvial element which is so amply documented in Aegean communities by Anita Seppilli.[43] The very same waters that are defiled by bridges exact tolls of appeasement. At archetypical and phylogenetic levels, their healing and regenerative powers can beckon to subjects in moments of utmost stress.

A series of songs by Radiohead conveys the supernatural attraction of such waters, associating them with transformative continuity and ontological renewal. One from *The King of Limbs* (2011) called "Codex" invites people to "jump off the end" with no one around, like dragonflies. The water is perfectly "clear and innocent," the song insists, and it suggests that the jump abolishes guilt ("No one gets hurt / You've done nothing wrong"). Is the jump in "Codex" really intended to end in death? Does its antiguilt gesture bring consolation or merely self-deception (by way of the "sleight of hand" the song mentions)? Or does the song voice a perspective that the singer does not share, which encourages the leap? All that is sure is the clear and restorative life associated with the aqueous dimension. When the song's verses are ended, the music modulates to a passage of utter serenity with sustained chords, suggesting an incipient new life beneath the waters.

Another Radiohead song—the "Pyramid Song" from *Amnesiac* (2001)—speaks in the first person and identifies entry into the waters more pointedly with liberation from torment: "I jumped in the river and what did I see? / Black-eyed angels swam with me." There in the water lay also "a moon full of stars and astral cars," along with "all my lovers [and] all my past and futures." The song's conclusion, "There was nothing to fear and nothing to doubt," is a preformulation of the later idea in "Codex" to the effect that "You've done nothing wrong" and "No one gets hurt." The only disquieting element among the good things in this place beneath the waters—from which "we all went to heaven in a little row boat"—lies in the black eyes of the angels, cast, one imagines, as fish.

The song's music video produces a revealing perspective to the narrative, replacing the paradisiacal transit of the collective "we" with a more complex and abstract ascension. First the video shows a penguin-like protagonist jumping into a broad body of water stretching as far out as one can see. We see it descend to the bottom where a great metropolis with skyscrapers, floating chairs, disembodied lights, empty cars, and human skeletons rise up. Here lie signs of a civilization that is no more, a city like Atlantis, which has met with an unspecified catastrophe. Before diving into the waters, the creature grabs an air tank. At the bottom of the sea it enters a front yard, and then a house, and eventually settles into a living room where the starlike lights grow thick. After a few moments the camera exits the house and floats back to the top of the water. An air tube accompanies it, now detached from the protagonist, who apparently has remained at the bottom. At the water's surface the scene changes to an orange, cloud-filled sky where one dancing star is slowly joined by a second, then a third, until there are five. They play with each other and waft through the sky in a delicate dance. Three stars bond in the center of the screen while two rotate at its edges. The stars vanish one after the other, leaving one in the middle.

When great sea tempests have passed, especially those placing sailors' lives at stake, dramatic lights are occasionally said to appear at the tops of boat masts. Perceived as good omens, these electromagnetic phenomena are called corposants (from *corpi sancti*, or holy bodies). They are traditionally identified with the souls of dead sailors. In a sublime description in "The Candles," chapter 119 of *Moby-Dick*, Melville instead depicts the corposants as infernal, boding no good at all. Either way, these illuminations—called St. Elmo's Fire when they appear in a flame-like blue or as violet glows—are iconographically akin to the astral divinities that mythological traditions describe as leaping into the sea. The head star of them all is Helios—that sun from which Emperor Hadrian Aelius took his name. Greek mythology recounts that Helios is hurled to his death into a river, a river leading out to the great ocean surrounding every known land on earth. From the same ocean the sun rises again each day. "Stars dive into the sea," comments Seppilli, "but . . . rebirth is what they appear to promise—in harmony with the character of Ocean, bestower of both death and life—to those who repeat their exemplary act."[44]

The lights at the end of Radiohead's song recall these corposant-stars, just as its title, "Pyramid Song," recalls the final resting place of Egyptian pharaohs from where they rejoin eternity, evoking a second association of the Helios with which this chapter began: the divinization of the Emperor Hadrian, in his analogous mausoleum, a structure approached by the bridge or, in this context, by the dive of the astral divinities. The final lights of Radiohead's music video develop the song's emphasis on seeing, and with it an even rarer association of Helios. The song's first question, "What did I see?" is supplied by all the things "I used to see / All my lovers were there with me / All my past and futures." These all return with the "moon full of stars and astral cars," alongside black-eyed angels who look back at the jumper swimming alongside. Helios—cast into the ocean—was said to have eyes everywhere.

The vision of a new life in the deepest ocean reappears in a third Radiohead song where, at the bottom of the sea, "your eyes / they turn me." Here, in "Weird Fishes/Arpeggi" (from *In Rainbows*, 2007), the singer says he would be crazy not to follow where those eyes lead—to the "edge of the earth" where he will fall off. Everybody leaves "If they get the chance / and this is my chance." The "I" will hit the bottom "and escape," eaten by worms and weird fishes.

Whose eyes are "your eyes"? Do they belong to a mermaid, to a drowned lover, to angel-eyed fish? The secondary title of the song is "Arpeggi": ensembles of tones of one unifying chord struck in succession, stretching out the harmony as they hang together. These eyes and tones tempt our singer to turn his attention "to phantoms" followed to the edge of the earth, where he will achieve some sort of new chance.

The Golden Gate

At the westernmost reach of the American continent, where the sun sinks into the Pacific, stands an august emblem of the unity of water, sun, death, and eternity. It is the Golden Gate Bridge, marking the last terrestrial destination of the new nation's march of civilization, once thought to be backed by divine providence. By 1846, long before the bridge was built, the name "Golden Gate" already named the straits of the San Francisco Bay, and not merely in recollection of the Golden Horn of Constantinople, but also in expectation of great riches to flow into the American continent from Asia—Crane's "Cathay"—through this gate. This Golden Gate offers the last, unobstructed view of the setting Helios, the sun, and of the boundless spaces beneath and beyond him.

The Golden Gate Bridge is the antithesis of the monument at the other shore of America. Hart Crane died too soon to articulate the difference between it and the Brooklyn Bridge. After evoking New York City, Crane's poetic hymn to the prodigious promises of the new nation and its art passes through a descriptive panorama of America without coming to rest in the west, at the end of the nation's gold rush and railroads. There the Golden Gate Bridge signals the border between the national territory and the great reign of nature, the immeasurable Pacific, the setting sun, and the night daily engulfing the day. There the tall reach of the bridge's red pylons (a word deriving from the Greek word *pulē*, gate) creates a ladderlike ascension into the heavens, often receding invisibly into the clouds. These pylons create the impression of an Axis Mundi joining Heaven and earth, there combining with the horizontal axis of the bridge's platform to overcome a primordial strife between land, water, and air.[45] The massive intersecting axes thrust themselves into telluric origins and sea destinations. Both the location and the design of the Golden Gate make it appear to be the very last bridge of the world, providing the land's utmost frame, beyond which it points like a gateway onto the immense cosmos on which all life depends. There, where the great star sinks into the waters, Greek and Near Eastern mythologies situated the transitional point between life and death, the turn "from the ordinary world to . . . imaginary lands."[46]

It is impossible to account for the spell such a site can cast over those in a condition of spiritual turbulence, a site alluding to the source of life's light and the universe beyond. Crane's *The Bridge* could only supply an indirect perspective on this life-and-death relation through the image of a sacredly deranged figure who jumps to his death in the great inaugural metropolis:

> Out of some subway scuttle, cell or loft
> A bedlamite speeds to thy parapets,
> Tilting there momently, shrill shirt ballooning,
> A jest falls from the speechless caravan.
>
> ("TO BROOKLYN BRIDGE," LINES 17–20)

People witnessing this act may well be speechless or make embarrassed jests, but the jump of the bedlamite is neither humorous nor desperate. It is related to a "search for rebirth" embedded in the word "bedlamite" itself, for the word evokes not only the famous asylum of Bedlam but also "Bethlehem and the birth of the Word made Flesh. . . . 'To be drowned in order to be born again.'"[47] These words by Richard Sugg cite the psychologist Rollo May as he discusses the generative associations "of going under water, being drowned and born again, a myth that is passed down in different religions and different cultures. . . . To be drowned in order to be born again."[48]

The bridges of this chapter are all bridges of separation, signaling differences between ontological realms. But they also signal a wish for transition, for redemption and expiation of guilt, as in the case of the son of Kafka's "The Judgment." These undertones are hard to overlook in deaths by water. The gallows at these cataclysmic sites is reserved for those who are "houseless by night," to quote Thomas Hood and his poem about a woman who throws herself to death in the London of 1844. But whether actually homeless, whether female or male, those houseless by night have been rendered

> Mad from life's history,
> Glad to death's mystery,
> Swift to be hurl'd—
> Anywhere, anywhere
> Out of the world![49]

The bridge as gallows is a site for a crossing, carrying the estranged away. For them there is no Cathay beyond the western shore, but only the water spanned, the water unspannable.

CHAPTER 7

Nietzsche's Bridges

No study of the conceptual implications of bridges would be complete without a discussion of a statement that has echoed for a century in the ears of millions: "Man is a rope, tied between animal and overman—a rope over an abyss. . . . What is great in man is that he is a bridge and not a goal."[1] This evocative declaration is one of the very first in Nietzsche's *Thus Spoke Zarathustra* (1883–85) and remains bedeviled by questions. Just what is this overman—or "more-than-man"—to which the rope of man is tied?[2] What does Nietzsche mean by animal (*Tier*)? In what way is humanity moving from animal toward more-than-man? And why does Nietzsche associate that humanity with a collocation in space, especially such a singular one? He speaks of humans as a rope, or a connective tissue. Yet a rope is already a human artifact. To be human in this way would be to tread over a humanity we have already created, on a trip to the extrahuman.

This statement about a rope-bridge as the foundation of human existence can only be tied to others in Nietzsche, and to the image of the bridge in his time, if we hope to understand its meaning. To begin acquiring a clearer sense of the statement it helps to take note of the philosopher's approach to the built space of human environments, of which the bridge is a type.

Architectural Soul

Few and far between, Nietzsche's remarks on architecture reveal a thinker continually reflecting on the spatial and subjective positioning of human beings. A recurring motif in those reflections is the way psyches are bridged with built environments. Any architect who takes good care in designing a building, writes the philosopher in a note of

1873, aims to provoke a “manifold unequal reflex, the repercussion of his work in many souls.”[3] The word “repercussion” suggests an acoustic effect, with a stimulus moving from a building to a psyche wherein it echoes.[4] Five years later, Nietzsche develops his intuition about the interaction of material and immaterial phenomena into an idea of buildings appearing to rise from the ground with a life of their own. The Greek temples at Paestum give a distinct impression that “a soul had been instilled in a stone by magic and now desired to speak through it.” The philosopher surmises that the temples’ makers sought to achieve instantaneous and overwhelming spiritual effects—“to attune the viewer’s or the hearer’s soul in such a way that it believes in the sudden emergence of perfection.”[5]

This idea of soul communicating with stone imagines cutting through the divide between subjective and objective phenomena. Up to the late nineteenth century, churches inspired reverie in those passing by them or entering them, Nietzsche remarks. By his own time this occurs only rarely, and the loss, he believes, should be redressed. Modern cities should be planned or redesigned to offer “still, wide, extensive places for reflection,” the type of places that churches and once religious spaces no longer provide. The word “reflection,” *Nachdenken*, signals the philosopher’s interest in intensifying the interaction of subject and space: “We wish to see *ourselves* translated into stones and plants,” his remark on reflection ends; “we want to take walks *in ourselves* when we stroll around these buildings and gardens.”[6] The title of this particular aphorism of Nietzsche—“Architecture for the Perceptive” (*für Erkennenden*)—accentuates the spiritual activation which can and should result from built space.

Architecture is thus seen as a mise-en-scène for subjective activity, particularly among those who are philosophically or spiritually inclined, who walk around knowing or perceiving. This abiding concern for the interchange of self and surroundings had already begun when the philosopher was only thirteen years old:

Ein Spiegel ist das Leben.
In ihm sich zu erkennen,
Möcht ich das erste nennen,
Wonach wir nur auch streben!![7]

Life is a mirror.
To recognize oneself in it,
May I be the first to say,
Is also what we strive for!

The name of this poem, *Rückblick*, "look back," anticipates the *Nachdenken*, or "thinking back," that Nietzsche later hopes that built space will foster (translated above as "reflection"), just as the poem's *erkennen*, "to recognize or perceive," prepares for the use of the same word in the "knowing" or "perceiving" that architecture stimulates.

The perception of an ensemble of self and space helps explain why Nietzsche became so attached to the hard and somber city of Genoa on the Ligurian coast: "to leave it behind is also to leave oneself behind," he writes in a letter of April 7, 1888, to Peter Gast.[8] If architecture is itself already a material embodiment of mind (an instilling of soul in stone), then it is perfectly appropriate for moods and inspirations of the perceptive to be kindled by amenable settings. The experience of self-in-world aims at a rapport of sympathy, of feeling together, of reciprocal reflection. Productive architecture creates passage. It gives spatial-existential character to the "content" of psychic form, enabling people to fit into their surroundings something like characters in the pages of a book. Being integrated with one's environment is being bridged.

Venice

A poem by Nietzsche speaks of music and built space in terms of these bonds:

An der Brücke stand
Jüngst ich in brauner Nacht.
Fernher kam Gesang:
Goldener Tropfen quoll's
Über die zitternde Fläche weg.
Gondeln, Lichter, Musik—
Trunken schwamm's in die Dämmrung hinaus . . .

Meine Seele, ein Saitenspiel
Sang sich, unsichtbar berührt,
Heimlich ein Gondellied dazu,
Zitternd vor bunter Seligkeit.
—Hörte jemand ihr zu? . . .[9]

Lately I stood at the bridge
in the brown night.
From afar there came a song:
a golden drop, it swelled
across the trembling surface.

Gondolas, lights, music—
drunken it swam out into the twilight . . .

My soul, a stringed instrument,
sang to itself, invisibly touched,
a secret gondola song,
trembling with iridescent happiness.
—Was anyone listening?

What affects the speaker's spirit in this way at this time is not the bridge on which he stands, nor a portico or a building facade, but rather a piece of music. It is a Venetian *barcarolle* wafting over to Nietzsche on the Rialto Bridge—in the spring of 1885, as he reports to Peter Gast on July 2.[10] Self-propelling or self-animating, like the temples at Paestum, the song transmutes itself into a liquid drop, swimming drunken over the quivering surface of the Venetian lagoon. The synesthesia of sound into sight affects the soul of the speaker in like manner, who is "touched by invisible hands," enough to be turned into a stringed instrument. Imperceptibly moved, he responds in sympathy with a song of his own.

The Venetian bridge *enables* the brown-evening contact, producing another bridge in turn, triggering a dynamics of call-and-response. Did anyone hear the song sung to himself, answering the one that he heard, this speaker wonders? Will the new song extend and multiply the song-generating ties? The poem implies no, but the answer is yes: The song Nietzsche heard in 1885 created a poem that people now read, replicating the reciprocating process of the bridge. The song is revived by each reading in a potentially infinite relay. That is the effect of art—when aiming at interaction.

A separate reference by Nietzsche to Venice creates a more complicated relay. "Together one hundred deep solitudes form the city of Venice—this is its magic," to which he adds: "An image for the human beings of the future."[11] The implication is that the interaction engaged in by the solitary Nietzsche in Venice might partake in a ramifying network of numberless solitudes. If one anonymous song can spur the response of another, a single person can bond with lone souls in a chain of relationships. The bridge-city of Venice brings solitudes together to compose a city, modeling the features of a future society. Will cities of the twentieth and twenty-first centuries have to learn to accommodate monadic subjectivities, to grapple with the political challenge of connecting them one to another in a space they share? Is that the suggestion of Nietzsche's "image of the human beings of the future"?

Anticipating several theories of community of the past three decades (particularly of Maurice Blanchot, Jean-Luc Nancy, Giorgio Agamben, and Roberto Esposito), Massimo Cacciari calls attention to a related passage in which Nietzsche discusses the state. Cacciari surmises that every politics of the future will be pressured to produce unity among individuals without a true state to represent them. Politics will face an "autonomous multiplication of subjects" sharing little other than the space each occupies in a different way.[12] To use a metaphor dear to Nietzsche, each will be a wayfarer in the midst of others, perhaps even a migrant, coexisting in contiguity. In glossing that passage at the end of the first volume of Nietzsche's *Human, All Too Human* (§638), Cacciari invokes this other one from *Thus Spoke Zarathustra*:

> Where the state ceases, there the unsuperfluous person begins; there the song of the necessary begins, that unique and irreplaceable melody. Where the state *ceases*—look there, my brothers! Do you not see them, the rainbow and the bridges to the more-than-man?
>
> (*ZARATHUSTRA*, "ON THE NEW IDOL")

That necessary, exceptional, and unsuperfluous person can no longer embody a typical or universal subject. Where persons are not homogenized by institutions like states or nations, but rather remain singular and "necessarily" essential, the possibility arises of a true engagement with differences, where humans emit statements or songs that can find resonance outside them. There, where the state no longer exists, appear rainbows and bridges to the "more-than-man"—channels to realities over and beyond a single, self-articulating people.

Although, by the philosopher's own reckoning, the art of Zarathustra remains solitary and monological, it produces strong responses in readers. Nietzsche's poem and the fragment on Venice, in particular, announce and perform the differential communication about which they speak. The fragment propagates the performance when it returns in an exchange of letters between Karl Jaspers and Martin Heidegger. It brings the estranged philosophical associates together across the strife-ridden years following World War II.

In a letter of August 6, 1949, Jaspers thanks Heidegger for three essays received in the mail. Jaspers also takes the occasion to criticize his junior philosopher, who has publicly tainted himself through firm affiliation with the Nazi party (a matter Jaspers does not reference in his letter, but we know how disillusioned he was). Jaspers takes particular exception to Heidegger's declaration that "Language is the house of Being." It seems too peremptory, too categorical an assertation, to Jaspers. Above all, the credo makes language, a medium of intellectual connection, appear too insular, gathering and subsuming all things within it. To Jaspers's mind Being is not *contained* in language, but takes place outside it—in open and ramifying contacts, in orientations and actions that language serves, especially in reciprocal human attachments. "Language as 'the house of Being,'" exclaims Jaspers: "—I bristle, because all language seems to be only a bridge to me. . . . I could almost say conversely: 'Where there is language, there Being itself is not yet or no longer.'"[13]

Heidegger's conception of language strikes the older philosopher as too monological in nature. It appears to downplay the relationships that language establishes between words and things, between persons, communities, and cultures. Jaspers's metaphor of a bridge in place of a house resounds deeply with Heidegger. It reminds him (perhaps via the poem above) of the Nietzschean fragment on Venice. In his answer to Jaspers, Heidegger might well have said directly that his apparently monological, self-contained language *enables* the intersubjective action that Jaspers has in mind. But he does not. Instead he *exemplifies* Jaspers's intersubjective language by citing the Nietzschean passage, "Together one hundred deep solitudes form the city of Venice—this is its magic. An image for the human beings of the future." What he may be saying indirectly is that this city joined by bridges gives evidence that monologue and dialogue are not mutually exclusive. Even one hundred deep monologues can—indeed must—connect across divides, especially in these times of cultural division and isolation. The fractious conditions of postwar Germany may presage a more generalized situation in the future of interpersonal distance and metropolitan estrangement. In isolating times like these, Jaspers's bridge-language might have to be enacted precisely through the call-and-response of these kinds of letters.

Put to this use, Nietzsche's solitary, monological fragment validates the claim that it makes. The fragment, evoked by familiarity with Nietzsche's poem and recalled by Jaspers's notion of language as a bridge, presses Heidegger to re-elaborate the relation between language and Being *beyond* his original house-metaphor. Three years later he draws language into the precinct of a bridge in a critical meditation he elaborates in the essay "Building Dwelling Thinking" (1952).

Between Space-Times

Nietzsche saw his vocation as a historical bridge-event, and the characterization was not lost on thinkers and artists to come. In 1906 Edvard

Munch imagines the philosopher steeped in thought on a bridge (plate 3). He emanates blue swaths of color sweeping out like wings from his shoulders and a broad band of yellow from his head. The bridge on which the thinker stands—down which he looks—creates imbalance, diagonally slicing the setting in two. Swirling and abstract activity animates the left part of the painting while the side of the bridge remains calm and monochromatic.

As he stands on the bridge, Nietzsche also *is* the bridge. Munch effectively represents Nietzsche's own idea of himself as a critical event in the history of the West, standing at the brink of a transition to a future that would be radically different from the two millennia inaugurated by another bridge-figure, Jesus. Whoever is born after this transition, the philosopher boasts, "will belong to a higher history than all history hitherto."[14] His devastating critique of philosophy and religion presents an "event without equal," making the thinker "a *force majeure*, a destiny—he breaks the history of mankind into two parts. One lives *before* him, one lives *after* him."[15]

The Nietzsche of Munch stands at a juncture between a shore that he has left behind and another that he contemplates before him. The bridge is an all-altering Rubicon crossing, even if its steep downward angle casts a shadow over the salubriousness of the new itinerary. Still, two generations of intellectuals galvanized their work around the Nietzschean prospect that the twentieth century would play out a new approach to the world at hand. The Futurists, Expressionists, and Vorticists, Gabriele D'Annunzio, George Bernard Shaw, and Robert Musil, with dozens of others, shared a conviction that new principles for living had finally surfaced.

Massive bridge constructions in concrete and steel had already underpinned the great railroads of Europe and North America, giving figurative expression to the imagined leap forward. With its "space-traversing form," suspension technology had accrued sublime connotations, defying what art historian Wilhelm Worringer called the "immense spiritual dread of space" that characterized this moment in time.[16] By 1930, when Crane published *The Bridge*, bridges of mind as well as industry offered formidable metaphors for the transformative force of culture. If Crane originally wanted painter Joseph Stella to illustrate his great epic, it was not just because Stella had devoted a series of dramatic and metamorphic paintings to the Brooklyn Bridge ten years earlier. He had also given the impetus for this poetry of the bridge, writing of standing before it as though "on the threshold of a new religion or in the presence of a new DIVINITY." To all appearances the miraculous construction "proclaimed the luminous dawn of A NEW ERA."[17] Although the poet settled instead for the very different effects of three

Figure 7.1. Ernst Ludwig Kirchner, *Program of the Artists' Group Brücke* (1906). Serge Sabarsky Collection, New York

photographs by Walker Evans, Crane himself, as we have seen, also thought of the Brooklyn Bridge as a "Tall Vision-of-the-Voyage," a sacred mediator between personal spirit and world.[18]

What exactly this divinity or the new era might consist of at this juncture was not always clear. But that was just a detail to audacious post-Nietzscheans ready for the crossing. "To draw together all the revolutionary and vibrant elements; this is what we mean by the word bridge," wrote the painter Karl Schmidt-Rottluff when he joined three others to form the avant-garde project called *Brücke,* or "Bridge," in 1905.[19] The title page of their manifesto shows them perilously perched on a connection clinging to cliffs above running waters (fig. 7.1). Schmidt-Rottluff and fellow painters and woodcutters Ernst Ludwig Kirchner, Erich Heckel, and Fritz Bleyl settled on the moniker "Bridge" to highlight the transitional ambition of their project. "One evening, as we were walking home," recounts Heckel, "we talked about it once more. Schmidt-Rottluff said we could call it 'Brücke,' that was a many-layered word, and didn't imply a programme, but in a sense implied going from one bank to the other. It was clear which bank we wanted to leave, but it was less certain where we wanted to end up."[20] Along their journey they amalgamated elements of African and Oceanic primitivism, gravid gothic spiritualism, and contemporary urban perspectives into their work, charging it with dynamic, expressionistic distortion.

The inspiration for the *Brücke* was precisely that prologue to Nietzsche's *Thus Spoke Zarathustra,* which opened with the words, "Man is a rope, tied between animal and overman—a rope over an abyss." In choosing their venture for the sake of venture, the artists reaped the implications of another image central to the thinking of their world-historical mentor: the wanderer without direction. After his reflections on the state at the end of *Human, All Too Human,* Nietzsche stressed that this wanderer is anything but "a traveler *towards* a final goal, for this does not exist." The open-ended act of ethical and artistic departure is even better expressed by a contemporary of the *Brücke* group, Robert Musil. Art is "a dependent condition," he wrote, "a bridge arching away from solid ground as if it possessed a corresponding pier in the realm of the imaginary."[21] Imaginative novelty departs from a historically and epistemologically certain shore. While it depends on that only firm base, it arches away from the solid ground *as though* it possessed another pier in the realm of the imaginary, which it does not. The balancing destination is only hypothetically posited, or aspired to, by productive action.

The journey can thus be anxious and risk loss of all starting security. Its implications are eloquently expressed by another Austro-Hungarian, slightly younger than Musil, who eventually become a leading interpreter of Islam. Born in Galicia to a long line of rabbis, Leopold Weiss (1900–1992) changed his name to Muhammad Asad and converted to Islam in 1926. On his way to this conversion he had a vision:

> In the silence of the desert, which was underlined rather than broken by the plopping of the camels' feet, the occasional calls of the beduin drivers and the low-toned singing of a pilgrim here and there, I was suddenly overcome by an eerie sensation—so overwhelming a sensation that one might almost call it a vision; I saw myself on a bridge that spanned an invisible abyss: a bridge so long that the end from which I had come was already lost in a misty distance, while the other end had hardly begun to unveil itself to the eye.

The fear that overtakes him in the middle of this bridge in North Africa, when the mist obscures his point of departure, is what is most telling:

> I stood in the middle: and my heart contracted with dread as I saw myself thus halfway between the two ends of the bridge—already too far from the one and not yet close enough to the other—and it seemed to me, for long seconds, that I would always have to remain thus between the two ends, always above the roaring abyss.[22]

This spiritual conversion allows for no return to the start of the bridge; the commitment is destined to erase its point of departure, making way for an unknown future. As the arrival begins to unveil itself, it seems still to lie forbiddingly far away, risking to leave Asad perpetually stranded at the halfway point. A similarly unsettling transitional experience characterizes Nietzsche's bridge-condition, too, more strongly than apocalyptic forecasts of what is to come.

The Human Rope

Zarathustra's allegory of man as bridge, inspiring as it was to ambitious artists and thinkers of the early twentieth century, lacks an endpoint. The way it constructs its bridge-image complicates both Musil's idea of an imaginary arch and Asad's notion of radical conversion by describing a precarious walk on a tightrope with imminent danger of falling. The passage in full reads:

> Der Mensch ist ein Seil, geknüpft zwischen Tier und Übermensch—ein Seil über einem Abgrunde. Ein gefährliches Hinüber, ein gefährliches Auf-dem-Wege, ein gefährliches Zurückblicken, ein gefährliches Schaudern und Stehenbleiben. Was groß ist am Menschen, das ist, daß er eine Brücke und kein Zweck ist: was geliebt werden kann am Menschen, das ist, daß er ein Übergang und ein Untergang ist.
>
> Man is a rope, tied between animal and overman—a rope over an abyss. A dangerous going-across, a dangerous on-the-way, a dangerous looking back, a dangerous shuddering and stopping. What is great in man is that he is a bridge and not a goal: what can be loved in man is that he is a *going-over* and a *going-under*.
>
> ("ZARATHUSTRA'S PROLOGUE," §4)

The crossing of this bridge evokes danger, potentially precipitating its traveler into a ravine. Its going across entails faltering movement, a looking back, a shuddering and coming to a standstill (fig. 7.2). The passage also suggests a strange kinship between coming to ruin or perishing (*Untergang*) and transcending or overcoming (*Übergang*). In addition, the ropewalk possesses only a vague *Übermensch* as its destination: something (more than man) toward which man tends, perhaps in the manner of a culturally variable construct. Apparently advocating an ethos of self-transcendence, this parable of the suspension bridge makes clear only the "animal" from which human projects depart, and to which the rope is tied, obliging humans to remain balanced *here* on the way to an indeterminate *there*.

Figure 7.2. Katsushika Hokusai, *The Suspension Bridge on the Border of Hida and Etchū Provinces* (1830). Woodblock, 258 × 380 mm.
Mann Collection, Highland Park, Illinois

The betweenness of this human condition is not new in the history of thought. Analogies lie as far back as the Platonic duality of body and soul, turning humanity into an uncomfortable conjunction of matter and spirit, finitude and the infinite, in a hybridity that makes coherent action difficult. The metaphorical exclamation of Shakespeare's Hamlet attributes his indecisiveness to precisely this divided condition: "What should such fellows as I do crawling between heaven and earth?" The metaphysical stretch of Hamlet, the student of philosophy, is vertical and probably more reassuring than Nietzsche's horizontal one. With his head in the clouds, Hamlet at least has his legs firmly planted on the ground, even if he there crawls like a worm. He lives in this place of ontological division and relationship. Another key expression of the intermediary nature of humanity lies at the beginning of Pico della Mirandola's *Oration on the Dignity of Man* (1486), describing man as a half-bestial, half-angelic creature that God made free to determine his own responsibilities. This hybrid species possesses the potential for both the best and the worst actions, and is charged to make choices. Familiarity with a wide range of scriptures convinced Pico that the special darling of God possessed no inherent or fixed essence, but pure tendencies, linked to the extremes of beast and angel. Here too *homo sapiens* stands on a bridge, able to move forward or backward as circumstances require; but Nietzsche's bridge is less steady than Pico's and less teleologically clear.

Retaining from his predecessors one end of the polarity (the animal), the philosopher replaces the other (the goal of human aspiration) with something considerably more open. The word *Übermensch* only adds a prefix to the phenomenon *Mensch*, a prefix operating more in the manner of a suffix ("man" + *X*). The far pier of the rope-bridge remains shrouded in mist. The uncertain destination of the transiting *Mensch* confers a kind of "surplus value" on the conjectural projects of human beings, a value that not only transcends everything that individuals have already achieved, but one that remains relative to what they themselves are. Given Nietzsche's general reluctance to speak about anything more fundamental to human essence than a kind of will or drive to power, it is all but impossible to form a clear idea about this quality-less *Übermensch*. As Peter Sloterdijk puts it, it is a "transcendence device that cannot be fastened at the opposite pole," designed "to test the ability to keep your balance on the slimmest foundation."[23]

Nietzsche's rope-bridge thus does not present an image of humanity as part animal and part overman. It rather figures humanity as a connector between a certain and a nebulous condition, a commitment to a vital, hypothetical connection. Even before speaking of man as a bridge, Zarathustra emphatically rejects the notion that humanity is composite, denouncing "even the wisest" of his contemporaries for embodying only "a dichotomy and hybrid [*nur ein Zwiespalt und Zwitter*]." The cleavage between body and soul is a critical fallacy that Zarathustra's own thinking is bent on undoing. That is why he follows this denunciation of human schizomorphism with the injunction, "*remain true to the earth* and don't believe those who speak to you of supraterrestrial hopes" ("Zarathustra's Prologue," §3). The earth pertains to the "animal" at the first end of the rope: a complex body of material, biological fact. Humanity is thus suspended between natural, inherited materials and the ideal, transcendent ends to which they are put. The connector of the rope-bridge is a post-Platonic strategy to reunify what has improperly been made bipolar.

Count on Kafka to illuminate this condition with a surreal literalization. If man is a bridge, then how does the suspension feel? And who passes over the man-bridge? The humorist gives us the following vignette:

> I was stiff and cold, I was a bridge, I lay over a ravine [*über einem Abgrund*]. My toes on one side, my fingers clutching the other, I had

> clamped myself fast into the crumbling clay. The tails of my coat fluttered at my sides. Far below brawled the icy trout stream. No tourist strayed to this impassable height, the bridge was not yet traced on any map. So I lay and waited; I could only wait. Without falling, no bridge, once spanned, can cease to be a bridge.

After lying and waiting a long time, the anxious man-bridge finally receives the pleasure of hosting the first passenger—although it hardly proves pleasant! The crosser arrives and, after plunging the iron point of his stick into the bushy hair of the bridge, he

> jumped with both feet on the middle of my body. I shuddered with wild pain, not knowing what was happening. Who was it? A child? A dream? A wayfarer? A suicide? A tempter? A destroyer? And I turned so as to see him. A bridge to turn around! I had not yet turned quite around when I already began to fall, I fell and in a moment I was torn and transpierced by the sharp rocks which had always gazed up at me so peacefully from the rushing water.[24]

The parable first shifts the focus of Nietzsche's text from the lofty bridge passage to how it feels to be so stretched—as a man-bridge over which one is expected to cross. Then it raises the question of *just who* passes over this bridge, without giving us an answer. It is, by definition, an "overman," about which no more is said. Kafka also does something else. He accentuates the violence done to the stepped-on man, developing the implication Nietzsche built into *Zarathustra* by relating *going-over* to *going-under*:

> I love those who do not know how to live, except by *going under*, for they are those who cross over [*als Untergehende . . . Hinübergehenden*] . . .
>
> I love him who loves his virtue, for virtue is a *will to downfall* [*Wille zum Untergang*] and an arrow of longing . . .
>
> I love him who justifies those to come and redeems those begone: for he wants to be destroyed [*zu Grunde gehen*] by those in the present . . .
>
> I love him whose soul is deep even in its ability to be wounded, and who can be destroyed [*zu Grunde gehen kann*] by a small experience: thus he is glad to go over the bridge.
>
> ("ZARATHUSTRA'S PROLOGUE," §4; EMPHASIS ADDED)

Kafka's parable elaborates the first step in the process of bridge transit discussed by Zarathustra: the coming-to-ruin through which self-making occurs, the outcome of following such an ethos of self-transcendence to begin with. Indeed Zarathustra's prologue stresses the human sacrifices to be endured by whoever lives as "a bridge and not a goal." The crossing, warns the prophet, will create innumerable casualties (including one before his eyes—the tightrope walker falling to his death just after Zarathustra conceives of his parable). Self-overcoming cannot be distinguished from *being* overcome. They are both aspects of a single bridge.

Kafka's tragicomical man-bridge embraces his condition as transit-venue without a clue about what overman to support, about the ontological coordinates of his fastened structure, or about the endpoint of this self-transcendence. All he has is a structure to *serve* transcendence, suspended with no piers beneath it. The parable returns us to the fact that the only clear thing in Nietzsche's text is the present condition of insecurity and its point of departure: one's material and inherited constitution, woven—one imagines through culture—into a rope. The overall conditions of the transit thus include (a) the earthly foundation of the first pier—the body, the animal, or the life we are given, (b) the human condition of the rope—woven out of historical givens, (c) the precarious equilibrium of the required crossing, and (d) the abyss over which it takes place. The last element—in German the *Abgrund*—looms largest in the whole equation. It is the closest the bridge comes to having a proper foundation. It is the reality over which the bridge is constructed and the reason for its suspension design.

Philosophically speaking, the *Abgrund* names the lack of firm theoretical support for the things humans do. Our beliefs and morals possess no necessary and sufficient reason for being shaped as they are. Political and practical power is not (necessarily) underwritten by knowledge. Even philosophy lacks culturally foundational force. "Every philosophy is [merely] a foreground philosophy," writes Nietzsche; it serves interests that it does not even acknowledge. One always finds "an abysmally deep ground [*Abgrund*] behind every ground, under every attempt to furnish 'grounds.'"[25]

This leaves all ethics in the lurch. Robert Musil, Nietzsche's most intelligent first-generation heir, elaborates the metaphorical logic in nearly Kafkaesque fashion: "'The morality that has been handed down to us,' he said, 'is like being sent out on a swaying high wire over an abyss, with no other advice than: 'Hold yourself stiff as you can!'"[26] You have a sensation of walking on air, an intellectual vertigo, a feeling of spatiotemporal insecurity. This is "a dangerous looking back, a dangerous shuddering," and potential coming to a moral standstill. There is no firm footing in time and space.

From this hovering perspective present action appears thoroughly "untimely"—an epithet Nietzsche repeatedly uses to characterize his own biography and thought (cf. the *Untimely Meditations*, or *Unzeitgemässe Betrachtungen*, the title of collected essays from 1873 to 1876). A bridge-person like the philosopher Nietzsche lives always with "one foot *beyond* life," belonging to "the day after tomorrow." He is one "who has found his advantage in standing aside and outside . . . who *looks back* when relating what will come." Since childhood he has been "always . . . on his way and in foreign parts." His middle-aged thinking, too, is a "*Stehn und Spähn und Warten*" (standing and scouting and waiting). This seer of new futures is a "wanderer . . . always on my way, but without any goal." He suffers a whereabouts-anxiety, continually battling with the solipsistic fears experienced on the bridges of Venice.[27]

All this pertains to the *Abgrund* and the uncertain bridge journey. To overcome that anxiety—and, more to the point, to make it *productive*—the atopic philosopher must not be daunted by the teleology of the bridge, or where it is leading. He must transform the transit into a *final* condition on which to discover his balance. He must learn how "to occupy rather than merely to penetrate space," in the words of Steven Connor, "to thicken the infinitesimally thin itinerary of the wire into a habitat."[28] To do so, though Nietzsche does not mention it, the tightrope walker must make critical use of a hefty long pole, perpendicular to the rope's axis and offsetting it with sways in lateral motion. Manipulating the pole is the work of the will and self-management. Two texts that Connors juxtaposes to Nietzsche's illuminate the topos of the ropewalk as well as its existential-ethical challenges. The first, Madame Blavatsky's *Isis Unveiled* (1877), observes that in the second half of the nineteenth century society stands balanced "on an unseen tight-rope stretched from our visible universe into the invisible one . . . uncertain whether the end hooked on faith in the latter might not suddenly break, and hurl it into final annihilation." The second, *The Secret Doctrine of the Rosicrucians* (1918), speaks of balancing desire and will. Needing to pit opposites "one against the other—balancing law by law—the Master traverses the slender tightrope thread which separates the world of desire from the world of will."[29] One can reassign meanings to these terms in a Nietzschean context: The desire is the world of the *Übermensch* to which one aspires in taking one's steps. The will instead focuses on the footwork and on balancing the walker's pole. Taken together, desire and will, the rope and the pole, form a great cross, protecting one from the fall.

To achieve balance, hovering self-transcendence must will forward as well as backward, left and right. Zarathustra understands this just after he has come off "a great bridge," and a hunchback accuses this man's crossing over to the future as amounting to an intolerance toward the present and the past—as an inability to put up with what the earth has until now been. The "arrows of longing" of this prophet of transcendence would appear to be driven only by a desire and demand for a different shore. Zarathustra, if he shares anything with the hunchback, is consumed by frustration and life-resentment. Does Zarathustra cross bridges only because he cannot stand the land of his time? Is his teaching of self-overcoming really grounded in negativity? The answer is partially yes, Zarathustra must admit. But this means that if his bridge serves just to take him to another place he will never inhabit his eternally transiting present.

Zarathustra must thus discover purpose in the atopic, untimely, disoriented present. We can do so, he realizes, only by *carrying forward* our resented past, and *carrying back* our desired future, into the present that we perpetually tread on our bridge. We legitimate our future and redeem our past losses only by gathering them together into an ineluctable, ongoing present. Bridge-life thus can be occupied by willing in a dual direction. Only in this way can we mold whatever fate we have been given (with the "earth" and the "animal") into *destiny*. Feeling melancholy and anger for our limitations guarantees only this: a future of more violence.

A Dancing Rainbow Wheel

Willing in this complex way activates bonds between things that are otherwise kept separate, that are hostile and discontinuous. Not self-assertion ("Thus I will it") but *this* would be the means to self-overcoming, or to an ethos and pathos of distance bringing transcendent perspectives into the present. By endorsing all that one does and has done in the past, in a process understood to be intimately dependent on individual choice, one renders both past and future omnipresent. A new understanding of the bridge would thereby attach to the one with which Zarathustra's preachings began. That bridge would free the will from its entrapment in unfulfilled desire, in compulsion to "overcome," deny, and get even for things one cannot change. Freedom from revenge, "that is for me the bridge to the highest hope, and a rainbow after long storms" (*Zarathustra,* "On the Tarantulas"). Liberation of the will makes the bridge a rainbow.

Storm-pacifying rainbows rise from the earth to sky and fall back again, in grounded transcendence, in a single, uninterrupted arc. Through backward-and-forward willing, every bridge becomes circular, and the circle a wheel, locked into a self-revolving Now. Nietzsche links the rainbow bridge not only to a circle, but also to the innocence of a child, as well as to singing and self-abandoning dance. The child is "a new beginning, a game, a self-propelled wheel, a first movement, a sacred 'Yes'" (*Zarathustra*, "On the Three Metamorphoses"). This childlike dance creates purposive action in purposeless becoming, artful motion in meaningless progression. Bridge, circle, rainbow, child, and dancer form a family of ideas celebrating the integration of the here and now.

Thus can a person exist "without goal, unless the joy of the circle is itself a goal; without will . . . unless a ring feels good will toward itself,"[30] actualizing a "necessary" and multifarious soul that is dramatically intertwined with the world,

> which out of sheer joy plunges itself into chance; the soul which, having being, dives into becoming; the soul which *has*, but *wants* to want and will; the soul which flees itself and catches up with itself in the widest circle . . . in which all things have their sweep and their counter sweep and ebb and flow.
>
> (*ZARATHUSTRA*, "ON OLD AND NEW TABLETS," §19)

Only in this way can "untimely" philosophers and artists of life reconfigure their misfortunes, balancing themselves as on a rope. A life spent in *amor fati*, molding fate into destiny, perceives the actual as a face of the possible.[31]

Only now do the unspoken implications of the pensive loner on Munch's bridge, and the singer on the Rialto, come into sight—standing out, ek-sisting, in and outside his surroundings, his seemingly estranged "I" freed for a potentially all-unifying experience of space and time. The ungrounded experience of this "I" is now fundamental, to borrow a phrase from Maurice Merleau-Ponty, "because it is not borne by anything . . . not fundamental as if with it one reached a foundation upon which one ought to base oneself."[32] It is a self-in-relation, multiply tied, in tragic joy, to what happens around it. Here "no 'Fixed bridges' can still exist," writes Alberto Giorgio Cassani; "each thing is a Bridge toward every other, every point and line. Bridges toward other forms, other figures . . . Bridges immediately interrupted, Instant-bridges in incessant becoming."[33]

From this self on a bridge we can go back to the question raised earlier about future communities. In prior periods of history one was able to refer to a collective people, remarks Nietzsche;

> but not with us, my brothers: here there are states. . . . Where the state ceases, there the unsuperfluous person begins; there the song of the necessary begins, that unique and irreplaceable melody. Where the state *ceases*—look there, my brothers! Do you not see them, the rainbow and the bridges to the more-than-man?
>
> (*ZARATHUSTRA*, "ON THE NEW IDOL")

The question raised in the wake of Nietzsche by Cacciari and others was whether one might be able to base a new form of community on a stateless relationship among unsuperfluous selves. Roberto Esposito suspects that this could be possible only once a society can appreciate "pure relation," the type of relation evidenced by "the tree that links the earth to the sky, the bridge that connects two banks, the threshold that joins inside with the outside." Recognition of this type of relation can envision the possibility of "a unity in distance and of distance; of a distance that unites, or a separation that brings near."[34] The question for such a society is whether an ethos of self-overcoming can help build deep, fundamental connections between separate and multiple selves. Might "monological" selves provide points of conjunction to a different sociality than the one fostered by the "state" and its identity politics, "where everyone, whether good or bad, loses himself [and] where the slow suicide of all is called—life"? (*Zarathustra*, "On the New Idol")

CHAPTER 8

Sea Bridges and Selves

The more ties I have the rarer and more particular my own identity becomes.

—AMIN MAALOUF, *IN THE NAME OF IDENTITY*

Coastal Ties

The Adriatic Sea has the shape of an elongated gulf between land banks cleaved apart by seismic activity many millions of years ago: the Italian and the Balkan peninsulas. One of several basins in the Mediterranean, it is narrow in width (120–150 kilometers) and easy to ford by boat. The western coast of the Adriatic is administered by a single country (Italy) and the east by five (Slovenia, Croatia, Bosnia-Herzegovina, Montenegro, and Albania). That is the most recent political partition of the region, and hardly the most fractured, but it hints at the cultural and political complexities converging around this unifying-dividing gulf.

So much coming and going down and across the Adriatic has occurred that it was inevitable that someone would eventually think of physically bridging this sea. At the beginning of the twenty-first century the architectural team of Giorgio De Romanis elaborated that plan, imagining a colossal construction calling for many millions of euros in funding and multinational approval. The stated rationale for the sea roadway was more economic than political. The Adriatic bridge from Croatia to Italy would support Europe's Pan-European transport routes and, more specifically, the east-west Corridor V, which crosses much of the continent already and which the European nations had projected to tie Lisbon to Kiev in 1994. The Adriatic bridge would be punctuated by great floating maritime stations capable of hosting two hundred ships at a time. It would service mass transit needs of the increasingly congested and connected economies of Europe.

A bridge of this magnitude would radically reconfigure the geopolitics of Italy and the Mediterranean Sea. We would see a nation firmly circumscribed by the sea transformed into a pier reachable across a vast aqueous border. Naturally cast in the form of an axis running north to south, the land-pier of Italy would begin to assume the traits of a cross. One hundred years ago the statesman Salvatore Barzilai had already incited Italian fantasies of political supremacy in the Mediterranean by seeing the peninsula as a *ponte lanciato*: a bridge cast from Europe to the shores of Africa and other southern territories.[1] The verb *lanciato*, commonly used for the launching of projectiles, also suggested that the recently unified nation possessed the aggressive force to fly through the air like a spear (spears that Italy itself had received during the ill-fated First Italo-Ethiopian War of 1895–96, a disaster it later sought to vindicate in the second such war of 1935–39). At the beginning of the twentieth century Italy was imagined to be an offensive frontline from Europe to both Africa and the Middle East.

The third millennium has seen these futuristic and imperialistic dynamics considerably tempered. Italy now appears to be more of a bridgehead than a frontline, a landing point for thousands of extranational immigrants each year. De Romanis's project of 2008 was formulated before the European Union began truly to be alarmed by migratory patterns. He thought of his east-west juncture as expanding on the centrifugal tendencies geologically favored by the peninsula and supplementing its southern gravitation. The Adriatic bridge would give Italy a privilege of place in European interconnections, making the country a "new gateway to the East."[2]

This engineer's vision is only one of dozens bolstering cultural interplays from coast to coast. Earlier Adriatic connections were more multiplex and mutable than the intentions at work in this bridge. Before nationalist and separatist movements of the nineteenth and twentieth centuries turned the Balkans into a metaphor for division and strife, the Adriatic was the scene of "bridge cultures" adept at traversing ethnic and religious borders.[3] At the top of the sea, the Republic of Venice had a long history in navigation and trade in the region. Another state that worked its way up from the opposite direction was the Ottoman Empire, a multinational and multifaith state that "possessed the foundation of its unity in diversity."[4] Despite armed conflicts and fierce reprisals against rebellions, the empire's interaction with other peoples in the Balkan peninsula was fairly stable and productive of lasting exchange. The Ottoman Turks were an assimilationist people, discovering themselves through contact with Slavs, Italians, Jews, Arabs, Orthodox and Catholic Christians. Their religion, language, technology, and music appropriated phenomena discovered in the lands and seas that they occupied, where they adapted local beliefs and customs to their own purposes and communicated their own as well. At peace or at war, the Ottomans never insisted on complete sovereignty over the Balkan lands. They coexisted in shifting balances of power with kingdoms, principalities, and vassal states administered by Venetians, Serbs, Bosnians, Albanians, Bulgarians, and Austrians, in units like Montenegro, the Republic of Ragusa (Dubrovnik), Kotor, and Felvidék (Upper Hungary).[5] Like the Romans whom they looked to as models, the Ottomans both accepted and authorized the diversity they discovered on the eastern coast of the Adriatic.

So great was the plurality of ethnicities cohabiting the lower Balkans that in Italian and French the name of one of its regions, "macedonia," eventually came to mean finely chopped fruit salad. People on the banks of the Adriatic had engaged in reciprocal religious and commercial exchange since at least the Corinthians in 700 BCE. Grain, salt, sugar, wine, wood, oil, fabrics, iron, technologies, myths, and cultural mores crisscrossed the Adriatic for many more centuries, more actively perhaps than in any other Mediterranean basin except the Aegean.[6] From the Middle Ages onward, these in-between lands on the Adriatic coast, writes Predrag Matvejević, born in Mostar seventy kilometers from the coast, constituted

> the meeting place of Latin and Byzantine culture and the scene of the major schism within Christianity, the boundary between the Holy Roman and Ottoman Empires and a battlefield for Christianity and Islam [developing] in a symbiosis with Mediterranean cultures as a "third component" among such oppositions as east/west, north/south, land/sea, Balkan/European, and others more homegrown.[7]

With boats pointing their prows toward foreign and sometimes unvisited shores, the cities of trade docking these boats were mobile enablers of bridge culture. Ragusa and Trieste were designated free ports and offered privileged customs regulations. They were not alone. Amalfi, Genoa, Livorno, and Pisa on the western side the Italian peninsula, and several others in the southern and eastern Mediterranean, performed similar functions. Well after the rise of "the rigid exclusivism of nationalisms and blocs"—which is to say, in the second half of the nineteenth century—"this Mediterranean of confluences and meetings" was incarnated in the "cosmopolitan world-cities [of] Istanbul, Smyrna, Beirut, Alexandria, Algiers, Trieste, and Marseilles."[8] Smyrna supported such rich and autonomous trade from

1600 through 1900 that a greater blend of Englishmen, Dutch, French, Italian, Greek, Armenian, and Jewish merchants could not be found in all of Europe.[9] Bridge-figures, too, proved crucial to this interlaced trade—scholars, journeymen, and diplomats; religious emissaries, artists, and cultural mediators called *dragomans,* all vital to these intricate economic networks. The illuminating story of one of them—"a Sephardic Jew born in Leghorn, established in Salonika, speaking Italian, French, Turkish, Greek and *dragoman* for the consulates of France and of Belgium"—is told by his grandson, the philosopher and polymath Edgar Morin.[10]

The flexible exchanges fostered by bridge-cities undercut claims to proprietorship of the land and sea that transformed nineteenth-century nationalism into the imperialistic ambitions of liberal and fascist Italy. Before the ascent of Benito Mussolini, Cassio's *Il Mare Adriatico* (1915) and Sillani's *Mare Nostrum* (1918) had already helped revive the old Roman idea of the Adriatic and indeed the entire Mediterranean as "our sea," suggesting that the waters surrounding Italy were the political prerogative of the country's *ponte lanciato*. The imposition of that view occurred after Mussolini came to power in the 1920s, with Italy annexing a long strip of coastline along the eastern Adriatic. It became policy to Italianize the inhabitants all the way down to Dalmatia, forbidding schooling in any other language, obliging Slavic residents to change their names into pseudo-Italian ones, and provoking an exodus of some 100,000 people from the coastal areas.[11]

This "ethnocide," as Bosetti calls it, created an inevitable backlash, as Italians themselves became victims. Many who had lived on the eastern shores of the Adriatic fled twenty years later, when the shores were bequeathed to Yugoslavia after the Second World War.[12] The idea of *Mare Nostrum* amounted to an obstinate and indefensible claim that the Adriatic was *not* fundamentally hybrid, not a multicultural region of habitation, but rather a birthright of imperial sovereignty.[13] No appeals to autochthony, or to ethnic, geocultural precedent, could help eliminate the plurality in question, however. Fascist leader Galeazzo Ciano justified the Italian invasion of Albania in 1939 as the inevitable "outcome of relations between Albania and Italy which go back for twenty-two centuries," suggesting that a pre-Christian dispute between Albanians and Italians was here being settled. The more thoughtful Simone Weil wasted no time to remind Ciano's audience that on the occasion to which he refers, back in 170–169 BCE, the Roman imperial militia reacted to a mere affront to their political sovereignty by despoiling seventy towns on the coast and selling 150,000 Albanians into slavery.[14]

Disappointed Bridges

In the year of Ciano's declaration, in 1939, Eugenio Montale addressed the quandaries of personal and national sovereignty in this part of the Mediterranean in a poem. While it leaves most of its historical message unspoken, "Dora Markus" begins as follows:

> Fu dove il ponte di legno
> mette a Porto Corsini sul mare alto
> e rari uomini, quasi immoti, affondano
> o salpano le reti. Con un segno
> della mano additavi all'altra sponda
> invisibile la tua patria vera.[15]
>
> It was where the wooden pier juts out
> on the high sea at Porto Corsini
> and rare men, almost immobile, sink
> or haul in their nets. With a wave
> of your hand you pointed at the unseen
> land across the sea—your true homeland.

This vague and withholding poem pictures an imaginary woman pining for her homeland from one shore of the Adriatic to another. It is "where the wooden pier juts out" at Porto Corsini that the poet has her pointing to this true but unseen homeland across the sea—to her *patria vera*. For James Joyce, who had lived fewer than two hundred miles north on this coast (in Trieste) from 1904 to 1915, a pier is nothing other than a disappointed bridge.[16] Jutting out from the land, it fails to reach the other side (fig. 8.1). Each pier, writes sociologist Franco Cassano, "offers the temptation to sail, to leave, to chase—without being able to grab it—the utopian line of the horizon."[17] In Montale's poem, neither this pier nor the wave of Dora's hand connects with its longed-for shore. Both have affinities with that other stand-in for a disappointed bridge which is the tower, a type of Jacob's ladder from earth to sky.[18] When he describes the wharf as "setting out" on the high sea (*mette sul mare alto*), Montale also evokes the idea of the bridge, or deck, of a ship, which also takes the name *ponte* in Italian.

Porto Corsini, the setting of this poem, locates us outside Ravenna. There Dora's hand and the pier point northeast toward the peninsula of Istria, now divided between the states of Slovenia and Croatia. From 1918 to 1926, when Montale wrote the first part of his poem, Istria belonged to

Figure 8.1. Matthew Hoser, *The Derelict West Pier at Brighton* (2017). Courtesy of the artist

the nation of Italy. Before 1918 it had been the property of the Austro-Hungarian Empire. Due north of Istria lies that *patria vera,* or true homeland, of Dora. The second part of the poem identifies it as Carinthia. At the date of this second part of the poem, when the whole thing is published (1939), Dora has come home:

> Ormai nella tua Carinzia
> di mirti fioriti e di stagni,
> china sul bordo sorvegli
> la carpa che timida abbocca . . .
>
> (LINES 29–32)

> Now in your own Carinthia
> of ponds and flowering myrtles,
> you lean at the brink to watch
> the shy carp gaping . . .

Today Carinthia is hardly more of a household name than Porto Corsini. It is a 150-kilometer swath of land straddling the border between Austria, Italy, and Slovenia (fig. 8.2), a place where lands meet—or rather, where one land is politically divided into three. That

Figure 8.2. Northern Adriatic.
Google Maps

this is the territory yearned for by Montale's fictitious Dora Markus across the watery basin is perfectly ironic, for between 1926 and 1939 the political identity of the ethnically mixed Carinthia was uncertain and strongly contested. After World War I, part of it had been annexed to the state of Italy (the southwestern Canale Valley), another part to the new Kingdom of Serbs, Croats, and Slovenes, and the rest was apportioned to the whittled-down remains of Austria.

At the time of Montale's poem, "Carinthia" thus signified anything but a clear homeland—at least not if "homeland" implies a firm national space with political sovereignty on the part of its inhabitants. The same problem affected much of the northeastern Adriatic following the watershed of World War I. In 1919, east of Istria, the Italian legionnaires of hero and poet Gabriele D'Annunzio occupied Fiume (Rijeka) just as soon as it became clear that President Woodrow Wilson and the Triple Entente were preparing to transfer the rule of the region to the Kingdom of Serbs, Croats, and Slovenes. A year later, Italy ousted D'Annunzio's militants from the contested coastal area and allowed it to be rendered independent, formally agreeing with the new kingdom to recognize "the complete freedom and independence of the State of Fiume and . . . to respect it for eternity." It was an eternity that lasted all of four years. In 1924 Mussolini persuaded the Yugoslavs to nullify the declared independence of Fiume. He annexed it to Italy in a move to control the northeastern shores of the Adriatic, which he went on to do through the thirties.

While Carinthia was not contested quite so dramatically as the area of Fiume, the Yugoslavs were not satisfied with their portion of the territory allotted them by the Treaty of Saint-Germain of 1919 and occupied the region assigned to Austria. The powers of the Triple Entente intervened, splitting the disputed region into Zone A, administered by the Slovenes, and Zone B, administered by the Austrians. It was decided that Slovenian Zone A should hold a plebiscite to let its citizens decide which of the two countries they wished to belong to. A surprising majority favored annexation to Austria, and so both Zone A and Zone B went to Austria. A month later—in the same Treaty of Rapallo that established the sovereignty of Fiume—the Kingdom of Yugoslavia ratified its new borders with Italy and ceded to its western neighbor 172 square miles of Carinthia. All these historical facts are embedded in that cipher of a homeland that Montale calls Carinthia.

The problem deepens with political upheavals to come. In 1939, when Montale wrote the second part of his poem, barely a year had passed since Hitler had annexed Austria (and Carinthia along with it) to the German Third Reich. By the end of the poem "Dora Markus" we become aware that Nazi rule is threatening the very existence of the woman who had returned home to Carinthia from the coast of Ravenna, a woman who, as we deduce from her name, is Jewish:

> Ravenna è lontana, distilla
> veleno una fede feroce.
> Che vuole da te? Non si cede
> voce, leggenda o destino.
> Ma è tardi, sempre più tardi.
>
> (LINES 57–61)

> Ravenna's a long way off, a brutal
> faith distills its poison. What
> does it want of you? Voice,
> legend, or destiny can't be surrendered . . .
> But it's getting late, always later.

The *fede feroce*—brutal faith or ferocious ideology—of Nazi racism had no place in Carinthia for Jews like Markus.

The spirit of Montale's homeward-pointing bridge is thus portentous from start to finish. While in Italy, Dora could still imagine her Carinthia as a greater place of belonging than Ravenna. (The setting of Ravenna—the former capital of the Byzantine Empire, nostalgically evoked in the same 1926 by W. B. Yeats's "Sailing to Byzantium"—only reinforces the vicissitudes of history.) When Dora actually rejoins her land, instead, she comes tragically under siege. Now, in the 1939 of the poem's second half, Montale offers images of a blackened mirror and a carp wary of being baited, enveloping them in references to "errors" or wanderings (probably of the Jews) in Carinthia's superficially idyllic landscape (lines 29–45). The images convey an unmistakable impression of life being suppressed. Carinthia, like Ravenna before it, is a unit that has been conceptually and politically superseded, sounding chords of a broken harmonica at dusk (lines 51–53). Dora's hour grows increasingly late. Given the destructive power of history, the poem concludes, one can hope for nothing more than to *preserve traces* of a life that is no more—in "voice, legend, and destiny" (line 60), which is as much as to say in poems like this one, reflecting on the implications of historical record.

One final historical irony can be noted about this pier at Porto Corsini. By Italian standards the Corsini Port is a recent construction (and by the 1960s the site of some of the biggest industrial refineries in Europe). One of the few interesting things reported today about Porto Corsini is that it features a semiweekly ferry service to a town in Croatia called Rovino.[19] This ferryboat service, conveying the impression of a bonding between the divided shores of the Adriatic, may give some consolation to the exilic pressures of Montale's poem. It reminds us that since Croatia joined the European Union in 2013, vacationing Italians flock to its beaches in Istria. Yet this feeling of comfort lasts only for a moment—until the name Rovino registers in the mind as the place earlier called Rovigno (*Ruveigno* in Istrian dialect and *Rovinj* in Croatian), which had been a center of Italian habitation for centuries. The coastline around Rovigno was invaded by the German military during World War II. By war's end the region had passed into the hands of the Yugoslavian forces of General Tito. At this point, as Istria and Fiume too changed hands from Italy to the Republic of Yugoslavia, 150,000 to 350,000 Italians residing on this coast of the Adriatic were evacuated to another (older) "homeland" of theirs: a nation now lying on the other side of a border.[20]

As an embarkation site for Rovino, Porto Corsini thus unwittingly exposes a wound in Italian, and not only Carinthian, history. The decks of its tourist ferries point—like the pier and Dora's own hand—toward the "destiny" and "legend" of the community on the Istrian peninsula which was politically and demographically Italian at the time of Montale's poem. (To be clear, then, the exodus was two-way; that of Italians after World War II replicated an earlier and smaller one of Slavs under Fascist Italy.) In 1911 the last census of the Hapsburg Empire reported that 97.8 percent of the population of Rovigno spoke Italian. A century later the situation has been reversed, with approximately 76 percent of the town's inhabitants now identifying as Croatian.[21] A ferryboat now transports vacationing Italians to a shore that no longer belongs to their country. Even the *new* destination of the wharfs at Porto Corsini undoes the myth of a true homeland around which Montale's poem revolves. The Second World War left exiles from both banks of the Adriatic gazing off toward a fatherland (*patria*) on an opposite, invisible shore.

Montale's poem bridges several stories of bridges burned. In this Balkan peninsula, where one ethnic group still insists on claiming priority over another, Dora-type subjects were produced well before and well after the poem was written. Taking a Jewish woman as its emblem of a political expatriate, the poem speaks for *all* people with reason to believe that an essential part of their identity lies geopolitically elsewhere. Historical vicissitudes whirl around the wound of *la patria vera*, a floating and empty signifier appropriately figured as the invisible object of a pointing wharf and named Carinthia—a contested, multiethnic, supranational region among many on the globe which is claimed as a homeland by rival communities, to which women like Dora do not belong except as members of subaltern groups.

From Wharf to Sea

The image of a wharf as point of departure for a passage over waters reminds us that the origin of *pons*, or bridge, was not a fixed structure at all, but the sea: the *pontos*.[22] The Mediterranean was just such a passageway for the Greeks and Phoenicians. Its geography extends beyond inlets, coves, and bays to maneuverable basins like the Aegean, Ionian, and Alboran Seas, each serving as a conduit between people living on different banks of its shores. According to one of the sea's celebrators, the very phenomenology of the Mediterranean impresses on its dwellers a sharp sense of "destiny and fatality, an architecture of spectacle and vision: a way of seeing the horizon and seeking the beyond."[23] That manner of seeing is already embedded in the etymology of the word "Medi-terranean"—a space in the midst of lands, indeed between three continents. The horizon visible from the sea's shores usually ends in a clear division between sky and water, often broken by bits of land, accompanied by knowledge or hearsay about what is different in these separate but proximate lands. This is the geographical basis for that sensation and understanding of mediation, plurality, and alterity that scholars associate with dwellers of the Mediterranean.[24] In contrast to unending stretches of hard and fatiguing earth, not to mention impassable mountains, the fluid separation between lands invites renewed and varied acts of bridging.

Sophocles's famous "Ode to Man" in *Antigone* celebrates the species that learns to plow the earth, snare birds, and build themselves houses. Before that it associates human life as a confrontation with the sea on bridges in motion:

> There is much that is strange, but nothing
> that surpasses man in strangeness.
> He sets sail on the frothing waters
> amid the south winds of winter
> tacking through the mountains
> and furious chasms of the waves.[25]

The strangest thing about this strangest of all species is its willingness to embark on maritime journeys, even under the most daunting conditions. The motivations seem as unnatural as the risks are high. The real challenge lies in passing through and beyond the unusual boundary of this aqueous element, calling out to be made navigable, to be mastered or made familiar, to be made continuous with the land. Two thousand years after Sophocles, when political theorists reflected on the binding principles of the new European Union, other implications of the Mediterranean came into view. Philosopher and Venetian mayor Massimo Cacciari proposed to conceive of the European nations as connected in an archipelago, with the sea serving as byway between separate and autonomous territories.[26] Venetian sailors, long reputed to be the world's best, had navigated the waters between Europe, Africa, and Asia more easily than most. A 1993 archipelago of contemporary, independent nation-states would require a more difficult passage, especially as the notion of an archipelago came to be undercut by conflicting metaphors of a "Fortress Europe," of the continent as a land with excessively porous borders, and of the Mediterranean as a solid or inelastic sea.[27] And what could one say of those in the Mediterranean who lacked the Venetian facility of navigation and the encouraging prospect of finding welcome on foreign shores? What about the non-European migrants who embarked on their hazardous voyages well before the European Union was formed?

A half-century after Istrians and Dalmatians left Yugoslavia, Albanians crossed the Adriatic to the shores of Italy in the tens of thousands. Considerably more sub-Saharan Africans, Syrians, Libyans, Romanians, Iraqis, and Tunisians also followed, to whom islands such as Lampedusa and those of Greece beckoned in the form of temporary, unstable, transitional piers. Migrant transduction across continents, in many ways more toward mirages than realities, is steered by a complicated set of economic, technological, and cultural practices subtending their voyages. Without solid institutional bridges, established and enforced by political treaties, the only bridges in operation are those cobbled together by the border-crossers themselves, on clandestine boats and makeshift roadways, rarely integrated or "insured" on the shores where they land.[28] When they are, they turn into bilingual and bicultural subjects, joining millions already populating most metropolises of the world. The mixed and liminal habitats they form will eventually make homogeneous lands of belonging obsolete.

Migration and Exile

Theoretical discussions of immigrant experience over the past thirty years cope at length with the question of cultural bridging. The status of the bridging metaphor has been particularly pronounced in discussions of the self-understanding of Turkish migration to Germany, the foundations of which were laid by agreements between the two countries in the 1960s. Bridge images arose just as soon as first- and second-generation immigrants converted their lives into narrative, the images appealing partially because geopolitical juncture has been so archetypical a notion for Turks living at the divide of continents. For centuries Anatolians have conceived of themselves as straddling Asia and Europe, East and West. The departure-culture of Turkish immigrants is so respectfully and firmly conceived in works like *The Bridge of the Golden Horn* by Emine Sevgi Özdamar (1998) that the limitations on their assimilation into the arrival-culture is perfectly comprehensible. It is therefore not surprising to find an image that is so rooted in Turkish culture as the bridge redoubling itself in autobiographical writings, with first-generation Turkish Germans in particular describing themselves as occupying a position between two places to which they do not consider themselves to fully belong. Images of betweenness recur in diasporic and repatriated subjects the world over, as though they were cultural islands floating in one and the same sea with other migrants, temporary or recurrent sea passages being provided by bridges between them.[29] Cultural differences resist fixed and standardized human relationships.

The interstitiality of such lives comes especially into relief in the *secondary* bridge-process which is writing, transposing the existential bridge-process into language. Bicultural experience stands in need of an idiom that not only incorporates the vocabularies of both lived spheres but also transcends them, making itself comprehensible to monolingual and multicultural readers alike. Translated into literary expression, the bilingual experience of the migrant writer itself becomes multi- or interlingual.[30]

As freely as interpretations of Turkish German writing invoke the metaphor of the bridge, several theorists of second- and third-generation writers view transcultural bridging as too narrow a conceptual framework to elucidate the complexity of transnational subjects. The pontile metaphor seems to constrict the very spaces that these self-questioning migrants multiply occupy.[31] Thus the exophonic Japanese German writer Yoko Tawada exclaims,

> The expression eine Brücke schlagen, "to strike a bridge," frightens me. The shore on which I'm standing suddenly becomes a hand, which holds a cudgel over the other shore. In this way, it is forced into a bond. This bond reminds me of a hyphen: German-French. The first and second world cannot be metamorphosed into a third with a magic wand.[32]

Even referring to transnational subjects as "hybrid" can give the impression of a too dyadic approach to cultural development, considering the fact that there are always more than two factors at play in human self-understandings, whether migrant or not, and whether multicultural or ostensibly monocultural. Yet the bridge metaphor does not suggest a welding together of two preconstituted substances (metamorphosed into a third through Tawada's magic wand) so much as a confrontation with interstitialities, encounters, and contacts. Hence the bridge metaphor never lies very far from discussions of identity articulation, and perhaps even subtends Tawada's vocabulary of "thresholds" and "transitional spaces" (*Zwischenraümen*) no less than the "hyphenated identities" of Gustavo Perez Firmat, the dialogue without fusion of Azade Seyhan, and the third spaces of enunciation of Homi Bhabha and Edward Soja.[33] These situations and processes entail many of the same transductive or transportive dynamics of cultural space that are actively created by a bridge (which may be why Tawada publishes English translations of both her statement about fearing a bridge *and* her collection of stories called *Facing the Bridge* in the same year, 2007). Far from being a neutral link between presumably autonomous spaces, cultures, or discursive zones that make contact in migration experience, a bridge is a medium that allows for their interaction. It draws disparate phenomena into a third, semi-non-place. It operates in and as a space that *gathers*, at a "passage that crosses," writes Heidegger.[34] It goes over from the near to the far, in simultaneous entry and exit. What Bhabha says of a cultural border applies even better to a bridge (and even he does not distinguish them categorically): It is a locus "from which *something begins its presencing*."[35] Producing access to another shore, it opens that territory up to the understanding.

The life of most migrants, then, is less an amalgam of two cultural bases than a susceptibility of one to the other which refashions both. When the cultural passage of a subject is particularly troubling, the stretch proves to be long and abstracting. To put it in the words of Salman Rushdie, the deepest process of intellectual migration will tend to produce postprovincial people

> who root themselves in ideas rather than places, in memories as much as in material things; people who have been obliged to define themselves—because they are so defined by others—by their otherness; people in whose deepest selves strange fusions occur, unprecedented unions between what they were and where they find themselves. The migrant suspects reality: having experienced several ways of being, he understands their illusory nature. To see things plainly, you have to cross a frontier.[36]

This does mean experiencing Firmat's "life on the hyphen" after all. Seeing things plainly from a vantage of distance means perceiving foreignness not only within the space one inhabits, but also within oneself.

Autobiography—a self-writing of life—crosses bridges that are more formative than those of territories. For those living in lands that have repeatedly changed political hands, nothing loses its cogency so easily as national identity. Predrag Matvejević's *Mondo Ex* is about being ex-Yugoslavian and ex-socialist, or coming to terms with a whole series of cultural changes beneath one's feet. "If anything," writes Rossana Rossanda in the book's preface, identifying with the author,

> I am Mediterranean and Adriatic. But is that a nation? It is a color, a passage between rocks and the sea; it is transit turned into geography. Maybe that is the only thing I would feel *Sehnsucht* for, if ever I should see it no more.[37]

By *Sehnsucht*, or longing, Rossanda means a palpable feeling of absence. It spurs a quest for articulate and ultimately definitive understandings—which political reshufflings and reconfigurations inspire but also hinder. To long for something like "transit turned into geography" is to favor an ethos of transition over those illusory objects of *Sehnsucht* which are homeland and nation. If anything, writes Rossanda, reflecting on what

Matvejević means about belonging to an ex-culture and ex-nation, it suggests that the notion of sovereign territories must be left behind. "I would sing the praises of the *apolide* condition" (the condition of being country-less), she affirms: "I am moved by the fact that after his return to Ithaca Ulysses departed yet again, never again to be heard from, unable to inhabit the same island, the same sky, the same sea."[38] When vacillation and mobility mediate one's sense of belonging, territory and bridge invert their roles; the bridge becomes a more basic residence. It is second nature in the bilingualisms and cultural negotiations of migrant writers like Gregor von Rezzori, Giorgio Pressburger, Carmine Chiellino, Yoko Tawada, and hundreds of others.

The *apolide* condition praised by Rossanda returns us to those bodies of water that bridges were devised to deal with. The Mediterranean historical novelist Amin Maalouf characterizes semiautobiographical settings as a key to postnational identity:

> My identity is constituted by multiple belongings, and this is precisely what makes for my specificity. . . . For me the sea is a pathway; for others it is a barrier, a border, but not for me. . . . I think this is an attitude already present in the culture within which I was formed. A culture that includes the trips of my ancestors, who, already three or four thousand years ago, got on boats and took sail to discover the world across the sea. For them the sea was an immense becoming, and when the war forced me to leave I got on a boat and reproduced their same attitude. For me the sea will never be a barrier, in this I am profoundly Mediterranean and even Phoenician. For me the sea is an immense pathway that connects all the countries of the world.[39]

Maalouf accordingly emphasizes the reciprocal formation, even when conflictual, of peoples around this Mediterranean: "a conciliatory belonging of cultures and wholes into which the current world is divided." Even Ismail Kadare, who is particularly unsettled by the ethnic and social strife that has marked his Albania on the Adriatic, believes that if one could achieve "a true integration of this sea into Europe, many problems would be resolved."[40]

Pons and Corpus Callosum

Analogues of these pathways of migrancy, boats, and seas enable relationships critical to other systems of operation. Several are found in the field of human cognition. Nerve cells convey electrical or chemical signals by way of synapses—junctions between neurons across which the communication occurs. The nineteenth-century neurophysiologist Charles Sherrington chose the term "synapse" (from the Greek *synaptein,* "to clasp, join together, tie or bind together") in order to stress the notion of union between separate elements. Electrical neurotransmitters connect with receptors across a gap-junction or synaptic cleft. That connection is significantly strengthened when the neurons on both sides of the cleft are active at the same time. As in a meeting of cultures, the more vital the activity already is on both sides of the neural pathway, the more information is registered and retained. Scientists distinguish bidirectional electrical neural communication across synapses from unidirectional coupling of neurons *not* separated by gaps. That unidirectional connection is called "ephaptic" (from the notion of "touching"). It invites analogy to domineering forms of cultural contact, and hence is also called "one way, "master-slave," or "unidirectional" synchronization.[41]

Synaptic neurotransmission is one thing. The "pons," or bridge, of the brain is another. The pons enables transit of localized impulses, signals, and what might casually be called protowishes, between the upper and the lower part of the brain. There in the pons, just above the medulla oblongata, is where the most expansive dream activity takes place during sleep. To say dream activity is to say an association between empirical perception and the imagination. Situated in front of the aqueduct of Sylvius (another organ named by referenced to aqueous passages), the pons also regulates the body's cycle of sleeping and waking, breathing, balance, hearing, and taste.

Higher up in the brain lies a thick band of nerve fibers serving another bridge-function. Called the "corpus callosum," it joins the right and left cerebral hemispheres. The right governs a majority of the body's spatial and nonverbal tasks, while the left specializes in speaking and writing. The left is primarily analytical and logical, the right synthetic, imaginative, and intuitive. By way of a crucial, or crossing, logic, the left hemisphere controls the right side of the body and the right the left. Joined by the nerve band of the corpus callosum, rather than separated by a gap like neurons, the differentiated hemispheres of the brain share information and influence each other.

Effective mental activity relies on relentless communication across that connective strip. Each of its millions of fibers ties a single spot on one side of the brain to another across the divide. Dividing but joining the brain, this callosal bridge transfers sensory, cognitive, and motor information from its native "homeland," where it first registered, to a different territory. There the datum is fed into another information system, processed by another language or code. Without continuous transference across this bridge, the brain would only be able to emit incoherent and unintegrated commands, making a task as simple as tying one's shoes, or naming an object recognized by the eyes, infinitely difficult.

Studies have suggested that the corpus callosum is thicker and neurologically more active in females than in males, supporting a longstanding belief in cognitive dimorphism (dual brain configurations) and thus sex differentiation.[42] Men appear to manifest more compartmentalization, or lateralization, of brain activity than women. A woman's thicker brain bridge would make her more bilateral and bicameral: more prone to perceiving phenomena as parts of wholes rather than in isolation, balancing more types and varieties of data in formulating responses to problems. Whatever the final word on these differences, for studies continue apace, in both sexes the corpus callosum coordinates interdependent cerebral activities into the coherent behavior of a single person. Seemingly automatic, reflex, or isolated acts of the body are actually complex, negotiated events, determined by invisible goings and comings across the bridge.

As the role of callosal bridges in the performance of human cognition may or may not carry implications for gendered behavior, so it may or may not have bearing on attitudes toward a politics of human community, where sympathetic identification with others and dialogical discussion of differences are at variance with authoritarian rule. The same variance sets particularists off from pluralists—or "those desiring culturally pure states and those desiring a multicultural state."[43] The very institution of bicameral politics mirrors one of these two ways of thinking, calling for the social integration of intellectual perspectives. It stipulates that the most efficient and sophisticated working of any legislative body should be predicated on the coordination of two independent assemblies (such as the Senate and House of Representatives in the United States), requiring majority consensus in *both* chambers for legislation.

Self and Antiself

As for a single person sitting within such an assembly, William Butler Yeats endorses an analogous pair of interlocking relationships. He calls them self and antiself, and considers the person to be a product of the distance between them. The "I" (a thinker like Georg Groddeck would call it the "it") straddles more space than is represented by what it believes or does.[44] It interacts with and often opposes undesirable internal inclinations (aggression, timidity, or laziness, for example) while pursuing traits not necessarily given to its natural disposition (altruism, courage, and so on). The psychic result is conflict, with inclinations, wishes, ideals, and needs vying among themselves for supremacy. No executive officer manages these disagreements. "The I," said Nietzsche, and Yeats read him carefully, is not "*one* being with respect to plural beings (instincts, thoughts, and so on); rather the ego is a *plurality of forces* of a personal type."[45]

Yeats is less interested in everyday processes of self-actualization than in the space of ethics and imaginative creation. The development of both depends on how proactively one responds to a recognition of potentiality—acknowledging personal and historical limitations, on the one hand, and the pull of emotional, intellectual, and existential projects, on the other. Yeats locates the tense effects of a self-opponent *within* that space of potentiality and calls it the "daimon." The original Greek word appears to derive from *daiomai*, "to divide or lacerate," suggesting, in the context of the psyche, a difference between the everyday "I" and the intangible force of an antiself within or beyond it. Early philosophers often formulated the force in terms of *pneuma* (spirit) or *nous* (soul), acting on the human animal in the manner of a mysterious psychic will. Heraclitus thought of *nous* as an intermediary between the minds of humans and a cosmic order of *logos*. Socrates regularly heard a daimon speaking to his reasoning mind from the sphere of divine justice; the daimon seemed to wish to harmonize the two. His internal dialogue with his daimon turned Socrates's innermost "I" into the space of what Hannah Arendt called the permanent "two-in-one" of thinking, as opposed to what one might call the expression of mere opinion, or the misnomer "pontification." This dialogue or interaction is not just the source of speculation and intellectual reflection; it is also what they aim to perfect. "What thinking actualizes in its unending process is [that] Socratic two-in-one," whose challenge is to grapple with "the infinite plurality which is the law of the earth."[46] That space is also the location of ethos and inarticulate passion. Other daimons in Greece came into this space regularly. One of them was Eros, in some ways the main intermediary between gods and humans, bridging the ineluctable distance between human desire (where I "want" or lack) and desire's satisfaction, which can never quite be achieved.[47]

For Yeats this "soul of man" (*anima hominis*) seeks an integration of self on which *mature* individuation, or the real right to say "I," depends. "By the help of an image / I call to my opposite," he writes in *Per Amica Silentia Lunae*,

> . . . summon all
> I have handled least, least looked upon. . . .
> I call to the mysterious one who yet
> Shall walk the wet sands by the edge of the stream
> And look most like me, being indeed my double,
> And prove of all imaginable things
> The most unlike, being my anti-self,
> And, standing by these characters, disclose
> All that I seek. . . .[48]

Reaching over from a world to which the ego deeply intuits itself to belong, this daimon explains literary, musical, philosophical, and artistic creativity. It is a "Ghostly Self," making consciousness a place of junction and discord, aiming to bridge the split self, whispering that the human person is productively unaccomplished and incomplete, and pushing it toward ever more remote and inclusive achievements.[49]

Those who ignore the discord are creatures of vague sentiment and lazy attainment, Yeats alleges, wedded to

> a hollow image of fulfilled desire. All happy art seems to me that hollow image, but when its lineaments express also the poverty or the exasperation that set its maker to the work, we call it tragic art. . . . The other self, the anti-self or the antithetical self, as one may choose to name it, comes but to those who are no longer deceived, whose passion is reality. The sentimentalists are practical men who believe in money, in position, in a marriage bell. . . .[50]

Out of our quarrels with others we produce rhetoric, he writes, "but out of the quarrel with ourselves, poetry." The dramatic, creative, potentiating appeal of a daimon places people in the intermediate space of ethical and aesthetic self-making. "The Daimon, by using his mediatorial shades, brings man again and again to the place of choice."[51] That place is irreducibly divided. When the choice one reaches within it is tragic, or irreducibly difficult, its causes and effects appear to be reciprocally bound—fated no less than chosen. The decision looks like a link in chains upon chains of connection, losing its presumable freedom, changing all past and future actions.

Productive states of mind are thus animated by their own incompletion, gripped by what they are not yet capable of grasping. Extraordinary achievements in art and social action follow from this bond-and-conflict. "Nations, cultures, schools of thought may have their

Daimons."[52] And Plato agrees: his daimons are also collective.[53] They beckon from another territory, like the homeland that Dora Markus cannot quite reach.

The Other End of the Bridge

At the space of political borders, the daimon spurs relationships between neighbors which can shift at barely a moment's notice, drawing mutual hostility out of situations of trusting conviviality. Yet even the hostility that surfaces, notes Cacciari, is "a conflict that unites . . . a *cum-fligere*" (a common infliction).[54] Communities cohabiting zones of contact rarely forget their differences; they just let them hang in the balance. That is why the border town of Trieste can as easily be called the "Berlin of the Adriatic" as a "bridge to the East."[55] It can be, and has been, both. The vacillation is endemic to gateway contacts. Depending on the degree of social and political instability, they "may figure as sites of coexistence or violent conflict, rigidity or fluidity, purity or hybridity."[56]

Even when stability is achieved, tensions remain, and rituals help diffuse them. Once a year, on the last Saturday of June, still today, the city of Pisa transforms the location of its oldest crossing over the Arno River into a community clash. The *Gioco del Ponte* casts members of opposing neighborhoods into a symbolic duel above the river on the Ponte di Mezzo—the Halfway Bridge, or Bridge In Between. The battle of the bridge reenacts the very ambivalence of the bridge as a structure, a space of belligerent excursions no less than dreaded incursions, rallying the collective strength of one community to push back those pressing over from the other side. The Ponte di Mezzo is well named, for the word *mezzo* suggests not only "halfway between" (two rivals), but also "means," as in "means to an end." The bridge is a vehicle to an end, which users themselves must determine.

The Pisan ritual is not unique. Formerly men of Testaccio on the left bank of Rome's Tiber River and those of Trastevere on the right enacted an annual bridge battle with significant casualties. Venice hosted similar bridge wars, calling them *battagliole*, and conducting them at the Bridge of Fists, at the Diedo Bridge, and at two Bridges of War.[57] Judging from paintings from the seventeenth and eighteenth centuries, these organized clashes were not so small as the diminutive *battagliole* suggests (fig. 8.3). Speaking of Italian cities, the patron spirit of Florence used to be Mars, the god of war. Until 1333, a statue of the god stood high on a pedestal at the entrance to Ponte Vecchio, and Dante

Figure 8.3. Joseph Heintz the Younger, *Contest on the Fist of Bridges in Venice* (1673). Germanisches Nationalmuseum, Nuremberg, Germany

and Boccaccio bemoaned its divisive effects, blaming it for the violence and bad blood reigning between the Florentine families to either side of the Arno River.[58] In the same spirit defensive towers of rival clans once guarded the four corners of Florence's main bridge (the Mannelli Tower, one of the four, still stands).

Several literary fictions illustrate how difficult it is for bridges to resolve the differences they bind in a deeper or underlying union. A novel about the troubles in Ireland, *The Other End of the Bridge* by Una Troy (1960), tells of a bridge built in County Cork with the express purpose of pulling together two rival, river-tied communities. Despite the best intentions of the peacemakers, the bridge does nothing to lessen their hostility. On the contrary, it stokes their aggression, becoming a flashpoint where the very project of social cohesion must be abandoned. The humanitarian ideologue of the bridge is called the Apostle. His efforts to mediate between the groups of different faiths prove so unsuccessful that, in desperation, he blows up his bridge and himself with it. The disheartening lesson of this novel is that heightened contact between dissimilar communities accentuates their animus. Or, to be more precise, the communities *shore up* their dissimilarity, which is ultimately a small element in a cluster of similarities they share. They are reluctant to reinterpret themselves from an external position, which is precisely what the bridge requires. "Standing outside oneself," entertaining other systems of reference, adopting double perspectives, recontextualizing identity from across the divide—all these prove intolerable to them.

Similar questions about the paradoxically divisive effects of a bridge motivate a play by the Hungarian Ferenc Herczeg. It concerns the spectacular and still standing Széchenyi Chain Bridge, which opened over the Danube between Buda and Pest a year after Hungarian aspirations for independence were dashed in 1848. *The Bridge* (*A híd*, 1925) tells the true story of Count István Széchenyi, the catalyst of Hungarian national unity and founder of the bridge bearing his name. His efforts to make Budapest a more inclusive space run into obstacles from the radical activist Lajos Kossuth, a militant promoter of Magyar nationalism. Kossuth eventually gets the better of Széchenyi. Deeply embittered by Hungarian politics, Széchenyi breaks down and is committed to an insane asylum. There at the end of the play, while holding his own actions responsible for a violent Magyar revolt against the Austrians, he regrets having attempted to conciliate the banks of the Danube. As he listens to Count Széchenyi plead for his bridge to be dynamited, the aristocratic vice-regent of the Hapsburg Empire invokes a metaphor we have seen before. He wryly notes that the Széchenyi Chain Bridge is not just a link between Buda and Pest; it is a bridge over the Styx, opening the gates from the underworld.

Boosting proximity, bridges produce the unsettling prospect of counterborders. Compartmentalization is easier, safeguarding simple, not complex, situations. When Troy's Apostle learns that members of the Irish Republican Army are heading off to assault "a customs post or two" at the border of Northern Ireland, he addresses them with these parting words: "'When you are on the border, remember . . . there are the same green fields on both sides of it, and it will go hard with you to know North from South.'"[59] Borders are barriers in a landscape that naturally lacks them; bridges connect spaces that are naturally divided. They produce evidence of distinctions by shortening the space between them. They bring notice of places outside one's protected habitat. Montale's *ponte* at Porto Corsini stretches toward one of these unseen, determining, and copresent places. The poet had the wisdom to allude to it through the image of a wharf from which boats take leave, steered by individual and mobile agents. Bridges proper instead fix access, enabling in addition two-way traffic. As transnational societies become increasingly migrant, it is likely that bridges of one shape or another will permanently replace boats, like De Romanis's projected construction over the Adriatic. Megabridges of vast international scope already encroach increasingly on once self-contained geopolitical places, defying divisions in a way boats and piers cannot. One can only hope that they will not annul the awareness that deep signs of a homeland beckon also from the *other end* of a bridge, in a space we share with others, who do not share our birthplace, but who have ever more access to our shore.

CHAPTER 9

Bridged Disconnection

My friends are my rivals; we dwell on opposite banks of the stream.

—HENRY DAVID THOREAU, *I TO MYSELF*

Tear Down This Bridge!

Bridges become walls and walls bridges with hardly a moment's notice. A short animated film produced in the age of the internet—at a time when our affective investments are increasingly remote, making distances seem near and nearness unclose—shows how easily one turns into the other. The plot of *Rinkta's Bridge* (2018, dir. Ray Jackson) is all based on computer-generated illusions and pursues an improbable narrative. But it dramatizes how a bridge registers separation, dividing what it seems to unite.

It features a Gabrielino Native American of the Uto-Aztecan tribe in California at a time Europeans still thought that land was an island. When Spanish conquistadores landed near the tip of the peninsula in 1534, they identified it with the territory described by the author of chivalric romances, Garci Rodríguez de Montalvo. On "the right-hand side of the Indies," he reports in chapter 157 of *The Labors of the Very Brave Knight Esplanadián* (1510), "there was an island called California, which was very close to the region of the Earthly Paradise." Ruled by the virgin queen Calafía, its only metal was gold. As late as 1768 the first *Encyclopedia Britannica* noted that it was uncertain whether that distant "California" was a peninsula or an island.[1]

Just as Cortes's Spaniards believed that here they had discovered their earthly paradise, so the Gabrielino was convinced he beheld the true referent of his heart's desire in another spirit who appeared to him from another set of isles across thousands of miles of sea. Rinkta, as she

Figure 9.1. Katsushika Hokusai, *Hanging-Cloud Bridge at Mount Gyōdō near Ashikaga* (1834). Woodblock, 262 × 385 mm.
Gerhard Pulverer Collection

was called, seemed to be the most wondrous of creatures. And the stars favored the leanings of the Indian's heart, helping him build a skybridge crossing the expanse between his home and hers. It was a most graceful and delicate bridge, similar to the one imagined by Hokusai (fig. 9.1)—but much longer and slender, fragile and bejeweled, yet sturdy enough to bear the weight of the two of them.

Rinkta first coyly observed him build this bridge. Then she rewarded his attention, meeting the Gabrielino every few months at the middle of the structure for four to five days at a time. She mitigated her loneliness through this contact, while bemoaning the abyss over which their love was spun. After two years she failed one day to appear on the bridge as planned. She hid behind trees as the Indian approached, and he did so repeatedly, retreading the bridge each week for another two years. From afar he sought an explanation for what was amiss but received no answer. He could only deduce that the junction had become too daunting, perhaps even too strange and beautiful, marred by the gap that it breached. Rinkta preferred cloistered security behind Hadrian's Wall in the other isles of Britannia. Occasionally she sent messages out onto the bridge, assuring the Indian brave that she had not forgotten him. She watched him quizzically from her mountain peak. Inconsolable, he

Figure 9.2. René Magritte, *Le pont d'Héraclite / Heraclitus's Bridge* (1935). Oil on canvas, 54 × 73 cm.

Private collection, © 2020 C. Herscovici / Artists Rights Society, New York

kept traveling the bridge without receiving a glimpse of Rinkta and took up the long journey back to his land. Finally he could not tell whether it was more distressing to engage in the failed contact or give up the effort to seek it. The bridge seemed only to span separation. It tied but did not unite. Empty and hosting no traffic, the bridge only commemorated loss. An inner voice cried out to the Gabrielino, "Tear down this bridge! Remove all trace of it!" And so he did, as Rinkta watched. Broken like the bridge he built, the Indian died two years later.

Seen in the mind's eye as whole, a bridge may not be so in fact, as in René Magritte's painting *Le pont d'Héraclite* (fig. 9.2). If it does not reach over to the other side, a bridge is as good as a wall. John Lennon, when estranged from Yoko Ono, did not know how else to title his album of 1974 than *Walls and Bridges*.

From Bridges to Walls and Back

The words "Tear down this bridge!" apparently play on the famous injunction of Ronald Reagan on his visit to Berlin in 1987, "Mr. Gorbachev, tear down this wall!" Two years later, once it had become intolerable to the Berliners it divided, the wall came down. A call rang out to replace it with a bridge. By 2002 that wish was fulfilled. A bridge was

Figure 9.3. Ponte Vecchio (Florence, Italy, 1345), topped by the Vasari Corridor with its three windows.
Sailko / Wikimedia Commons

built over Berlin's Spree River just where the wall had come down to the water and rose up from the other side. A passage was created in the space of division.

The preconditions for that space of passage go back to when John Lennon was not yet four years old and the tide of World War II was turning against the Germans. Beating a retreat from Florence in August, 1944, they destroyed every bridge over the Arno with one exception: the picturesque fourteenth-century Ponte Vecchio (1345), attributed to Taddeo Gaddi. Originally the Germans had slated even that bridge to be demolished. What spared it was a quaver of fine feeling in Adolf Hitler. On his visit to Italy in 1938 the Führer had been much taken by this covered bridge and its views of the city. Legend has it that in order to enhance the statesman's outlook on Florence, Benito Mussolini hollowed out three broad windows over the archways in the middle of the bridge (fig. 9.3).[2] True or not, by 1944 it appears Hitler had a sweet spot for the Ponte Vecchio, and this affection came into play when the Germans hastily drew up plans to demolish all bridges over the Arno in the face of rapidly advancing Allies.

Hitler's consul on the ground at the time was a great admirer of Renaissance architecture called Gerhard Wolf. Remembered as "the man who saved Florence," he pleaded with the Führer to spare one bridge in Florence—not the Ponte Vecchio at all, but the superlative Santa Trinita, the supreme invention of Bartolomeo Ammanati (1569). Wolf's arguments about the extraordinary value of the bridge fell on deaf ears. Hitler agreed to make one exception but had no interest whatsoever in the art historical opinions of his underlings. The Ponte Vecchio was "the Führer's *Lieblingsbrücke,* his favourite bridge," and this is the one he condescended to spare.[3]

By sparing Hitler's *Lieblingsbrücke,* the German forces wreaked more damage than if they had blown it up. To allow this bridge to stand they were obliged to demolish all access to it from across the Arno, razing dozens of medieval buildings. All of the other bridges of Florence were rebuilt with most of their original stones, which was unfortunately impossible with the complex structures at the foot of the Ponte Vecchio. Another historical irony is that Hitler's sentimental bridge-sparing provided clandestine enemy passage into the city along the same Vasari Corridor from which Hitler looked out of his one or three windows. That corridor along the second story of the bridge runs from the Pitti Palace on the far bank of the Arno to the Uffizi Museum in the city center. An episode of Roberto Rossellini's war film *Paisan* (1946) reconstructs the infiltration of the city over the Ponte Vecchio after the sinking of the other bridges. The decision to let Ponte Vecchio stand proved doubly wrong.

The German demolition of bridges in Florence was no local exception. Pushed from the territories they occupied during the 1940s, the Nazis exploded bridges as assiduously as they punished their enemies. They even dynamited the local bridge in Heidelberg so treasured by Hölderlin on one of the final days of the war, March 29, 1945. As with their reprisals against partisan resisters, these Nazi decisions did not always serve a useful military objective. Most were purely vindictive, denying the confraternity of combatants.

The collateral hostilities of that Second World War eventually issued into the construction of the Berlin Wall in 1961. It rose as an impregnable barrier within a city now fractioned into regions separately administered by different countries. The head of East Germany, Walter Ulbricht, walled off Berliners from one another *not* to stop West Germans from pressing into the east, but to force his own citizens to stay. Ulbricht feared that his state's integrity could not be assured without a wall. One bridge between the west side of the city and East Germany was left to host exceptional exchanges: the Glienicke Bridge, the "Bridge of Spies" featured in the 2015 Spielberg film by the same name.

German bridge-bombing during the war and the construction of the Berlin Wall sixteen years later are consecutive acts in a single political

Figure 9.4. Skybridge and the Marie-Elisabeth-Lueders-Haus in the Band des Bundes, Berlin.
Jo Chambers / Shutterstock.com

drama. The third act—the transformation of the wall into a bridge—was designed to signal the catastrophe's resolution. When the border between the two Germanies came down in 1989, the communities united in a mission of integration. The state commissioned a symbolic architectural complex to span the city's river and redeem the Cold War wall. Aligned on the same axis as the torn-down wall now rise two connected parliamentary buildings, visually affirming the mended difference. One is named after the last democratic president of the German Reichstag (Paul Löbe), the other after a feminist parliamentarian of the same Weimar Republic, who like Löbe was also jailed by Hitler: Marie-Elisabeth Lüders. The parliamentary buildings are attached over the Spree River by a pedestrian bridge and topped with wings protruding over the water in a gesture of spanning (fig. 9.4). Glass-framed halls and elevators, transparent stairwells and glazed facades on the riversides publicize openness, reinforcing the theme of accountability and cooperative links. This *Sprung über die Spree,* or Leap over the Spree as it is called, devolves into a ribbon of government buildings (*Band des Bundes*) and footpaths stretching 200 meters and housing more than nine hundred German parliamentary offices. One can hardly imagine a more appropriate repudiation of the bridge-wrecking xenophobia of two earlier state regimes. A matter of small irony is that only authorized personnel are allowed to cross the pedestrian bridge of the *Band des Bundes* that has replaced the wall.

This might have been the third and final act of the play, complemented by the imaginary bridges that appear on each of the seven denominations of euro banknotes launched in the same year of 2002. Instead, a fourth act begin to be written some fifteen years later, with a determined, international installation of border-barriers both inside and outside Europe, barbed-wire fences and sea interceptions, in a rush to stem immigration into the economically fairly stable countries of the European Union from impoverished and often war-torn communities. "After the Berlin Wall," notes Donatella Di Cesare, "the new millennium began with a new age of walls."[4] This fourth act is currently unfolding, with still too volatile a plot to configure.

Grand Acts of Pontification

The Germans were not the only agents of bridge-bombing converted to bridge-building. They were by no means Ur-destroyers atoning through a *mea culpa*. The American military has more routinely and more assiduously targeted bridges in more cities and many more wars. The first three acts in this political drama—beginning with the severing of links, then erecting high walls of civic partition, then forging cooperative bridges—composed an international story from 1944 to the end of the twentieth century. Flexible new unions throughout continents in the era of globalization celebrated a collective, and virtually universal, ethical transformation. After the end of the Cold War the world became ever more intent on linkage. Communications technology, supported by invisible and incalculable powers of transnational capital, imperiously run by "free market enterprise," makes the bridge-building gesture of Berlin seem to be a cipher of wider and more far-reaching trends. Newly walled states combat these trends with rudimentary, generally regressive, and often quite limited means.[5] Whether we are entering a new age of walls remains to be seen; in the meantime territories and islands that once seemed all but inassimilable geopolitically appear to be so yoked together that their architectural icon is the megabridge. The *Sprung über die Spree*, in its modest and local proportions, is just a tiny link in a heavy and tangled chain.

Megabridges capitalize on an ethos of planetary bonds. Nations use them to vie with one another for economic influence as well as to stress how much each is doing to make the world one. Their spectacular sight often obscures their function. The world's tallest bridge has masts rising higher than 300 meters (fig. 9.5). Its two-kilometer road deck, however, is relatively short by contemporary standards. Other bridges extend 100 kilometers and more. The five longest bridges—all in China or Taiwan—are designed for high-speed rail transport, or

Figure 9.5. Millau Viaduct Bridge, France (2004).
Pxhere.com

Figure 9.6. Jiaozhou Bay Bridge, China (2011).
Dr. Bernd Gross / Wikimedia Commons

purposes of sheer transit. Another colossal construction with 5,000 concrete piles supporting its roadway (fig. 9.6) is just a sixth as long as the 164-kilometer Danyang–Kunshan Grand Bridge. China boasts not only the world's longest bridges, but also the five highest, one standing 500 meters above the ground (fig. 9.7). The world's longest fully suspended, multispan, cable-stayed bridge is stretched across the Gulf of Corinth in Greece (fig. 9.8). The isthmus at the end of the gulf had already been cut through in the nineteenth century so that boats would not need to circumnavigate the Peloponnese peninsula. The new bridge across the gulf's mouth does something analogous, sparing cars circuitous journeys. Within minutes it lands them within miles of Patras, from which they can board ships to elsewhere (fig. 9.9). The most iconic, symbolic, and paradigmatic megabridges remain those that are suspended

Figure 9.7. Siduhe River Bridge, China (2009), the world's second highest in elevation.
Eric Sakowski / Wikimedia Commons

Figure 9.8. Rio-Antirrio Bridge, Greece (2004).
Eusebius / Wikimedia Commons

Figure 9.9. Gulf of Corinth, with the bridge and Patras near the left.
Google Maps

over a single span, their decks supported by cables hung from only two piers at the ends. No fewer than twelve of these suspension bridges with spans longer than the Golden Gate have been built since 1981. A half dozen that will be longer are currently under construction.

Given this spate of productive activity, one must conclude that great acts of bridging have become as compelling to progressive and self-respecting governments as to morally conscientious citizens. They engage in out-performance, vying to break technological records. Rival economies and corporations bridge profits and admiration by building the most daring constructions, using them to brand cities and cultures.[6] The longest road-and-rail bridge in Europe transports travelers from Denmark to Sweden through a tunnel under water and then swoops them over the Öresund Bridge to reach the dazzling precinct of Santiago Calatrava's Turning Torso (fig. 9.10). The bridge passageways of the past twenty years have become so much more complex than any produced in the prior five thousand years that their proper dimensions can only be gauged from high up in the sky.

Two centuries ago these structures would have struck spectators as monuments of antinatural arrogance. They were inaugurated, no doubt, by the Brooklyn Bridge, which, legitimating their scale in advance, demonstrated how much power could be pressed out of an alliance of science + capital + engineering. The wizardry of the Golden Gate Bridge raised the technological bar higher. Yet even the sincere appreciation of Kevin Starr in his study of this feat of engineering ends on a note of apprehension.[7] How well can a structure perched on such seismically susceptible rocks withstand the assaults of nature and time? And at what cost to the location, both natural and social? Measured by the geological rhythms of its site, generated over millions of years, the lifespan of the Golden Gate Bridge, however long, will amount to

Figure 9.10. Santiago Calatrava's Turning Torso with the Öresund Bridge (2000) in the background, Malmö, Sweden.

something on the order of a nanosecond. At a cost of $20 billion, or one billion dollars every six years, the Hong Kong–Zhuhai–Macau Bridge (2018) has been designed to last just 120 years. The Morandi Bridge in Genoa (1967) collapsed after fifty-one. "Without falling," as Kafka wrote, "no bridge, once spanned, can cease to be a bridge."[8]

There was a time when bridges were devised to serve limited needs and objectives. Tree trunks were dropped over brooks to help people forage more widely for food; obstacles along roads were bridged for the journeys of pilgrims. Of course, even the most modest footbridge must have seemed utterly audacious to its astonished first users, perhaps as much as mile-long suspension bridges do today. Yet great alterations in the order of nature have suggested impiety in virtually every culture that has preceded us, threatening to rain doom down onto the heads of men. The desecrating acts of bridge-building documented by Anita Seppilli evoke tales of natural retribution toward the haughtiness of men that are legion.

River Resentment

Stories of a river's rebellion against its bridge fill ancient texts. In book 8 of Virgil's *Aeneid* Vulcan forges a magnificent shield for Trojan hero Aeneas, on which the blacksmith dazzles viewers with carved pictures of human ingenuity. The last image on this shield is the most revealing: It shows the world's mightiest rivers, beginning with the Egyptian Nile and "his giant body mourning." Personified, the river is mourning the tragedy that so many "vast crowds of vanquished nations" on the Nile's banks (*Aeneid* 8.711, 722) have been harnessed to the purposes of an imperial will. The next rivers after the Nile are the

> Euphrates, moving now with humbler waves;
> the most remote of men, the Morini;
> the Rhine with double horns; the untamed Dahae;
> and, river that resents its bridge, the Araxes [*pontem indignatus Araxes*].
>
> (*AENEID* 8.726–28)

The final words about the Araxes allude to the bridge that the emperor Alexander the Great attempted to build over the mighty Armenian river. The Araxes was so enraged by this intention of subjugation that it dashed the bridge's deck and piers to pieces. Centuries later the emperor Caesar Augustus—Virgil's contemporary—succeeded where Alexander failed, installing a bridge over the same river. Thus the Araxes is now *indignatus*.

Imperial bridge-building had offended many since at least Herodotus. He gives us the example of Xerxes. Bent on invading the Greek mainland, the Persian ruler had a brilliant idea for transporting his troops across the waters dividing Greece from Asia Minor. The narrowest crossing was at the Hellespont, or Dardanelles, 1.2 kilometers wide. Xerxes's scheme for bridging this distance called for attaching flax and papyrus cables across the straits of the Hellespont, bound tightly enough to support planks of wood bearing the weight of thousands of infantry men. The Hellespont, unconsulted, did not consent. It bucked and unleashed its waves, breaking up the wooden sticks. Enraged, Xerxes beheaded his engineers who provided this design and ordered his men to whip the sea furiously with three hundred lashes. He dropped shackles into the deep strait to subdue its rebellious spirit; he branded

Figure 9.11. Pontoon bridge at Dardanelle, Arkansas (1900–1918).
US National Archives and Records Administration, NARA-516537

it with hot irons. The lashes and iron cuffs gave clearer evidence of Xerxes's barbarity, Herodotus noted, than the murder of his engineers: It showed that the leader of men had no inkling that the great body of nature was more powerful and divine than any mortal king, even one at the head of a two-million-man army. To the historian the episode illustrates the astonishing *hybris* of those pressed to control, engineer, and commandeer the planet.

Yet the implacable Xerxes would not be deterred and took steps to build another bridge, this time a pontoon made of boats, anchored in both front and back, and aligned parallel to the shore. Side by side, the fastened boats filled the span of the strait. Indeed a similar design had worked for his father Darius further north, at the top of the Bosphorus. We get an idea of what Xerxes's pontoon bridge might have looked like from another such bridge built at a place with virtually the very same name (Dardanelle, in the state of Arkansas). Once touted as being the "longest pontoon bridge in the world over moving water," this half-mile bridge was considerably shorter than Xerxes's (fig. 9.11). It was the property of the Dardanelle Railroad Company, but never carried a single train car across the Arkansas River. Perhaps some were afraid of the example of Xerxes.

Xerxes's second bridge did get his men over the divide between Asia and Europe, and there he lost nearly his entire army to the Greeks. In *The Persians* the playwright Aeschylus prefigures Xerxes's spectacular defeat in an imaginative metaphor. As Xerxes is engaged in his expedition, his mother Atossa dreams of two quarreling sisters, one dressed as a Persian, the other as a Greek. The emperor appears and yokes them both to a single chariot. The Asian sister submits to his rule, but the European rebels, upending the chariot and dashing the tyrant to the ground. Aeschylus repeats the word "yoking," or forced binding, throughout the play, expressing his contempt for a policy of forced unions. He explicitly identifies this with the threatening, ethnically different Persians, but tacitly associates with it analogous and indigenous manifestations of tyranny in Greece. Other imperial Persian yokings anticipated similar political failures in the tellings of Greek historians, as with the bridge Darius built over the mighty Danube and yet another bridge over the Araxes, the first, built before Alexander's, by the most illustrious Persian of all, Cyrus the Great.[9] History, as they say, repeats itself. Twenty-five centuries after Xerxes's crossing of the Dardanelles, the same strait on the coastline of Turkey now prepares to host the largest suspension bridge ever built on earth. Funded by nine states, the Çanakkale Strait Bridge will consolidate the International E-Road Network, connecting the O-3 motorway in East Thrace to the O-5 in Anatolia.

Reprising Xerxes's example in times less sober, a Roman emperor constructed a pontoon for the sheer pleasure of galloping his horse across the waters. Emperor Caius Caligula made his army sequester as many merchant boats as they could find near Naples and then line them up to form a pier stretching more than two miles across the Gulf of Baiae. He then rode his horse across, duly dazzling his onlookers. The next day he outdid his performance, charging back from Puteoli to Baiae on a two-horse chariot. Was this all? No, says the historian Suetonius: Caius Caligula wanted to strike fear in the hearts of his enemies and to defy a soothsayer who had vilified his claim to the imperial throne. Caligula had inherited his rule from Tiberius, his adoptive grandfather, who on his deathbed asked a seer whether Caius would succeed in replacing him on the throne. He received this derisive reply: "Caius would no more be emperor, than he would ride on horseback across the gulf of Baiae."[10] To prove the soothsayer wrong, Caligula made technological ingenuity thwart common sense.

Another Roman emperor paid an incalculable price for trafficking in pontoon bridges. The battle that Maxentius lost against Constantine at the Milvian Bridge cost him his rule, but also left the entire Roman Empire in the hands of a new religion. By failing to repel the God-driven

Constantine from Rome, the pagan Maxentius enabled one of the most decisive events in political theology. Still today what he did at the Tiber River has military strategists stumped.

Roman general Constantine descended on the capital with a battle-seasoned army to take the city in the year 312. The night before the battle, encamped across the Tiber, he had a vision of the Christian cross in the sky where he read the words, *In hoc vinces*: "under this [sign] you will prevail." The next morning, with divine backing, Constantine continued down the Flaminian Way toward the northern entry to Rome at Ponte Milvio. To halt the usurper's advance, Emperor Maxentius had made the bridge impassable and slightly upstream constructed a pontoon bridge. Whether he intended it to act as a collapsible trap for Constantine's troops or simply as passage for his own soldiers is now difficult to say. What remains certain is that, with 60,000 more men at his disposal, Maxentius met his adversary Constantine on the far side of the Tiber in front of these bridges. And there he was pounded ferociously back to the river with no place to regroup. Constantine cut down most of Maxentius's men on the riverbank. Others, like the emperor himself, were forced onto one of the two bridges and drowned in the river (fig. 9.12).[11] Had it not been for his bridge meddling, Maxentius might easily have held Rome. Instead he cut it off from its pagan roots. Incapacitating one bridge and cobbling together another, Maxentius helped create one of the most resounding bridge-events in history.

Satanic Unions

Legends about the catastrophic effects of bridge-building travel from Armenia, Greece, and Rome to English literature. The work of the devil, in John Milton's view, lay in attaching separate and diversified products of the Lord. In book 2 of *Paradise Lost* Satan and his rebel angels have been cast out of Heaven and wake up chained to a great lake of fire in Hell. They break free and with great technological ingenuity build a council chamber called Pandemonium. In their conference they resolve to corrupt the new creatures that God has assigned to a wondrous new world called "earth." Satan embarks personally on this mission. On his grueling expedition to join Adam and Eve through expanses of Chaos in the pitch black of night, with no conceivable indication of direction, Satan forges a path with the dexterity of an evil Prometheus.

His children Sin and Death later follow his tracks on this pathway through Chaos. They

Figure 9.12. Pieter Lastman, *Battle of Constantine and Maxentius* (1613). Oil on canvas, 161.5 × 170 cm.

Kunsthalle, Bremen, Germany

> Pav'd after him a broad and beat'n way
> Over the dark Abyss, whose boiling Gulf
> Tamely endur'd a Bridge of wondrous length
> From Hell continu'd reaching th'utmost Orbe
> Of this frail World; by which the Spirits perverse
> With easie intercourse pass to and fro
> To tempt or punish mortals . . .
>
> (*PARADISE LOST* 2.1026–32)

Satan's connection with humans lays the foundation for a sturdy bridge (fig. 9.13) over which all demons can henceforth cross, tempting and punishing mortals through "easie intercourse" (whose sexual connotations appear deliberate, years before Sándor Ferenczi's association of bridge with penis).

Milton denounces the hellish bridge again in book 10 of his epic. There passageways pure and simple are part of the problem, as the poet likens Sin and Death to polar blizzards struggling to dislodge icebergs

Figure 9.13. John Martin, *The Bridge over Chaos* (1826).

blocking "th'imagined way" from Europe to Asia (*Paradise Lost* 10.291). That imagined way was the Northeast Passage from the first continent to the second, complemented by quests for an alternative Northwest Passage, the British Empire's objective at the time being to reach the same Cathay (China) and its riches to which Crane's *Bridge* imagined America as the means. The frosty search for a route through the desolate expanses of Canada had caused untold affliction to sailors. As would have still been fresh in the memory of Milton's readers, Henry Hudson lost his life with all but eight of his men to this quest for a Northwest Passage in 1611.

As Milton conceived it, the passage from Hell to earth, like one through icebergs from Europe to Cathay, breaks a more primordial link between mortals and the divine. *Paradise Lost* presents it in the form of a gold chain attaching earth to Heaven like a hanging pendant. Satan and his children created an alternative, demonic connection to earth, tying it to Hell through a concourse that allowed perverse spirits to debase the higher inclinations of God's creatures: "a Bridge / Of length prodigious joining to the Wall / Immovable of this now fenceless [defenseless] world" (10.301–3). Milton repeats the word "easie" in this second description of Satan's bridge, where, by means of "a passage broad, / Smooth, easie, inoffensive [without obstacles] down to Hell," the earth is altered forever (10.304–5). To drive home the scandal of this bridge, Milton calls up the much-vilified Xerxes:

So, if great things to small may be compar'd,
Xerxes, the Libertie of Greece to yoke,
From Susa his Memnonian Palace high
Came to the Sea, and over Hellespont
Bridging his way, Europe with Asia joyn'd,
And scourg'd with many a stroak th' indignant waves.

(*PARADISE LOST* 10.306–11)

The passage does not stop at demonizing the Europe-threatening Persian ruler. It impugns the popes of Rome as well, for Sin and Death construct

by wondrous Art
Pontifical, a ridge of pendent Rock
Over the vext Abyss, following the track
Of Satan . . .

(*PARADISE LOST* 10.312–15)

By using the word *pontifical*—an epithet for the Vatican pontiffs—Milton links Satan's bridge to what Protestants considered to be the invasive routes of the Catholic Church. Although they called themselves Catholic—"universal" or faith-unifying—the loathed foes of England seemed to bond sinners and nothing more, creating communities of the unfaithful. One senses in Milton's polemic against bridges something like island-animus for mainlands as well, even when those islands (like England) are themselves colonizing powers. It may not be by chance that the derogatory verb "pontificate" (to proclaim or preach with pompous authority) is more widespread in the British Isles than in any country in Europe.

Men Wasted So Badly: Five War Films

If "great things to small" may be compared once more, Satan's bridge in *Paradise Lost* receives a distant echo in a scene of Sergio Leone's film, *The Good, the Bad, and the Ugly* (1967), where forces from the Union and the Confederacy are arrayed on either side of a bridge during the American Civil War. They have entrenched themselves to fight for the bridge and storm it twice daily to no avail, losing what seems like hundreds of soldiers each time. As they happen on the scene, two maverick gunslingers called Blondie and Tuco stand aghast at the scale and senselessness of the devastation. While young boys of the Union charge the bridge under the orders of a desperately drunk captain, are mowed down, and then repulsed by counterattacks, Blondie exclaims, "I have never seen so many men wasted so badly!" The word "wasted" means killed but also deprived of worth. At least Blondie and Tuco are motivated individually and muster up judgment, skill, and intelligence in their duels. The mass warfare around the bridge instead serves the interests of a distant and still abstract nation. Accomplishing their sole political act in the film, Blondie and Tuco relieve this collective suffering, dynamiting the bridge and bringing a smile to the face of the dying captain. The next morning the sun rises on an empty river landscape: the troops have withdrawn, abandoning their unburied soldiers. Tuco sardonically remarks, "Now these idiots will go somewhere else to fight!"

Wars turn bridges into infernal scenes. In *Apocalypse Now* (1979) Willard, a latter-day Marlow in a more contemporary heart of darkness, reaches a bridge battle in the Vietnam War and fails to discover who is directing it. "Do you know who is in command here?" he asks a common soldier. The bruised, dirtied, red-eyed black combatant, towering at the top of the shot's frame against lurid explosions and smoke, with eyes bulging out of his head, looks back long and hard. "Yeah!" he answers. That's all he says, but we know who he means. This scene by Francis Ford Coppola builds on the one by Leone, who already had Vietnam in mind in *The Good, the Bad, and the Ugly*.

Bridging the times of the Civil and the Vietnam Wars—and even World War I, given the style of entrenchment in his war scene—Leone's work also marks the point of arrival of an arc of bridge films made by ex-members of the Axis states of World War II. His signature style—psychologically tense expressions and gestures, shot in extreme close-ups, punctuated by suspenseful inaction, by dead time in empty panoramas—is sharply influenced by a film he would have watched carefully, for its director Bernhard Wicki was well known in Roman circles. He played the part of Tommaso, the reader of Adorno, dying in the hospital in the first scene of Michelangelo Antonioni's *La notte* (1961). Two years before *La notte*, Wicki, an Austrian, devoted a film based in history to the topic of a bridge and gave it that name: *The Bridge* (*Die Brücke*, 1959). Its protagonists are teenage German conscripts in the war's last days who defend a useless bridge in their village against the advancing Allies. All but one of these teenagers is killed. The lone survivor is Gregor Dorfmeister, the author of the semiautobiographical, homonymous novel on which the film is based (1958), in which Dorfmeister works through his feelings of guilt for surviving the catastrophe.

The return to bridge-trauma in both film and novel is a comprehensible attempt to redeem the historical affliction. By means of his film Wicki replaces the bridges of war with those of art, fostering social and moral coherence in those who survived the calamity. In fact his film is one in a series, reassessing the trauma of a film in which Wicki had starred as actor five years earlier: *The Last Bridge* (*Die letzte Brücke,* 1954). Directed by Helmut Käutner, *The Last Bridge* is itself an act of revisitation, where the German director returns to a theme he had broached in a film he had made while World War II was still in progress: *Under the Bridges* (*Unter den Brücken,* 1946). In this earlier film two bargemen along the Spree River of Berlin take onboard and befriend a woman who was poised to jump to her death from the Glienicke Bridge. Eight years later Käutner addressed this war that once raged head-on, setting his new film, *The Last Bridge,* in Bosnia-Herzegovina, where Tito's partisans fight the occupation of Italian and German fascists. Just as Leone's bridge scene in *The Good, the Bad, and the Ugly* harks back in style to *The Bridge* of Wicki, so Wicki's film develops out of that second bridge film of Käutner in which he had acted. The three directors held a common interest in redeeming the tragedies of a war that put them on the wrong side. The actress Maria Schell, who plays a lead role in *The Last Bridge* of 1954, helps extend the series of bridge films by former Axis citizens by participating in a fourth bridge film that also points the way to the aforementioned works of Leone and Coppola: Luchino Visconti's *White Nights* of 1957 (discussed earlier in these pages). Visconti's film, like Käutner's *Last Bridge,* also dramatizes the story of a failed romance in a final scene at a bridge. In both, Schell plays the role of a woman who staves off commitment to one man out of allegiance to another, affirming the distance between them.

Of these four films, the one that most explicitly addresses the wall-like effect of bridges is Käutner's *Last Bridge.* As the film opens at the iconic Stari Most in Mostar, the voice-over narrator informs us that locals call it the "Turkish bridge." He thereby puts us on notice. In the five centuries that have passed since the Ottomans erected this structure, he says, "Many foreign conquerors had crossed it from one bank of the Neretva to the other." He thus underscores the valence of the bridge as means of invasion and subjugation. Any hope that the Stari Most might do otherwise now, in the present of the film, is dashed in the film's second scene, where the German nurse Helga, played by Maria Schell, crosses the bridge to commit to a marshal she has just fallen in love with. As the couple is halfway across the bridge, fascists chase an enemy partisan to its midpoint. Cornered, the partisan jumps and is shot in midair. Traumatized, Helga reverses her decision to consummate her affair with her fellow countryman. The adversity and the death here witnessed make the union lose its conviction.

Figure 9.14. Stills from *The Last Bridge* (1954), dir. Helmut Käutner.

That surprising second scene is carefully prepared by the first. There Helga, with considerable misgivings, told this marshal Martin that she would *not* spend the night with him because she was destined to lose him the next day when he rejoined the war front. As they speak and draw close, the camera pushes in toward them, but it continues right on, moving through and between them to highlight the bridge as an icon of division in the background (fig. 9.14). The transition to the second scene reinforces the severing effects. Helga, having apparently reconsidered her fear of love, here takes a decisive step to cross the bridge with Martin. The move from the first scene to the next is visually jarring. The image of the Mostar Bridge, with which the first scene ends and which is held for a second or two, dissolves into a shot of the same bridge *taken from the other side* (fig. 9.15). This signals a moral, psychological reversal. The large tower on the right now reappears on the left. A few moments later a second dissolve makes it clear why we have this reversal, for Helga crosses the bridge with Martin (fig. 9.16). When the partisan is shot, however, her decision is annulled. Here and throughout the rest of the film, no bridges are crossed except at the cost of life.

This pattern is underscored later when, further downstream, the German Wehrmacht plows through the river on gunboats and one affirms that each bridge over the Neretva River has been destroyed. But just as the soldier says this, they reach a rickety plank bridge over which partisans are carrying their wounded. Instantly the bridge becomes the scene of battle and the symbolic connection is shattered. Eventually we reach the *last bridge* alluded to by the film's title, which is to say, the one beyond which no passage or interaction will be allowed. The bridge is "last" by providing a scene for a final gesture of reconciliation—the nurse Helga's—which war itself does not respect.

The last bridge divides the Wehrmacht from the antifascists. Helga is

Figure 9.15. Stills from Käutner's *The Last Bridge.*

Figure 9.16. Stills from Käutner's *The Last Bridge.*

on the German side from which she intends to transport medical supplies to the other. Discovering her fiancé Martin among the Germans, Helga promises she will return immediately after making this exceptional delivery. Martin allows her to go. As Helga is halfway over the bridge, a gun battle breaks out across the stream and she is caught in the middle. She attempts to take cover but appears to be wounded. The enemies cease fire. Helga slowly rises and walks even more slowly to the partisan side, then returns to the bridge to rejoin her German compatriots. Enveloped in the silence of these hostile witnesses, Helga collapses on the bridge. Within seconds the gun battle resumes over her body, no friend or lover coming to her rescue.

The Last Bridge denies the hope and the promise of bridges, presenting them as unreliable guarantors of passage. From start to finish they threaten dissolution, division, misunderstanding, and death. The nurse Helga, the healer and mender of wounds, the bipartisan bridge, is their casualty. Committed to the common humanity of foes, and cherished equally by both, she cannot be shared. Better, in the eyes of these foes, no bridge at all than one that creates reciprocity.

Bridging Over What Matters

Unions possess no value in themselves; they must be judged by what they achieve. By providing connection, a bridge poses the question of what this connection is for and how to manage its effects. Issues attending the connections of Europe and Asia in Turkey provide a brief example.

The first great Eurasian suspension bridge was built in 1973 when car ferries were deemed inadequate to meet Istanbul's transit requirements. Instead of satisfying demand, the megabridge only increased it. Ten times more people took to crossing the Bosphorus straits than before. The outcome spawned the wish for another bridge. A second was duly built and opened fifteen years later (1988). In five years the neighborhoods located at its feet (Kagithane and Ümraniye) more than doubled their populations.[12] By 2007 the populations had doubled again, to say nothing of the effects of bulldozing traditional dwellings, urban blight, and impacted living conditions. Thanks to its bridges, Istanbul turned into the fifth largest city in the world, with a population of fifteen million. To cope with the crowds, a third bridge over the Bosphorus was deemed necessary. By 2031, or fifteen years after the opening of this Yavuz Sultan Selim Bridge (2016), the car traffic it fosters has been projected to increase fourfold, with few plans for ancillary roads to feed into the clog. The bridge also happens to be located at the heart of the water resources and life-support systems of Istanbul, threatening the city's biosustainability.

Another 122 million passengers pass *beneath* the straits between Europe and Asia along thirteen kilometers of suburban train lines. Plans are also afoot by the government of the current Justice and Development Party to supplement the bridges and the tunnel by a canal joining the Black Sea to the Sea of Marmara. Its purpose? To create more space for oil tankers going up and down the Bosphorus each day—and thereby forcing them to pay Turkey revenues. Just as the third bridge over the Bosphorus emulates the construction of Darius the Great at the very same spot, so the digging of this canal re-elaborates Xerxes's project to cut through the Mount Athos isthmus. What the emperor had in mind, reports Herodotus, was "a channel broad enough for two triremes to be rowed abreast"; he concludes that it could only be "ostentation that made Xerxes have the canal dug—he wanted to show his power and to leave something to be remembered by."[13] When Ottomans took possession of Constantinople in 1453, they were also determined to prove themselves worthy of its splendors. Sultan Bayezid II invited designs by Michelangelo and Leonardo to bridge the Golden Horn. (Leonardo sketched one in his notebooks, while Michelangelo built an actual model.) Architectural historian Gülru Necipoğlu sizes up the sultan's progressive program with wry irony: "Bayezid II's attempt to procure the services of two leading Renaissance artists for its construction shows his global outlook and his willingness to mobilize international networks."[14]

Beneath grandiose projects and megabridges lurk less conspicuous geopolitical intentions: to bring provinces under the control of centralized governments, granting themselves the power to control them; to yoke them to larger economic systems, which thus tighten their tentacular grip; to disconnect communities from reliance on local production and traditions. These projects are not designed to produce an encounter with difference so much as to subjugate it. These are not bridges but ephaptic contacts and unidirectional transmissions.

Yoking things together also raises the question of what such unions exclude. Viaduct bridges in the occupied West Bank tie Israeli settlements to one another in such a way as to bypass Palestinian towns and camps at a protective height. In this political space, writes Eyal Weizman, "separate security corridors, infrastructure, bridges and underground tunnels have been woven into a bewildering and impossible Escher-like territorial arrangement that struggles to multiply a single territorial reality."[15] The Israeli viaducts are backed up by a meandering, 700-kilometer-long structure of walls and fences (the West Bank Barrier), buffered by vehicle-prevention trenches and wide swaths of no-man's-land. Separating Israeli settlements from Palestinian lands, these engineering strategies tie isolated and fragmented communities to one another only by creating yet more of them. When Donald Trump and Benjamin Netanyahu presented a peace plan for two separate states on January 28, 2020, an American spokesman assured a BBC reporter that there would be no problem in cobbling together a state for the Palestinians out of the "bits and pieces" remaining outside Israeli settlements. "The disjointedness of the areas that are in the West Bank can easily be resolved by tunnels and bridges."[16]

Landscapes technologically replotted by motorways, bridges, and tunnels—like gerrymandered electoral districts in American congressional races—involve a dialectic of inclusion and exclusion potentially as oppressive to insiders as outsiders. Even excessive connections in the brain further depression, as multiple passageways produce complexities hard to navigate.[17] Visitors to bridge-cities like Venice, Amsterdam, and Saint Petersburg know how difficult it is to negotiate the turns of alleyways and water channels where posted directions, like links on the Web, rarely lead where one expects. "Brooklyn Bridge, the Manhattan Bridge, the George Washington Bridge, and the Verrazzano Bridge connect all New Yorkers with each other and with the outside world," writes one spiritual holist;[18] yet this does not stop Manhattanites from talking of nonlocals as "bridge and tunnel people." Scant comfort lies in acknowledging that the world's ranks of bridge and tunnel people grow by the millions each year, becoming "foreign residents" with no easily recognizable or certain dwelling.[19] Greater numbers of people exit and return to the places they occupy hundreds of times a day through the

Figure 9.17. Giovanni Battista Piranesi, *The Drawbridge* (1745). Etching on white laid paper, 55.7 × 41.3 cm.

internet and social media—accessed, tracked, targeted, and interpolated by agents and systems beyond their ken.

Containment within these proliferating networks is often more worrisome than being outside them. They are the structural foundation for the dystopic elaborations of Piranesi's *Imaginary Prisons* (figs. 9.17 and 9.18). Depression is the lesser risk of this hyperconnectivity; the greater one is paranoia, where the world's phenomena appear all to be conspiratorially linked in hypertrophied rational relationships.[20] An opposite effect can lead to dissociation and even borderline psychosis, a syndrome the psychoanalyst Wilfred Bion describes as pressing patients to make destructive attacks "on anything which is felt to have the function of linking one object with another."[21] In the realm of philosophy Heidegger is analogously alarmed by "universal symbolics," where no X can still simply be called itself, but appears only as a function of A and B, and Y and Z.[22]

Labyrinthine interrelations have long been celebrated by enthusiasts of the fantastic like Jorge Luis Borges and Italo Calvino, who praises novels that articulate an unending "network of connections between

Figure 9.18. Giovanni Battista Piranesi, *The Smoking Fire* (1745). Etching on white laid paper, 54.2 × 40 cm.

the events, the people and the things of the world."[23] He practices the principle to excellent effect in *Invisible Cities* (1972), an amalgam of sketches of imaginary urban architectonics whose correlations and connotations are impossible to define or desymbolize. A prose poem by Arthur Rimbaud does something similar, envisioning London's material and musical connections—he calls them bridges—transformed into a skein of ethical and philosophical abstraction:

LES PONTS

> Des ciels gris de cristal. Un bizarre dessin de ponts, ceux-ci droits, ceux-là bombés, d'autres descendant ou obliquant en angles sur les premiers, et ces figures se renouvelant dans les autres circuits éclairés du canal, mais tous tellement longs et légers que les rives, chargées de dômes, s'abaissent et s'amoindrissent. Quelques-uns de ces ponts sont encore chargés de masures. D'autres soutiennent des mâts, des signaux, de frêles parapets. Des accords mineurs se croisent et filent, des cordes montent des berges. On distingue une veste

> rouge, peut-être d'autres costumes et des instruments de musique. Sont-ce des airs populaires, des bouts de concerts seigneuriaux, des restants d'hymnes publics? L'eau est grise et bleue, large comme un bras de mer. - Un rayon blanc, tombant du haut du ciel, anéantit cette comédie.

THE BRIDGES

> Skies the gray of crystal. A strange design of bridges, some straight, some arched, others descending at oblique angles to the first; and these figures recurring in other lighted circuits of the canal, but all so long and light that the banks, laden with domes, sink and shrink. A few of these bridges are still covered with hovels, others support masts, signposts, frail parapets. Minor chords cross each other and disappear; ropes rise from the shore. One can make out a red coat, possibly other costumes and musical instruments. Are these popular tunes, snatches of seignorial concerts, remnants of public hymns? The water is gray and blue, wide as an arm of the sea. A white ray falling from high in the sky destroys this comedy.[24]

Overcrowded like Piranesi's prisons, Rimbaud's poem anchors the painterly, musical, and theatrical gestures of these bridges to the graven shores that weigh them down, sinking and shrinking as the former seem to rise. Then suddenly a great bolt of light from the sky obliterates the "comedy" of this transcendent, ethereal interaction.

In a more concrete way, tunnels, viaducts, and megabridges can pull—or literally "ab-stract"—subjects out of civic contexts traditionally made up of affective and material ties into a condition of potentially unending suspension. Many new feats of engineering appear to be governed by the same invasive-evasive intentions as imperial projects of old, reaching into territories only in order to append them to something else. To what exactly? An answer could provide one bridge to the future.

ACKNOWLEDGMENTS

I would like to thank a *frère pontife* who has supplied me with more bridge references than any person could ever have coordinated into a single book: Kelly Zinkowski, a close friend in Rome. Another bridge pier—and peer—is Alberto Giorgio Cassani, who worked through many similar issues in his *Figure del ponte. Simbolo e architettura* (Bologna: Edizioni Pendragon, 2014). He generously shared his findings when his work and mine were both in process and since then has gone on to elaborate his thinking in important additional essays. I am grateful to Guglielmo Bilancioni for putting us in contact, and to another mutual friend, Alessandro Dal Lago, for mediating that contact, too, when the three of us were working on the Watts Towers of Los Angeles.

Several of the ideas in this book took preliminary shape in two previous essays: "The Architectural Word," in *Inquieto pensare: Scritti in onore di Massimo Cacciari*, edited by Emanuele Severino and Vincenzo Vitiello (Brescia: Morcelliana, 2015), 271–82; and "Istrian Italy and the Homeland: The Lessons of Poetry," *Forum Italicum* 47, no. 2 (2013): 324–35.

Excellent studies of bridges that I would have liked to reference with the attention they deserve should be mentioned here. They include Frank Brangwyn and Walter Shaw Sparrow, *A Book of Bridges* (London: John Lane, 1915); Wilbur J. Watson and Sara Ruth Watson, *Bridges in History and Legend* (Cleveland: J. H. Jansen, 1937); F. W. Robins, *The Story of the Bridge* (Birmingham: Cornish Brothers, 1947); and Joseph Gies, *Bridges and Men* (New York: Grosset & Dunlap, 1963).

The reproduction of some images in this book was supported with the help of university subventions, for which I am indebted to David Schaberg, Dean of Humanities, and Dominic Thomas, Chair of the Department of European Language and Transcultural Studies, both at

UCLA. Authors and copyright holders of photographs, as well as facilitators of their reproduction, have been very generous in supporting their use in this book, especially Sarah Balmond, Noel Chiappa, Elisabetta Corni, Paolo Delle Monache, Tom Hill, Matthew Hoser, Alain Janssoone, and Alessandro Lanzetta.

Finally, I would like to thank my eager, outreaching, and synaptically fired students at UCLA, both graduate and undergraduate, along with another handful at Stanford. Although we have never studied bridges explicitly, this topic has in many ways been the unspoken theme of well more than one course. Given that these students will decide which cultural connections to strengthen, among those they inherit, and which new ones need yet to be forged, they deserve more humanistic support for the work on which those decisions depend. They are our bridges to the future.

NOTES

Introduction

1. Andrić, *Bridge over the Drina*, 208–9.

2. Ruskin, "The Nature of Gothic," in *The Stones of Venice*, 2:174.

3. The quotations here and in the following paragraphs are from Simmel, "Bridge and Door," 67, 68. I will continue to reference page numbers in the Ritter translation contained in *Rethinking Architecture* although my translations sometimes differ from his (as well as those of Michael Kaern and the unidentified translator of Simmel's essay in *Lotus International*) in small ways. The Kaern and *Lotus* translations are referenced in my bibliography.

4. Cassani, *Figure del ponte*.

5. Daniel C. Strack has commented on nearly two dozen implications of the bridge in metaphorical speech, and no doubt one could find others. See his "The Bridge Project." Strack has posted several other illuminating studies of bridges on his website, https://www.dcstrack.com/.

6. Heidegger, "Building Dwelling Thinking"; Gordon, *Bridges*, 6-7.

7. Paul Valéry, quoted in Bauman, *Liquid Modernity*, 1.

8. Thoreau, *I to Myself*, 174 (journal entry of January 16, 1853).

9. Nietzsche, *Gay Science*, 90; "Over the Footbridge," bk. 1 §16.

10. Lukács, "On Poverty of Spirit," 44, translation slightly revised. The essay is also included in another translation in Lukács's *Soul & Form*, 201–14.

Chapter One

1. Hearn, *Romance of the Milky Way*, 40.

2. Hearn, *Romance of the Milky Way*, 5–6.

3. Hearn, *Romance of the Milky Way*, 48–49.

4. Sturluson, *Edda*, 15.

5. Lindow, *Norse Mythology*, 81; Simek, *Dictionary of Northern Mythology*, 36. On folk-cultural beliefs about rainbows in other cultures, see Savi-Lopez, *Leggende del mare*, 127–28.

6. See Palmer, "The Liminality of Hermes," and Carravetta, *The Elusive Hermes*.

7. Sproul, "A Bridge Between Cultures."

8. "Natural Bridges," *National Park Service.*

9. Luckert, *Navajo Mountain,* 60–72, 134.

10. Beckwith, *Hawaiian Mythology,* 38, 528.

11. Brown, "Little Wing," 160.

12. Luckert, *Navajo Mountain,* 108.

13. Al-Bukhâri, *Sahîh Al-Bukhâri,* bk. 97, no. 7439, p. 324.

14. Patch, *Other World*; Dinzelbacher, *Die Jenseitsbrücke im Mittelalter.*

15. Bagliani, "Il ponte fra simbolismo e rappresentazione," 48.

16. Van Haeperen, *Le collège pontifical*; Seguin, "Remarques sur les origines des pontifices romains."

17. On the Christianization of the title *pontifex* see Pascal, "Mediaeval Uses of Christianity," 193–97. Three popes had assumed the title *pontifex maximus* between 384 and 604 (Siricius, Leo, and Gregory) but it was not until the fifteenth century that the appellation became a standard, honorary title for the head of the Roman Church. On Gratian's refusal to wear the pontifical robe and the testimony of Zosimus see Knight, "Bridges."

18. This was Quintus Scaevola, *pontifex maximus* in 89 BCE. Notwithstanding his idiosyncratic view, historians mindful of the crucial function of bridges in sacred waters and the water-logged lands of Etruria do not doubt that it lies at the root of the Collegium's foundation. The philologically astute Varro himself disagrees with the pontiff Scaevola, and most scholars today accept *pons* rather than *posse* as the root of the spiritual title. An alternative that has been proposed to *pons* as the etymon for *pontifes* is the Italic word *pompe,* meaning "five." This thesis, first advanced by the Italian philologist Francesco Ribezzo in 1931, points to another possible origin of the Collegium: a board of five men performing sacred rites in Rome centuries prior to Varro and Scaevola, during the reign of the Sabine king and maybe even of the first pontiff, Numa Pompilius. This view has been systematically reproposed by Kavanagh, "Pontifices, Bridge-Making and Ribezzo Revisited." For additional studies of the association of *pontifex* and the construction of bridges see Crifò, "A proposito di *pontifices*"; Champeux, "Ponts, passage, religion à Rome"; and Hallett, "'Over Troubled Waters': The Meaning of the Title Pontifex."

19. Holland, *Janus and the Bridge,* 69.

20. Coomaraswamy, "Perilous Bridge of Welfare," 196; Benveniste, *Problèmes de linguistique générale* 297–98. A half-dozen scholars referenced in van Haeperen's *Le collège pontifical* (including Herbig, Latte, Fugier, and Dumézil) agree that *pánthāh* is where the most ancient source of the *pontifex*'s function should be sought.

21. Van Haeperen, 40.

22. Boniface VIII, "Unam Sanctam."

23. Alighieri, *Divine Comedy: Inferno,* 18.25–33. All subsequent references to the *Inferno* will be to this translation, with canto and line numbers indicated parenthetically.

24. Frothingham, *Roman Cities*; Frazer, *Fear of the Dead,* 1:181–82, 2:46–50; Cumont, *After Life in Roman Paganism.*

25. Eliot, *The Waste Land,* "The Burial of the Dead," lines 60–63.

26. Doré, *Researches into Chinese Superstitions,* 7:301–2.

27. Ellis, "Canto XXI: Controversial Comedy," 292; Baglivi and McCutchan, "Dante, Christ, and the Fallen Bridges"; Singleton, "The Vistas in Retrospect."

28. St. Catherine of Siena, *A Treatise of Discretion,* 21–22.

29. Blake, *Jerusalem: The Emanation of the Giant Albion,* 232, plate 77.

30. Roe, *Blake's Illustrations,* 100.

31. See De Santis, *Blake and Dante.*

32. Lanchester, "Flashes of Flora."

33. Arendt, "No Longer," 122.

34. Arendt, "No Longer," 124, 125. In the first quotation Arendt cites words of Broch.

35. Broch, *Death of Virgil*, 388. Key passages to the same effect appear on pages 321, 373–78, and 384.

Chapter Two

1. Natirbov, "*The World Is A Bridge*, by Christine Weston," 364.

2. Arendt, *Life of the Mind*, 1:200. On Jesus's position in Islam see *The Muslim Jesus*, ed. Khalidi.

3. Wilder, *Conversations with Thornton Wilder*, 88.

4. Wilder, *The Bridge of San Luis Rey*, 97. Subsequent quotations from this novel are referenced parenthetically.

5. Larkin, "Bridge for the Living," 203–4.

6. Makaš, "Representing Competing Identities," 203.

7. Tacitus, *Annals* 13.47.

8. Höfferer, *A Literary Journey to Rome*, 16–17.

9. This translation is an adaption of the one by Richard Wilbur, *New and Collected Poems* (New York: Harcourt, Brace and Jovanovich, 1988), 28.

10. Chaplin excised the near suicidal scene on the bridge from his 1971 reedit of *The Kid* perhaps because the film inspired real jumpers from the same Arroyo Seco Bridge. For a good study of numerous functions of bridges in film see Nafus, "Celluloid Connections: The Bridge in Cinema." See also Dupré, *Bridges*, 93.

11. See Nicoletti, "Downward Mobility."

12. Rizzo, *Ponti di Venezia*, 284–86; Smith, *Cultural Encyclopedia of the Breast*.

13. Jadhav, "Under Dadar Bridge," 11:147.

14. Juvenal, *Satires* 14, line 134: *inuitatus ad haec aliquis de ponte negaret*.

15. Oudin, *Curiositéz françoises, pour supplément aux dictionnaires*, 438; James-Raoul, "Le pont dans les locutions," 304.

16. France, *Red Lily*, chap. 7.

17. Roth, *The Legend of the Holy Drinker*, 43. Subsequent quotations from this edition will be referenced parenthetically.

18. Zurawsky, User Review, "Nirvana, Nevermind."

19. Delli, *Ponti di Roma*, 66. A copious sourcebook for inhabited bridges throughout the ages is "(Ponti abitati)," a special issue of *Rassegna*, ed. Dethier and Eaton. Other useful studies are *Living Bridges*, ed. Murray and Stevens, and Biau, *The Bridge and the City*.

20. Alberti, *On the Art of Building*, 262.

21. Andrić, *Bridge over the Drina*, 14, 15.

22. Di Siena, *Due ponti pedonali sul Tevere*, 44–72.

23. Biau, *The Bridge and the City*, 41–42. See also Keil, *Pedestrian Bridges*.

24. These and several other modernist projects are outlined in Dethier and Eaton, "(Ponti abitati)," 54–55, 82–88.

25. Bishop, *Bridge*, 203. Two excellent sourcebooks on ingenious and spectacular bridges of the past twenty years are Dupré, *Bridges*, and Binney, *Bridges Spanning the World*.

26. "I did not know about the local legend," writes Cecil Balmond. "The mayor told me at the groundbreaking ceremony." Balmond, *Crossover*, 244.

Chapter Three

1. These three quotations come from Nancy, *Listening*, 6, 14. Studies of the phenomenology of sound establishing similar points include Bowman, *Philosophical Perspectives on Music*, and Clifton, *Music as Heard*.

2. Burrows, *Sound, Speech and Music*, 91; Weil, "Human Personality," 71.

3. These two quotations are from Burrows, *Sound*, 21, and Nancy, *Listening*, 8.

4. Arendt, *Life of the Mind*, 1:47.

5. Clifton, *Music as Heard*, 290.

6. Nancy, *Listening*, 52–53.

7. Burrows, *Sound*, 38.

8. Giacomo Leopardi, "Ricordi d'infanzia," 1102. On other functions of the voice in this passage see D'Intino, *La caduta e il ritorno*, 39–40. On the poetics of sound in Leopardi generally see Brose, "Leopardi and the Power of Sound."

9. Leopardi, *Zibaldone*, 57.

10. Leopardi, "Ricordi d'infanzia," 1101.

11. Leopardi, "L'infinito," 106–7, translation modified.

12. Harrison, "Offscreen Space"; Peretz, *The Off-Screen*.

13. Hölderlin, "Heidelberg," lines 5–8, in *Selected Poems*, 20–21.

14. The two levels are articulated by Emil Staiger and Wilhelm Schneider, both discussed by Sitz, "Hölderlin's 'Ode to Heidelberg,'" 156.

15. Ungaretti, "Nostalgia," in *Vita d'un uomo*, 54. An alternate translation of this poem is offered by Tony Kline at https://www.poetsofmodernity.xyz/POMBR/Italian/FiveItalianPoets.php#anchor_Toc326225696.

16. Camus, *The Fall*, chap. 6.

17. Crane, "To Brooklyn Bridge," lines 17–20, in *The Bridge*, 3–4. When not identified by poem and line number, citations from this work will indicate pages in this edition.

18. Fontana, *Oscillating Steel Grids along the Brooklyn Bridge*, 1983. A forty-six-minute extract from this live "sound sculpture" can be heard at http://resoundings.org/Pages/Oscillating.html.

19. Fontana, "Environment." Twenty-five years later, on the occasion of the bridge's seventy-fifth anniversary, Fontana followed up with *Acoustical Visions of the Golden Gate Bridge* (2012).

20. Fontana, "Environment."

21. Fontana, *Cologne*.

22. Cage, "Future of Music: Credo," 25.

23. Fontana, *Cologne*.

24. Rose, "Project Outline."

25. Serres, *Angels* and *L'Art des ponts*.

26. John Cage, quoted in Revill, *Roaring Silence*, 52.

27. Gambacurta, *Autophones*.

28. Gambacurta, *Autophones*.

29. Schopenhauer, *World as Will*, vol. 2, chap. 13.

30. Akin, *Crossing the Bridge*, chap. 3, 7:35–8:10.

31. Randel, *New Harvard Dictionary of Music*, 113–14.

32. Golson, *Playboy Interviews with John Lennon & Yoko Ono*, 183. The only song in which Lennon references a chorus is "Can't Buy Me Love," also on page 183.

33. Alberti, *On the Art of Building*, 107, 262.

34. These incipits are from Robert Johnson, "Terraplane Blues," 1936; Jules Bihari and B. B. King, "It's My Own Fault," 1961; Preston Foster, "Got My Mojo Workin'," 1956; Muddy Waters, "Blow Wind Blow," 1953; Tracy Chapman, "Give Me One Reason," 1989. On the performative contexts of the blues, which I discuss further in the pages that follow, see Ferris, *Blues from the Delta*, 101–3; Keil, *Urban Blues*, chapters 6 and 7.

35. McClary, "Thinking Blues," in *Conventional Wisdom*, 32–62. On the erotic and self-assertive styles of the female blues see Jackson, *A Bad Woman Feeling Good*; Davis, *Blues Legacies and Black Feminism*; and Carby, "It Jus Be's Dat Way Sometime."

36. Barretta, "Southern Expressions of the Blues Revival."

37. Schwartz, *How Britain Got the Blues*. Other excellent critical studies on the crossover from the U.S. to the U.K. include Milward, *Crossroads*; Adelt, *Blues Music*; Kellett, "Fathers and Sons"; McStravick and Roos, *Blues-Rock Explosion*; and Bane, *White Boy Singin' the Blues*.

38. Alvin Lee, quoted in Yardley, "Alvin Lee."

39. Eric Clapton, quoted in Adelt, *Blues Music*, 61.

40. Doyle, *Commitments*, 9.

41. Danny Kirwan, quoted in Celmins, "A Rare Encounter."

Chapter Four

1. Grégoire, *Recherches historiques*, 62.

2. Paulus, *Indulgences*, 86.

3. Georg Ratzinger, quoted in Paulus, *Indulgences*, 77–78.

4. Bruguier-Roure, "Les constructeurs de ponts," 232.

5. Brodman, *Charity and Religion*, 123.

6. Paulus, *Indulgences*, 79. The description of the order between 1196 and 1208 comes from Boyer, "Bridgebuilding Brotherhoods," 640.

7. All three citations are from J. Becker, "Die religiöse Bedeutung des Brückenbaues im Mittelalter," *Archive für Frankfurter Geschichte*, Neue Folge, 4:10 (Frankfurt, 1869), quoted in Paulus, *Indulgences*, 68.

8. Several early hospices are documented by Pellegrini, *Gli xenodochi di Parma*.

9. Kadare, *Three-Arched Bridge*, 29–30.

10. Kadare, *Three-Arched Bridge*, 5–26.

11. Sigler, "Crossing Folkloric Bridges." For legends of the pact with the devil see Galanti, "La leggenda," and Cocchiara, *Il diavolo nella tradizione popolare italiana*.

12. Eliade, "Master Manole," 184. See also Pinza, "Conservazione delle teste umane," and Sainéan, "Les Rites de la construction."

13. Gould, "Allegory," 211.

14. Andrić, *Bridge over the Drina*, 16.

15. For a tentatively feminist reading of wife immurement in this ballad see Mandel, "Sacrifice at the Bridge of Arta." A more expansive analysis of female foundation-sacrifice can be found in Schott, "Sexual Violence Sacrifice." The genealogy and variations of the wife-and-bridge ballad in the Balkans from the twelfth century forward are illuminated

by Villalba, "Arches of Discord"; Leontis, "Bridge Between the Classical and the Balkan"; Dunes, *Walled-up Wife*; Cocchiara, *Il Paese di Cuccagna*; Vargyas, "Origin of the 'Walled-Up Wife.'" See also Stanesco, "Du pont de l'épée au pont eschatologique."

16. On this question in Kadare see Claude Thomasset, "La Construction du pont medieval," and Cassani, "Distruggere i ponti?"

17. See Kadare, *Three-Arched Bridge*, 110, 145, 170. From here on, citations from this novel are referenced parenthetically by page number.

18. See Reynolds, "Bridge to Nowhere." A compassionate fictional film has been made about this border conflict by Kezele, *My Beautiful Country*, and an informative documentary by Bialis and Ealer, *View from the Bridge*.

19. Garrod, foreword to Yarwood, *Rebuilding Mostar*, ix.

20. Yarwood, *Rebuilding Mostar*, 4.

21. Hedges, *War Is a Force*, 73. See also Pašić, *The Old Bridge*, and Bishop, *Bridge*, 157–61.

22. Andrić, *Bridge over the Drina*, 25. Subsequent citations from this novel are referenced parenthetically.

23. Comprone, "Alterity, Violence, and History."

24. Andrić, *Bridge over the Drina*, 208–9.

25. Andrić, *Bridge over the Drina*, 210–11. The quotations about substantial and functional-structural connections are from Milutinović, "Andrić's Strategy of Redemption."

26. Comprone, "Alterity," 265.

27. Hedges, *War Is a Force*, 64. On Bosniak opposition to Andrić's work see Rakić, "The Proof Is in the Pudding."

28. Hedges, *War Is a Force*, 112.

Chapter Five

1. Roth, "Avignon," in *The White Cities*, 100–101.

2. This and the next three quotations are from Nietzsche, "The Convalescent," §2, *Thus Spoke Zarathustra*, in *The Portable Nietzsche*; further quotations from *Thus Spoke Zarathustra* will be referenced parenthetically in the text. In the interests of international readers, quotations from works by Nietzsche will, when possible, be referenced by chapter and paragraph section (§) rather than page number. Unless otherwise specified, all *Zarathustra* quotations use the Kaufmann translations in *The Portable Nietzsche*.

3. Actually Sloterdijk did, in *You Must Change your Life*, 9. Heidegger's dictum comes from his "Letter on Humanism," 217.

4. Nietzsche, "On Truth and Lie," 46–47.

5. Friedrich Nietzsche, "Nur Narr! Nur Dichter!" in *Dionysos-Dithyramben*, online at the Nietzsche Channel, http://www.thenietzschechannel.com/works-pub/dd/dd-dual.htm. For variations on this poetic composition see Nietzsche Source: Digital Critical Edition (eKGWB), http://www.nietzschesource.org/#eKGWB.

6. Nietzsche, *Human, All Too Human*, vol. 1, §189.

7. Nietzsche, *Nachgelassene Fragmente/Posthumous Fragments*, eKGWB/NF-1884,28[20], accessible online at Nietzsche Source, http://www.nietzschesource.org/#eKGWB/NF-1884,28[20].

8. Valéry, "Poésie et pensée abstraite," a lecture delivered at Oxford University in 1939, in *Oeuvres I*, 1317–1318. English translation in Valéry, *Art of Poetry*, 55–56.

9. Calvino, *Six Memos*, 77.

10. Gadamer, *Truth and Method*, 469.

11. Ricoeur, "Metaphor and the Main Problem of Hermeneutics."

12. Dictionary.com.

13. Lakoff and Johnson, *Metaphors We Live By*, 28–31.

14. Kövecses, *Where Metaphors Come From*, ix–x.

15. Gadamer, *Truth and Method*, 406.

16. Gadamer, *Truth and Method*, 431.

17. Derrida, *Heidegger*, 190.

18. Gadamer, *Truth and Method*, 429.

19. Fenollosa, "An Essay on the Chinese Written Character," 377.

20. Samuel Johnson, quoted in Richards, *Philosophy of Rhetoric*, 93. The following quotations from Richards are referenced parenthetically.

21. Breton, *Communicating Vessels*, 109.

22. Lodge, *Modes of Modern Writing*, 109.

23. Ricoeur, "Listening to the Parables of Jesus," 239.

24. Sloterdijk, *Change Your Life*, 205.

25. Buber, "Teaching of the Tao," 35.

26. Ricoeur, "Parables," 242.

27. Ricoeur, "Parables," 242.

28. Ricoeur, "Parables," 244.

29. Picasso, quoted in Gilot and Lake, *Life with Picasso*, 51. An illuminating discussion of the statement in the context of metaphor is conducted by Rogers, *Painting and Poetry*, 125–27.

30. Stevens, *The Palm at the End of the Mind*, 240.

31. Parker, "The Motive for Metaphor," 87.

32. Dickinson, *Poems*, 70. Poem 721, lines 1–3.

33. Howe, *My Emily Dickinson*, 97.

34. Nietzsche, *Beyond Good and Evil*, §126.

35. Mengaldo, "Strategie di reticenza e demistificazione," 37.

36. Nietzsche, Letter to Elisabeth Nietzsche, May 20, 1885, *Briefe/Letters*, http://www.nietzschesource.org/#eKGWB/BVN-1885,601a.

37. *Gedanken und Gedankenstriche eines guten Europäers*; *Fragen und Gedankenstriche*; *Vorläufige Gedanken und Gedankenstriche von Friedrich Nietzsche*; *Gedankenstriche eines Psychologen*; Nietzsche, *Nachgelassene Fragmente*, NF-1885,1[232]; NF-1885,2[43]; NF-1885,35[8]; NF-1885,36[55], http://www.nietzschesource.org/#eKGWB/NF-1885,1[1] and http://www.nietzschesource.org/#eKGWB/NF-1885,35.

38. Richards, *Philosophy of Rhetoric*, 131.

39. All these quotations are from Crane, *The Bridge*, "The Harbor Dawn," lines 21–23. When not identified by poem and line number, other quotations from *The Bridge* will be referenced by page numbers in this edition.

40. Crane, "General Aims and Theories," 163.

41. See Beckett, "The (Il)logic of Metaphor in Crane's *The Bridge*."

42. Crane, quoted in *The Bridge*, 9; letter to Otto Kahn.

43. Hammer, "Hart Crane's View from the Bridge." The play on the terms "fusion" and "con-fusion" in the reception of Crane's poem goes back to its earliest readers, with Tate glossing confusion as "a phase of the inner cross-purposes of the time." See Tate, "On the 'Intensity of Sensation,'" 103.

Chapter Six

1. See Davies, *Death and the Emperor*, 10–11, 82–83, 159–63.

2. D'Onofrio, *Gian Lorenzo Bernini*, 80; Weil, *History and Decoration*, 89–103.

3. Delli, *Ponti di Roma*, 79. Body parts were often strewn on London Bridge as well, a place recognized in the song "London Bridge Is Falling Down" as a site for the foundation sacrifice of children. "Prisoners' heads were put on the bridge after execution down to modern times," writes Gomme, *Traditional Games*, 347.

4. Her name is Beatrice Cenci and her tragic story is told by Falconi, *I fantasmi di Roma*, 54–63.

5. D'Onofrio, *Il Tevere*, 232.

6. Burroughs, "Below the Angel," 97.

7. Boccacio plays on this theme in the story "Ponte dell'Oca," where it is sadly a wife being beaten and the bridge name associates her with a goose, a metaphor for a dimwit. See Boccaccio, "Ponte dell'Oca," *Decameron* 9:9. On the expression about beating donkeys at bridges see James-Raoul, "Le pont dans les locutions," 300.

8. Delli, *Ponti di Roma*, 82.

9. Little, "Life and Afterlife," 31–32.

10. Gardet, *Islam*, 87.

11. Dionysius of Halicarnassus, *Roman Antiquities* 1.38.

12. The Frazer quotation is from his "Commentary on Book V," 82. Dionysius of Halicarnassus discusses the rituals of the Argei in his *Roman Antiquities*. Plutarch's view of the *depontani* and marriages in or around the month of May is referenced by Seppilli, *Sacralità dell'acqua e sacrilegio dei ponti*, 67. The meaning of the phrase *sexagenarios de ponte* has been debated since at least Sextus Pompeius Festus in the second century (Knight, "Bridges," 849; Frazer, "Commentary," 74–110; and Klotz, "Sexagenarii"). On the purifying purposes of the Argei ceremony, see Ziółkowski, "Ritual Cleaning-Up of the City"; Wallace-Hadrill, *Rome's Cultural Revolution*, 260–64; and Mancini, "*Pietas* e *superstitio*." Considering that the Latin expression *de ponte dejici* (cast off the bridge) designated citizens who had lost the right to vote, it may also be that *depontani* did not reference anyone thrown to death off a bridge at all, but just those, perhaps the elderly, who were kept off the bridge leading to the polling booth in Rome. On this point see James-Raoul, "Le pont dans les locutions," 317.

13. Amadei, *I ponti di Roma*, 9.

14. The anecdote of Cicero is related by Seppilli, *Sacralità*, 73, who on pp. 74–78 also discusses the ritual killing of elders in diverse cultures.

15. Delli, *Ponti di Roma*, 102–3.

16. See Sells, *The Bridge Betrayed*, 165.

17. Bierce, "An Occurrence at Owl Creek Bridge," 9. Subsequent page numbers will be referenced parenthetically.

18. Strack, "When the Path of Life Crosses the River of Time," 6.

19. Biedermann, *Dictionary of Symbolism*, 249–50.

20. Connochie-Bourgne, "Le pont de Virgile," 50. On the bridge as signifying a rite of passage see Coomaraswamy, "Perilous Bridge"; Chevalier and Gheerbrandt, "Ponts," 47–49; Boyer, *Medieval French Bridges*; and Pastré, "Se battre sur le pont."

21. See two works by Ferenczi: "Symbolism of the Bridge," and "Bridge Symbolism and the Don Juan Legend." Also see Gordon, *Bridges*, 69–84, where she writes that in order to allow the penis "to function as a bridge, a person must, I suggest, have felt and

become aware of the anxiety and the depression of his essential separateness," perceiving and experiencing "that which divides and cuts one off" (71). See also Róheim, *Animism, Magic, and the Divine King*, 44–57.

22. Sloterdijk, *Spheres*. Vol. 1: *Bubbles, Microspherology*, 295, 320.

23. Von Beit, *Symbolik des Märchens*. Reimbold distinguishes Jungian from Freudian approaches to the bridge in "Die Brücke als Symbol."

24. Kafka, "The Judgment," 16.

25. Kafka, *The Trial*, 283.

26. Kafka, *The Trial*, 285.

27. See Kafka, "The Bridge," 411.

28. Horace, *Satires* 2, 3, lines 32–41.

29. Juvenal, *Satires* 6, lines 28–32.

30. Goethe, *Italienische Reise*, October 27, 1786 abends.

31. Leavitt, *Florence: A Delicate Case*.

32. Magherini, *La sindrome di Stendhal*.

33. Cook, "The Case against Saying 'Suicide Is a Permanent Solution to a Temporary Problem.'"

34. These estimates are from Paul Gromosiak, quoted in Hudson, "Suicide Season."

35. On the frequency of different modes of suicide see http://webappa.cdc.gov/cgi-bin/broker.exe and http://www.suicide.org/suicide-statistics.html. On people traveling to Marin County to end their lives see http://www.miller-mccune.com/culture-society/golden-gate-bridge-suicides-then-and-now-25290/.

36. Steel, "Interview, Part I."

37. Theroux, "Letter to the Editor."

38. Koenig, "Favored by Suicides."

39. Pater, "Conclusion" to *The Renaissance*, 114.

40. Leopardi, "Dialogue of a Physicist and a Metaphysician," 87.

41. Pliny the Elder, *Naturalis Historia* 4:89.

42. Leopardi, "Dialogue of Christopher Columbus and Pedro Gutierrez," 161.

43. Seppilli, *Sacralità*, 130–219.

44. Seppilli, *Sacralità*, 171–74.

45. On this thematic dimension of the Golden Gate Bridge see Cassani, *Figure*, 148.

46. Beaulieu, *The Sea in the Greek Imagination*, 10.

47. Sugg, *Hart Crane's "The Bridge,"* 25–26.

48. May, *Psychology and the Human Dilemma*, 103.

49. Thomas Hood, "The Bridge of Sighs."

Chapter Seven

1. Nietzsche, "Zarathustra's Prologue," §4, *Thus Spoke Zarathustra*, in *The Portable Nietzsche*. In this chapter, too, most quotations from Nietzsche's work will be referenced by chapter and paragraph section (§) rather than page number.

2. "More-than-man" is the quite appropriate translation of *Übermensch* that is made by Stanley Appelbaum in his edition of Nietzsche, *Thus Spoke Zarathustra (Selections)*. I will often substitute it for the term "overman," used by Kaufmann's translations, in citations to follow.

3. Nietzsche, *Writings from the Early Notebooks*, 184. The original can be found in Nietzsche, *Sämtliche Werke*, 2:141.

4. The observation is at the core of the study by Buddensieg, "Architecture as Empty Form." The entire collection in which his essay appears is dedicated to Nietzsche and architecture: Kostka and Wohlfarth, *Nietzsche and "An Architecture of Our Minds."*

5. Nietzsche, *Human, All Too Human*, vol. 1, §145.

6. Nietzsche, *Gay Science*, §280.

7. Nietzsche, "Rückblick," in *Werke*, 3:747.

8. Nietzsche, *Sämtliche Briefe*, 8:285.

9. Nietzsche, "Why I Am So Clever," §7, *Ecce Homo*; trans. slightly revised.

10. The biographical background for this poem can be reconstructed from Grundlehner, *Poetry of Friedrich Nietzsche*; Hollinrake, "A Note on Nietzsche's *Gondellied*"; and Lösel, "Nietzsche's 'Venice': An Interpretation." Goethe and Rousseau had been moved by the same *barcarolles* intoned by Venetian gondoliers in the moderate tempo of 6/8. "Indescribably plaintive," in Goethe's view, they involved a "distinctive antiphonal rendition of poetry and music by two gondoliers, frequently . . . situated at a considerable distance from each other" (paraphrased by Hollinrake, 141). Richard Wagner also focuses on the Venetian *barcarolles* in an essay on Beethoven of 1870, speaking of a "strange, melancholy dialogue" of gondoliers echoing each other's songs. It is the same "duologue" that appears in Nietzsche's poem, Hollinrake concludes (145). Wagner's experience in Venice is also referenced by Plant, *Venice: Fragile City, 1797–1997*, 195, where she examines the importance of Venice for Nietzsche (195–98), a topic explored philosophically by Cacciari in "Viaggio estivo," 127–40.

11. Nietzsche, *Nachgelassene Fragmente*, eKGWB/NF-1880,2[29], accessible online at Nietzsche Source, http://www.nietzschesource.org/#eKGWB/NF-1880,2[29].

12. Cacciari, "Nietzsche and the Unpolitical," 98.

13. Heidegger and Jaspers, *Heidegger-Jaspers Correspondence*, 169.

14. Nietzsche, *Gay Science*, §125.

15. Nietzsche, *Ecce Homo*, "Why I Am a Destiny," §8.

16. The first phrase is Sweetman's in his *The Artist and the Bridge 1700–1920*, 131. The second is from Worringer's *Abstraction and Empathy*, 15.

17. Joseph Stella, quoted in Crane, *The Bridge*, xvii.

18. Crane, *The Bridge*, "Atlantis," line 42. The phrase "sacred mediator" is from Cassani, *Figure*, 135.

19. Karl Schmidt-Rottluff, quoted in Selz, *German Expressionist Painting*, 95.

20. Lorenz, *Brücke*, 8.

21. Nietzsche, *Human, All Too Human*, §638; Musil, "Towards a New Aesthetic," 208.

22. Asad, *Road to Mecca*, 362. Asad retells the episode a couple of more times in this work (308, 375) as well as on p. 132 of his *Unromantic Orient*. I am indebted to Daniel Stein Kokin for bringing Asad's bridge-experience to my attention.

23. Sloterdijk, *You Must Change Your Life*, 63. Nietzsche's resistance to essentialist conceptions of the *Übermensch* is repeatedly underscored by Gianni Vattimo, most lately in his "Cristianesimo senza verità," 203–10. Where human behavior is conjectural and self-realization amounts to something more like striving, Roberto Esposito takes an analogous perspective: "Only conjectures that face up to their own inability to seize Truth are in a position to approach it," he writes in "L'Europa di Cacciari," 173.

24. Kafka, "The Bridge," 411–12. Interesting readings are given of this parable in Cassani, *Figure*, as well as his "Il ponte e il suo angelo," 213–30.

25. Nietzsche, *Beyond Good and Evil*, §289.

26. Musil, *The Man Without Qualities II*, 836.

27. The six citations in this paragraph, from first to last, are: Nietzsche, "Why I am

So Wise," §3, *Ecce Homo*; foreword to *The Anti-Christ*, 114; preface (Nov. 1887–March 1888), §3, *Will To Power*; *Beyond Good and Evil*, §295; "Aus Hohen Bergen/From High Mountains," line 2, *Beyond Good and Evil*; "The Shadow," *Zarathustra*. For an extended analysis of the "whereabouts anxiety" of this solitary philosopher, see Harrison, "Have I Been Understood?"

28. Steven Connor, "Man Is a Rope," at http://stevenconnor.com/rope.html. Cf. the words of Roberto Morese on the back cover of the publication by the bridge-scholar and architect Enzo Siviero: "The 'human bridge' is the becoming-place of non-place." Morese also introduces this interesting volume of reflections by Siviero, *Il ponte umano*.

29. Blavatsky, *Isis Unveiled*, 1:3; Atkinson [Magus Incognito], *Secret Doctrine*, 246.

30. Nietzsche, *Will to Power*, §1067.

31. See Nietzsche, *Gay Science*, §277.

32. Merleau-Ponty, *Signs*, 21.

33. Cassani, *Figure*, 305. Cassani properly ties these implications of Nietzsche's bridge-thinking to Zen Buddhism and other reflections of post-Nietzschean Viennese culture as expounded by Massimo Cacciari in his "The Art of Archery."

34. Esposito, "Community and Nihilism," 48.

Chapter Eight

1. Barzilai, *Vita internazionale*, 74.

2. De Romanis, *Il ponte sull'Adriatico/The Bridge over the Adriatic*, 22.

3. Tucci and Chiarini, *A chi appartiene l'Adriatico?* 37.

4. Tucci and Chiarini, *A chi appartiene l'Adriatico?* 41.

5. See Abulafia, *The Great Sea*, and Bosetti, *De Trieste à Dubrovnik*.

6. Studies on this subject are numerous. Some of the most salient are Fusaro, Heywood, and Omri, *Trade and Cultural Exchange*; Abulafia, *The Great Sea*; Goody, *Islam in Europe*; Cabane, *Histoire de l'Adriatique*; Motta, *I Turchi, il Mediterraneo e l'Europa*; Braudel, *The Mediterranean and the Mediterranean World*.

7. Matvejević, *Mediterranean: A Cultural Landscape*, 85–86.

8. Bromberger, "Bridge, Wall, Mirror," 292. On these cities see also Driessen, "Mediterranean Port Cities," and Haller, "The Cosmopolitan Mediterranean."

9. Mansel, *Levant*, 20–36.

10. Bromberger, "Bridge, Wall, Mirror," 293. The book referenced is Morin, *Vidal and His Family*. On *dragomans* in the Ottoman Empire, see Lewis, *From Babel to Dragomans*, 21–29.

11. Hametz, "Naming Italians"; Sluga, *Problem of Trieste and the Italo-Yugoslav Border*; Bosetti, *De Trieste à Dubrovnik*, 301.

12. See Bosetti, *De Trieste à Dubrovnik*, 298–303.

13. On Italy's modern embrace of *Mare Nostrum* as project see Fogu, "From *Mare Nostrum* to *Mare Aliorum*"; Trinchese, *Mare nostrum*; Maranelli and Salvemini, *La questione dell'Adriatico*.

14. Weil, "The Great Beast," 140–41.

15. The translation is mine, but excellent bilingual versions of the poem are provided by Montale, *The Occasions*, 31–34, and Montale, *Collected Poems 1920–1954*, 180–83. Hereafter line numbers are included parenthetically in the text.

16. James Joyce, *Ulysses*, 25–26.

17. Cassano, *Southern Thought*, 11.

18. On the theme of the tower as a primordial bridge or ladder aiming to connect earth to sky see Gordon, *Bridges*, 7; Harrison, "Without Precedent: The Watts Towers"; Cassani, *Figure*, 122–23. The association is also implicit in Crane's *The Bridge*, 2.

19. See http://portocorsini.info/.

20. I recount the political vicissitudes of this Istrian peninsula in greater detail in Harrison, "Istrian Italy." The estimated sums of exiles are compiled from Bosetti, *De Trieste à Dubrovnik*, 363; Cattaruzza, *L'Italia e il confine orientale*, 311; Petacco, *A Tragedy Revealed*, 133; Pupo, *Il lungo esodo*, 13; Valussi, *Il confine nordorientale d'Italia*, 172–73.

21. See http://en.wikipedia.org/wiki/Rovinj.

22. Benveniste, *Linguistique générale*, 296–97; Nagy, *Best of the Achaeans*, 337–47; Pralon, "La Méditerranée des grecs anciens," 17.

23. Matvejević, "Per una talassopoetica," 259.

24. See, e.g., Cassano, "Repubbliche mediterranee"; Bouchard, "Italy's Geophilosophies of the Mediterranean," 347–49. "Mutual visibility," write Horden and Purcell, "is at the heart of the navigational conception of the Mediterranean, and is therefore a major characteristic of . . . the multiple lines of communication that follow those of sight." Horden and Purcell, *Corrupting Sea*, 126. The sea, they continue, "is no barrier to communications, but the medium of all intercourse from one region to another" (133).

25. Sophocles, *Antigone*, as translated in Heidegger, *An Introduction to Metaphysics*, 123.

26. Cacciari, *L'arcipelago*.

27. See Cocco, "Territori liquidi," and Ballinger, "Liquid Borderland."

28. The need to "insure" migrants in new lands is discussed in Duffield, "Global Civil War."

29. On this betweenness see Dal Lago, *Non-Persons*, and Sayad, *The Suffering of the Immigrant*.

30. On multi- and interlinguality see Bond, Bonsaver, and Faloppa, eds., *Destination Italy*; Burns, *Migrant Imaginaries*; and Yıldız, *Beyond the Mother Tongue*.

31. Adelson, "Against Between: A Manifesto"; McGowan, "Brücken und Brücken-Köpfe"; Jordan, "More Than a Metaphor."

32. Tawada, "I Did Not Want to Build Bridges," 416. On Tawada as exophonic writer see Perloff, *Unoriginal Genius*, 136–45, and Wright, "Writing in the 'Grey Zone.'"

33. See Adelson, *The Turkish Turn*; Seyhan, *Writing Outside the Nation*; Firmat, *Life on the Hyphen*; Bhabha, *The Location of Culture*; Soja, *Thirdspace*.

34. Heidegger, "Building Dwelling Thinking," 153.

35. The words are by Heidegger, "Building Dwelling Thinking," 154, and are cited by Bhabha, *The Location of Culture*, 7.

36. Rushdie, *Imaginary Homelands*, 125.

37. Rossanda, preface to Matvejević, *Mondo Ex*, 6.

38. Rossanda, preface to Matvejević, 7.

39. Maalouf, "Il viaggiatore delle due rive," 210–14.

40. Maalouf, 217. Kadare, "L'Adriatico visto dalla cittadella," 161. Elsewhere Maalouf notes that those with complex, multilocal identities "who live in a sort of frontier zone . . . have a special role to play in forging links, eliminating misunderstandings. . . . Their role is to act as bridges, go-betweens, mediators between the various communities and cultures." Maalouf, *In the Name of Identity*, 4–5.

41. For more on ephaptic coupling, see https://en.wikipedia.org/wiki/Ephaptic_coupling.

42. De Lacoste-Utamsing and Holloway, "Sexual Dimorphism." This early study suggests that men tend to divorce their analysis of a problem from how they feel about it

(separating left-brain activity from right) while women integrate analytical and emotional responses to the situations they face, engaging in interaction between left and right hemispheres. Subsequent studies did not consistently corroborate this assessment of cognitive dimorphism. Some revealed that the corpus callosum grows at different rates and in different ways in men and women, making conclusions about sex-gender distinction difficult to reach. Others reasoned that growth in the brain is influenced by the environment, fostering gender-differentiated education and leading to greater development of certain skills in each gender. On key issues in this research see Westerhausen, Kreuder, Dos Santos Sequeira, et al., "Effects of Handedness and Gender"; Gorman and Nash, "Sizing up the Sexes." For a broader and wide-ranging study that transcends the *callosum* and gender altogether, but makes an eloquent plea for the need to enhance intrapsychic cognitive relationships, as well as to integrate more right-brained activity in human culture, see McGilchrist, *The Master and His Emissary*.

43. Makaš, "Representing Competing Identities," 210.

44. Groddeck, *The Book of the It*.

45. Nietzsche, *Nachgelassene Fragmente*, eKGWB/NF-1880,6[70], http://www.nietzschesource.org/#eKGWB/NF-1880,6[70]. For a compelling study of the vast number of intrapsychic bridges that need to be built for the maintenance of mental health see Gordon, *Bridges*.

46. Arendt, *Life of the Mind*, 1:187.

47. Plato, *Symposium*, 202e–203b.

48. Yeats, *Per Amica Silentia Lunae*, 324.

49. Yeats, *A Vision*, 193, and see also 214.

50. Yeats, *Per Amica Silentia Lunae*, 329–31.

51. Yeats, *Per Amica Silentia Lunae*, 331, 361.

52. Yeats, *A Vision*, 209.

53. Plato, *Statesman* 271d sq. and *Phaedo* 107e.

54. Cacciari, *The Withholding Power*, 175.

55. The phrase "Berlin of the Adriatic" is from Petacco, *A Tragedy Revealed*, 135, while the other is discussed by Ballinger, *History in Exile*, 164.

56. Ballinger, *History in Exile*, 423.

57. On the Roman bridge battle see Delli, *Ponti di Roma*, 110, and on the *battagliole* of Venice, Rizzo, *Ponti di Venezia*.

58. Alighieri, *Paradiso* 16.145–47; Boccaccio *Esp. litt., Inf.* 13.143–45; https://dante.dartmouth.edu/search_view.php?doc=137351131430&cmd=gotoresult&arg1=9. Giovanni Villani (1274–1348), the chronicler of Florence, also references the statue of Mars, which was carried away by the great flood in 1333, and which, unbeknownst to Dante's contemporaries, may originally have represented a Germanic king. See the pages by Robert Davidsohn anthologized in Paolini, *Ponte Vecchio*, 56–61.

59. Troy, *Other End of the Bridge*, 240.

Chapter Nine

1. Teel, *Sunday Morning*, "Encyclopedia Britannica."

2. This tale about the Italian dictator modifying the Ponte Vecchio to impress Hitler is widely diffused over the internet, where it is sometimes reported that the restructuring occurred in 1939 (which would have been a year too late). The erroneous date is even carried over into Denison and Stewart's *How to Read Bridges*, 121. In point of fact, the Ponte

Vecchio had three windows for centuries before 1938, and these were reduced to one on the occasion of *another* state visit to Florence—by King Victor Emmanuel II in 1860. The windows were returned to three after the Second World War, most likely in 1957 or 1958, when the bridge was also closed to vehicular traffic. I am grateful to the Florentine historian Mario Bencivenni for digging into the archives to help solve this mystery.

3. Tutaev, *The Man Who Saved Florence*, 206. In 2016 another story surfaced which attributed the saving of the Ponte Vecchio to an "ugly, lame, but very intelligent" local Florentine called Burgasso, who, according to a certain Lucia Barocchi to whom he told his story, detached wires to the explosives on the bridge. See Ferri, *Storie e leggende del Ponte Vecchio*, 61–62. So far this remains only hearsay.

4. Di Cesare, *Foreign Residents*, 168.

5. See the study *Walled States* by Wendy Brown, released before many events in "act four."

6. See Bishop, *Bridge*.

7. Starr, *Golden Gate*.

8. Kafka, "The Bridge," 411.

9. Herodotus, *Histories* 1.201–14, 4.83–143, 7.33–37.

10. C. Suetonius Tranquillius, "Caius Caesar Caligula," *Lives of the Twelve Caesars*.

11. For a complete telling of the tale see Carboniero and Falconi, *In hoc vinces*.

12. Azem, dir., *Ecumenopolis*. On the consequences of these bridges in Istanbul see also Yeşiltepe and Kubat, "The Effect of Bridges."

13. Herodotus, *Histories* 7.24–25.

14. Necipoğlu, *Age of Sinan*, 88. For an evaluative overview of the canal, tunnel, and bridge projects of Istanbul, some traced as far back as the time of Justianian (482–565), see Çekmiş Görgülü and Hacıhasanoğlu, "Water Crossing Utopias."

15. Weizman, *Hollow Land*, 182. See also his "Politics of Verticality"; Benvenisti, "An Engineering Wonder"; and Bishop, *Bridge*, 173–74.

16. Franks, "President Trump Releases 'Deal of the Century.'"

17. Wheeler, "Hyperactivity in Brain."

18. Erickson, "On the Town with Georg Simmel."

19. Di Cesare, *Foreign Residents*.

20. Freud, *Totem and Taboo*, 123.

21. Bion, "Attacks on Linking," 308. In *The Master and His Emissary*, 406–7, McGilchrist discusses borderline attachment dysfunction in terms of a manifestation of inadequate integration of left and right hemispheres of the brain. Gordon, *Bridges*, also engages in fertile discussions of these issues of psychic dissociation and integration, engaging productively with the work of Bion and D. W. Winnicott.

22. Heidegger, *Phenomenology of Intuition and Expression*, 11.

23. Calvino, *Six Memos*, 105.

24. Rimbaud, *Illuminations*, 55.

BIBLIOGRAPHY

Abulafia, David. *The Great Sea: A Human History of the Mediterranean*. Oxford: Oxford University Press, 2011.

Adelson, Leslie A. "Against Between: A Manifesto." In *Unpacking Europe: Towards a Critical Reading*, edited by Salah Hassan and Iftikhar Dadi, 244–55. Rotterdam: Nai, 2001.

———. *The Turkish Turn in Contemporary German Literature*. New York: Palgrave Macmillan, 2005.

Adelt, Ulrich. *Blues Music in the Sixties: A Story in Black and White*. Rutgers, NJ: Rutgers University Press, 2010.

Agamben, Giorgio. *The Coming Community*. Translated by Michael Hardt. Minneapolis: University of Minnesota Press, 1993.

Akin, Fatih. *Crossing the Bridge: The Sound of Istanbul*. Film. 2005.

Al-Bukhâri, Muhammad Ibn Ismaiel. *Sahih Al-Bukhâri: The Translation of the Meanings of Sahîh Al-Bukhâri*, Arabic-English. Vol. 9. Translated by Muhammad Muhsin Khan. Riyadh: Darussalam, 1997.

Alberti, Leon Battista. *On the Art of Building in Ten Books*. Translated by Joseph Rykwert, Neil Leach, and Robert Tavernor. Cambridge, MA: MIT Press, 1988.

Alighieri, Dante. *The Divine Comedy: Inferno*. Translated by Allen Mandelbaum. New York: Bantam Books, 1982.

———. *The Divine Comedy: Paradiso*. Translated by Allen Mandelbaum. New York: Bantam Books, 1986.

Amadei, Emma. *I ponti di Roma*. Rome: Fratelli Palombi, 1948.

American Heritage Dictionary of Indo-European Roots. 2nd ed. Revised and edited by Calvert Watkins. Boston: Houghton Mifflin, 2000.

Andrić, Ivo. *The Bridge on the Žepa*. Sarajevo: Oslobođenje, 1971.

———. *The Bridge over the Drina*. Translated by Lovett F. Edwards. London: Harvill Press, 2007.

Antonioni, Michelangelo. *L'avventura*. Film. 1960.

Arendt, Hannah. *The Life of the Mind*. Vol. 1: *Thinking*. Vol 2: *Willing*. New York: Harcourt Brace Jovanovich, 1978.

———. "No Longer and Not Yet." In *Reflections on Literature and Culture*. Edited and with an introduction by Susannah Young-Ah Gottlieb, 121–25. Stanford, CA: Stanford University Press, 2007.

Asad, Muhammad. *The Road to Mecca*. Louisville, KY: Fons Vitae, 1980.

———. *The Unromantic Orient*. Ann Arbor: University of Michigan Islamic Book Trust, 2004.

Ashbrook, John. "Politicization of Identity in a European Borderland: Istria, Croatia, and Authenticity, 1990–2003." Nationalities Papers. *Journal of Nationalism and Ethnicity* 39, no. 6 (2011): 871–97.

Atkinson, William Walker [Magus Incognito, pseud.]. *The Secret Doctrine of the Rosicrucians*. Chicago: Advanced Thought; London: L. N. Fowler, 1918. Online at https://www.sacred-texts.com/sro/sdr/index.htm.

Azem, Imre, dir. *Ecumenopolis: City without Limits*. 2011; Hamburg, Germany; Filmförderung Hamburg Schleswig-Holstein/York Street Productions, 2012. DVD.

Bachmann, Ingeborg. "Die Brücken." In *Darkness Spoken: The Collected Poems*, translated by Peter Filkins, 46–47. Brookline, MA: Zephyr Press, 2006.

Bagliani, Domenico. "Il ponte fra simbolismo e rappresentazione." In *Il ponte e l'architettura*. Edited by Enzo Siviero, with Stefania Casucci and Antonella Cecchi, 35–58. Milan: CittàStudi Edizioni, 1995.

Baglivi, Giuseppe, and Garrett McCutchan. "Dante, Christ, and the Fallen Bridges." *Italica* 54, no. 2 (Summer 1977): 250–62.

Ballinger, Pamela. *History in Exile: Memory and Identity at the Borders of the Balkans*. Princeton, NJ: Princeton University Press, 2003.

———. "Liquid Borderland, Inelastic Sea? Mapping the Eastern Adriatic." In *Shatterzone of Empires: Coexistence and Violence in the German, Habsburg, Russian, and Ottoman Borderlands*, edited by Omer Bartov, 423–37. Bloomington: Indiana University Press, 2013.

Balmond, Cecil. *Crossover*. Munich: Prestel, 2013.

Bane, Michael. *White Boy Singin' the Blues*. New York: Penguin Books, 1982.

Baraka, Amiri (LeRoi Jones). *Blues People: Negro Music in White America*. New York: Perennial, 2002.

Barretta, Scott. "Southern Expressions of the Blues Revival." *The Bohemian South: Creating Countercultures, from Poe to Punk*. Edited by Shawn Chandler Bingham and Lindsey A. Freeman, 165–80. Chapel Hill: University of North Carolina Press, 2017.

Barzilai, Salvatore. *Vita internazionale*. Florence: A. Quattrini, 1911.

Bauman, Zygmunt. *Liquid Modernity*. Cambridge: Polity Press, 2012.

Beaulieu, Marie-Claire. *The Sea in the Greek Imagination*. Philadelphia: University of Pennsylvania Press, 2016.

Beckett, Angela. "The (Il)logic of Metaphor in Crane's *The Bridge*." *Textual Practice* 25, no. 1 (2011): 157–80.

Beckwith, Martha. *Hawaiian Mythology*. Honolulu: University Press of Hawaii, 1970.

Benveniste, Émile. *Problèmes de linguistique générale*. Paris: Gallimard, 1966.

Benvenisti, Meron. "An Engineering Wonder." *Ha'aretz*, June 5, 1996.

Bertolozzi, Joseph. *Bridge Music*. Delos, 2009. CD.

Bhabha, Homi K. *The Location of Culture*. London: Routledge, 2004.

Bialis, Laura, and John Ealer. *View from the Bridge: Stories from Kosovo*. Film. 2007.

Biau, Daniel. *The Bridge and the City: A Universal Love Story*. Plantation, FL: Llumina Press, 2015.

Biedermann, Hans. *Dictionary of Symbolism: Cultural Icons and the Meanings Behind Them*. Translated by James Hulbert. New York: Meridian, 1994.

Bierce, Ambrose. "An Occurrence at Owl Creek Bridge." In *Tales of Soldiers and Civilians*, edited by Donald T. Blume, 9–16. Kent, OH: Kent State University Press, 2004.

Binney, Marcus. *Bridges Spanning the World*. London: Pimpernel Press, 2017.

Bion, W. R. "Attacks on Linking." *International Journal of Psychoanalysis* 40, nos. 5–6 (1959): 308–15.

Bishop, Peter. *Bridge*. London: Reaktion Books, 2008.

Blake, William. *Blake's Dante: The Complete Illustrations to the "Divine Comedy."* Edited by Milton Klonsky. New York: Harmony Books, 1980.

———. *Jerusalem: The Emanation of the Giant Albion*. In *The Complete Poetry and Prose of William Blake*. New rev. ed. Edited by David V. Erdman, 144–258. Berkeley: University of California Press, 2008.

Blanchot, Maurice. *La Communauté inavouable*. Paris: Éditions de Minuit, 1983.

Bland, J. "About Gender: Sex Differences." Last modified August 19, 2003. http://www.gender.org.uk/about/07neur/77_diffs.htm.

Blavatsky, H. P. *Isis Unveiled: A Master-Key to the Mysteries of Ancient and Modern Science and Theology*, 2 vols. New York: J. W. Bouton, 1877.

Bloom, Harold. *Hart Crane: Comprehensive Research and Study Guide*. Philadelphia: Chelsea House, 2003.

Boccaccio, Giovanni. *Esp. litt., Inf.* (*Esposizioni sopra la Comedia di Dante: Inferno*). Accessible at https://dante.dartmouth.edu/search_view.php?query=&cmd=Search&commentary%5B%5D=13735&language=any&cantica=0&canto=13&line=.

Bond, Emma, Guido Bonsaver, and Federico Faloppa, eds. *Destination Italy: Representing Migration in Contemporary Media and Narrative*. Oxford: Peter Lang, 2015.

Boniface VIII. "Unam Sanctam." *Catholic Library*. 1302. http://www.newadvent.org/library/docs_bo08us.htm.

Bono, Salvatore. *Il Mediterraneo. Da Lepanto a Barcellona*. Perugia: Morlacchi, 2000.

Borges, Jorge Luis. "The Garden of Forking Paths." In *Labyrinths: Selected Stories and Other Writings*. Edited by Donald A. Yates and James E. Irby, 19–29. New York: New Directions, 1964.

Bosetti, Gilbert. *De Trieste à Dubrovnik: Une ligne de fracture de l'Europe*. Grenoble: ELLUG, Université Stendhal, 2006.

Bouchard, Norma. "Italy's Geophilosophies of the Mediterranean." *Annali d'italianistica* 29 (2011): 343–62.

Bowman, Wayne D. *Philosophical Perspectives on Music*. New York: Oxford University Press, 1998.

Boyer, Marjorie Nice. "The Bridgebuilding Brotherhoods." *Speculum* 39, no. 4 (October 1964): 635–50.

———. *Medieval French Bridges: A History*. Cambridge, MA: Mediaeval Academy of America, 1976.

Brangwyn, Frank, and Walter Shaw Sparrow. *A Book of Bridges*. London: John Lane, 1915.

Braudel, Fernand. *The Mediterranean and the Mediterranean World in the Age of Philip II*. 2 vols. Translated by Siân Reynolds. New York: Harper & Row, 1972.

Breton, André. *Communicating Vessels*. Translated by Mary Ann Caws and Geoffrey T. Harris. Lincoln: University of Nebraska Press, 1990.

Broch, Hermann. *The Death of Virgil*. Translated by Jean Starr Untermeyer. New York: Grosset & Dunlap, 1965.

Brodman, James William. *Charity and Religion in Medieval Europe*. Washington, DC: Catholic University of America Press, 2009.

Bromell, Nick. *Tomorrow Never Knows: Rock and Psychedelics in the 1960s*. Chicago: University of Chicago Press, 2000.

Brose, Margaret. "Leopardi and the Power of Sound." *California Italian Studies* 4, no.1 (2013): 1–35.

Brown, Matthew. "Little Wing." In *Understanding Rock: Essays in Musical Analysis*. Edited by John Covach and Graeme M. Boone, 155–70. New York: Oxford University Press, 1997.

Brown, Wendy. *Walled States, Waning Sovereignty*. Brooklyn, NY: Zone Books, 2010.

Bromberger, Christian. "Bridge, Wall, Mirror; Coexistence and Confrontations in the Mediterranean World." *History and Anthropology* 18, no. 3 (2007): 291–307.

Bruguier-Roure, M. "Les constructeurs de ponts au moyen âge," *Bulletin monumental* 41 (Paris, 1875): 225–49.

Buber, Martin. "The Teaching of the Tao." In *Pointing the Way: Collected Essays*. Translated by Maurice Friedman, 31–58. Atlantic Highlands, NJ: Humanities Press International, 1990.

Buddensieg, Tilmann. "Architecture as Empty Form: Nietzsche and the Art of Building." In *Nietzsche and "An Architecture of Our Minds."* Edited by Alexandre Kostka and Irving Wohlfarth, 259–84. Los Angeles: Getty Research Institute Publications and Exhibitions Program: Issue and Debates, 1999.

Bugatti, Giovanni Battista. *Mastro Titta, il Boia di Roma: Memorie di un carnefice scritte da lui stesso*. Sassuolo, Italy: Libreria Incontri, 2010.

Burns, Jennifer. *Migrant Imaginaries: Figures in Italian Migration Literature*. Oxford: Peter Lang, 2013.

Burroughs, Charles. "Below the Angel: An Urbanistic Project in the Rome of Pope Nicholas V." *Journal of the Warburg and Courtauld Institutes* 45 (1982): 94–124.

Burrows, David. *Sound, Speech and Music*. Amherst: University of Massachusetts Press, 1990.

Cabane, Pierre. *Histoire de l'Adriatique*. Paris: Seuil, 2001.

Cacciari, Massimo. "The Art of Archery." In *Posthumous People: Vienna at the Turning Point*. Translated by Rodger Friedman, 157–69. Stanford, CA: Stanford University Press, 1996.

———. ed. *Crucialità del tempo. Saggio sulla concezione nietzschiana del tempo*. Naples: Liguori, 1980.

———. *L'arcipelago*. Milan: Adelphi, 1997.

———. *La città*. Villa Verucchio: Pazzini, 2004.

———. "Nietzsche and the Unpolitical." In *The Unpolitical: On the Radical Critique of Political Reason*. Edited by Alessandro Carrera and translated by Massimo Verdicchio, 92–103. New York: Fordham University Press, 2009.

———. "Viaggio estivo." In *Venezia Vienna. Il mito della cultura Veneziana nell'Europa asburgica*. Edited by Giandomenico Romanelli, 127–40. Milan: Electa, 1983.

———. *The Withholding Power: An Essay on Political Theology*. Translated by Edi Pucci. London: Bloomsbury Academic, 2018.

Cage, John. "The Future of Music: Credo." In *Audio Culture: Readings in Modern Music*. Edited by Christopher Cox and Daniel Warner, 25–28. New York: Continuum, 2004.

Calvino, Italo. *Six Memos for the Next Millennium*. Translated by Patrick Creagh. Cambridge, MA: Harvard University Press, 1988.

Camus, Albert. *The Fall*. Translated by Justin O'Brien. New York: Vintage, 2012.

Carboniero, Bruno, and Fabrizio Falconi. *In hoc vinces. La notte che cambiò la storia dell'Occidente*. Rome: Edizioni Mediterranee, 2011.

Carby, Hazel. "It Just Be's Dat Way Sometime: The Sexual Politics of Women's Blues." *Radical America* 20 (1987): 9–22.

Carravetta, Peter. *The Elusive Hermes: Method, Discourse, Interpreting*. Aurora, CO: Davies Group, 2012.

Cassani, Alberto Giorgio. "Distruggere i ponti? Note su due romanzi di Ismail Kadaré e Carlo Repetti." *Italianistische Zeitschrift für Kulturwissenschaft und Gegenwartsliteratur / Rivista d'italianistica e di letteratura contemporanea* 3 (2018): 26–59.

———. *Figure del ponte. Simbolo e architettura*. Bologna: Edizioni Pendragon, 2014.

———. "Il ponte e il suo angelo. Mito e simbolo di una figura archetipica." *Memoria e ricerca* 55, no. 2 (2017): 213–30.

———. "Ponti che crollano." *Gizmoweb*, July 24, 2015. https://www.academia.edu/15425037/Ponti_che_crollano_in_www.gizmoweb.org_24_luglio_2015.

Cassano, Franco. "Repubbliche mediterranee." In *Ethos repubblicano e pensiero meridiano*. Edited by Federica Frediani and Fernanda Gallo, 29–47. Reggio Emilia: Diabasis, 2011.

———. *Southern Thought and Other Essays on the Mediterranean*. Edited and translated by Norma Bouchard and Valerio Ferme. New York: Fordham University Press, 2012.

Cassio, Gellio. *Il Mare Adriatico*. Milan: Hoepli, 1915.

Cattaruzza, Marina. *L'Italia e il confine orientale*. Bologna: Il Mulino, 2007.

Cavarero, Adriana. *For More Than One Voice: Toward a Philosophy of Vocal Expression*. Stanford, CA: Stanford University Press, 2005.

Çekmiş Görgülü, Asli, and Isıl Hacıhasanoğlu. "Water Crossing Utopias of Istanbul: Past and Future." *Istanbul Technical University, Faculty of Architecture* 9, no. 2 (2012): 67–88.

Celmins, Martin. "A Rare Encounter with Danny Kirwan." *Guitar Magazine* 7, no. 9 (July 1997). http://bla.fleetwoodmac.net/index.php?page=index_v2&id=38&c=16.

Champeux, Jacqueline. "Ponts, passage, religion à Rome." In *Les Ponts au Moyen Âge*, edited by Danièle James-Raoul and Claude Thomasset, 216–76. Paris: PUPS, 2006.

Chaplin, Charlie. *The Kid*. Film. 1921.

Cheesman, Tom. *Novels of Turkish German Settlement: Cosmopolite Fictions*. Rochester, NY: Camden House. 2007.

Chevalier, Jean, and Alain Gheerbrandt. "Ponts." *Dictionnaire des symboles: mythes, rêves, coutumes, gestes, formes, figures, couleurs, nombres*, 4:47–49. Paris: Ed. Seghers and Ed. Jupiter, 1974.

Chion, Michel. *Audio-Vision: Sound on Screen*. New York: Columbia University Press, 1994.

Clayson, Adam. *Beat Merchants: The Origins, History, Impact, and Rock Legacy of the 1960's British Pop Groups*. London: Blandford, 1985.

Clifton, Thomas. *Music as Heard: A Study in Applied Phenomenology*. New Haven, CT: Yale University Press, 1983.

Cocchiara, Giuseppe. *Il diavolo nella tradizione popolare italiana*. Palermo: Palumbo, 1945.

———. *Il Paese di Cuccagna e altri studi di folklore*. Turin: Boringhieri, 1980.

Cocco, Emilio. "I territori liquidi. Forme e confini di un immaginario adriatico." In *Immaginare l'Adriatico. Contributi alla riscoperta sociale di uno spazio di frontiera*, edited by Emilio Cocco and Everardo Minardi, 11–26. Milan: Franco Angeli, 2007.

Cohen, Robin. *Global Diasporas: An Introduction*. Seattle: University of Washington Press, 1997.

Comberiati, Daniele. *Scrivere nella lingua dell'altro. La letteratura degli immigrati in Italia (1989–2007)*. Brussels: Peter Lang, 2010.

Comencini, Luigi. *Till Marriage Do Us Part* (Mio Dio, come sono caduta in basso). Film. 1974.

Comprone, Raphael. "Alterity, Violence, and History in Ivo Andrić's *Na Drini Cuprija*."

Serbian Studies: Journal for the North American Society for Serbian Studies 20, no. 2 (2006): 259–77.

Connochie-Bourgne, Chantal. "Le pont de Virgile: une *merveille* technique." In *Les Ponts au Moyen Âge*, edited by Danièle James-Raoul and Claude Thomasset, 49–63. Paris: PUPS, 2006.

Cook, Franklin. "The Case against Saying 'Suicide Is a Permanent Solution to a Temporary Problem.'" *The Mighty*, September 19, 2016. https://themighty.com/2016/09/suicide-is-a-permanent-solution-to-a-temporary-problem/.

Coomaraswamy, Doña Luisa. "The Perilous Bridge of Welfare." *Harvard Journal of Asiatic Studies* 8, no. 2 (August 1944): 196–213.

Crane, Hart. *The Bridge: An Annotated Edition*. Edited by Lawrence Kramer. New York: Fordham University Press, 2011.

———. "General Aims and Theories." In *Complete Poems and Selected Letters*. Edited by Langdon Hammer, 160–64. New York: Literary Classics of America, 2006.

Crifò, Giuliano. "A proposito di *pontifices*." *I riti del costruire nelle acque violate. Atti del Convegno Internazionale Roma, Palazzo Massimo 12–14 giugno 2008*. Edited by Helga Di Giuseppe and Mirella Serlorenzi, 115–27. Rome: Scienza e Lettere, 2010.

Crotti, Sergio, "Il ponte tra retorica e logica." *Casabella* 469 (May 1981): 10–16.

Cumont, Franz. *After Life in Roman Paganism*. New York: Dover, 1959.

Dal Lago, Alessandro. *Non-Persons: The Exclusion of Migrants in a Global Society*. Translated by Marie Orton. Vimodrone, MI: IPOC, 2009.

Davies, Penelope J. E. *Death and the Emperor*. Cambridge: Cambridge University Press, 2000.

Davis, Angela. *Blues Legacies and Black Feminism*. New York: Vintage, 1998.

de Certeau, Michel. *The Practice of Everyday Life*. Translated by Steven Rendall. Los Angeles: University of California Press, 1984.

DeJean, Joan. *How Paris Became Paris: The Invention of the Modern City*. New York: Bloomsbury, 2014.

de Lacoste-Utamsing, C., and R. L. Holloway. "Sexual Dimorphism in the Human *Corpus Callosum*." *Science* 216 (June 25, 1982): 1431–32.

De Montalvo, Garci Rodríguez. *The Labors of the Very Brave Knight Esplanadián*. Translated by William Thomas Little. Binghamton, NY: Center for Medieval and Early Renaissance Studies, 1992.

Denison, Edward, and Ian Stewart. *How to Read Bridges: A Crash Course Spanning the Centuries*. London: Herbert Press, 2012.

De Santis, Silvia. *Blake and Dante: A Study of William Blake's Illustrations of the "Divine Comedy" Including His Critical Notes*. Rome: Cangemi Editore International, 2018.

De Romanis, Giorgio. *Il ponte sull'Adriatico/The Bridge over the Adriatic*. Milan: Edizioni l'Archivolto, 2008.

Del Boca, Angelo. *L'Africa nella coscienza degli italiani*. Milan: Mondadori, 2002.

Delli, Sergio. *I ponti di Roma*. Rome: Newton Compton Editori, 1977.

Derrida, Jacques. *Heidegger: The Question of Being and History*. Edited by Thomas Dutoit, with Marguerite Derrida, and translated by Geoffrey Bennington. Chicago: University of Chicago Press, 2016.

Dethier, Jean, and Ruth Eaton, eds. "(Ponti abitati)," special issue of *Rassegna. Problemi di architettura dell'ambiente* 48, no. 4 (December 1991).

Di Cesare, Donatella. *Foreign Residents: A Philosophy of Migration*. Translated by David Broder. Cambridge: Polity Press, 2020.

Di Siena, Vincenzo, ed. *Due ponti pedonali sul Tevere. Concorso internazionale di progettazione*. Florence: Alinea, 2001.

Dickinson, Emily. *Poems*. Selected by Helen McNeil. New York: Barnes & Noble, 2002.

D'Intino, Franco. *La caduta e il ritorno. Cinque movimenti dell'immaginario romantico leopardiano*. Macerata: Quodlibet Studio, 2019.

Dinzelbacher, Peter. *Die Jenseitsbrücke im Mittelalter*. Vienna: Verband der wissenschaftlichen Gesellschaft Österreichs, 1973.

Dionysius of Halicarnassus. *Roman Antiquities*. http://penelope.uchicago.edu/Thayer/E/Roman/Texts/Dionysius_of_Halicarnassus/1B*.html#38.2.

D'Onofrio, Cesare. *Gian Lorenzo Bernini e gli angeli di ponte Sant'Angelo. Storia di un ponte*. Rome: Romana Società Editrice, 1981.

———. *Il Tevere*. Rome: Romana Società Editrice, 1980.

Doré, Gustave, and Blanchard Jerrold. *London: A Pilgrimage*. London: Grant, 1872.

Doré, Henri. *Researches into Chinese Superstitions*. Vol. 7. Translated by M. Kinnelly. Shanghai: T'usewei Printing Press, 1914–26.

Doyle, Roddy. *The Commitments*. New York: Vintage, 1989.

Driessen, Henk. "Mediterranean Port Cities: Cosmopolitanism Reconsidered." *History and Anthropology* 16, no.1 (March 2005): 129–41.

Duffield, Mark. "Global Civil War: The Non-Insured, International Containment and Post-Interventionary Society." *Journal of Refugee Studies* 21, no. 2 (2008): 145–65.

Dunes, Alan, ed. *The Walled-up Wife: A Casebook*. Madison: University of Wisconsin Press, 1996.

Dupré, Judith. *Bridges: A History of the World's Most Spectacular Spans*. New York: Black Dog & Leventhal, 2017.

Eliade, Mircea. "Master Manole and the Monastery of Arges." In *Zalmoxis, The Vanishing God*. Translated by Willard R. Trask, 164–90. Chicago: University of Chicago Press, 1986.

Eliot, T. S. *The Waste Land and Other Poems*. New York: Harcourt, Brace & World, 1962.

Ellis, Steve. "Canto XXI: Controversial Comedy." In *Lectura Dantis: Inferno*. Edited by Allen Mandelbaum, Anthony Oldcorn, and Charles Ross, 287–96. Berkeley: University of California Press, 1998.

Emerton, Ephraim. "Altopascio—A Forgotten Order." *American Historical Review* 29, no. 1 (October 1923): 1–23.

Enrico, Robert. *La Rivère de hibou* (*Occurrence at Owl Creek Bridge*). Film. 1961.

Erickson, Victoria Lee. "On the Town with Georg Simmel: A Socio-Religious Understanding of Urban Interaction." *Cross Currents* 51, no. 1 (Spring 2001). http://www.crosscurrents.org/erickson0151.htm.

Esposito, Roberto. "Community and Nihilism." In *The Italian Difference: Between Nihilism and Biopolitics*, edited by Lorenzo Chiesa and Alberto Toscano, 37–54. Melbourne: re.press, 2009.

———. "L'Europa di Cacciari." In *Inquieto pensare: Scritti in onore di Massimo Cacciari*, edited by Emanuele Severino and Vincenzo Vitiello, 165–74. Brescia: Morcelliana, 2015.

Evans, David. *Big Road Blues: Tradition and Creativity in Folk Blues*. Berkeley: University of California Press, 1982.

Falconi, Fabrizio. *I fantasmi di Roma*. Rome: Newton Compton, 2010.

Farooq, Umar. "Will Istanbul's Massive New Canal Be an Environmental Disaster?" *National Geographic*. March 28, 2018. https://www.nationalgeographic.com/news/2018/03/istanbul-canal-project-bosporus-environmental-impacts/#close.

Fenollosa, Ernest. "An Essay on the Chinese Written Character." In *Instigations of Ezra Pound, Together with an Essay on the Chinese Written Character by Ernest Fenollosa*, 357–88. New York: Boni and Liverwright, 1920.

Ferenczi, Sándor. "Bridge Symbolism and the Don Juan Legend." In *Further Contributions to the Theory and Technique of Psychoanalysis*, 356–58. New York: Basic Books, 1952.

———."The Symbolism of the Bridge." *International Journal of Psychoanalysis* 3 (1922): 163–68.

Ferri, Marco. *Storie e leggende del Ponte Vecchio*. Florence: Angelo Pontecorboli Editore, 2017.

Ferris, William. *Blues from the Delta*. New York: Doubleday Anchor, 1978.

Finkel, Caroline. *Osman's Dream: The Story of the Ottoman Empire, 1300–1923*. London: John Murray, 2005.

Firmat, Gustavo Perez. *Life on the Hyphen: The Cuban-American Way*. Austin: University of Texas Press, 1994.

Fleetwood Mac. *Mr. Wonderful*. Blue Horizon, 1968.

Fogu, Claudio. "From *Mare Nostrum* to *Mare Aliorum*: Mediterranean Theory and Mediterraneism in Contemporary Italian Thought." *California Italian Studies Journal* 1, no. 1 (2010): 1–23. http://escholarship.org/uc/item/7vp210p4.

Fontana, Bill. *Cologne San Francisco Sound Bridge*, 1987. http://echosounddesign.com/media/Cologne_San_Francisco_Soundbridge.mp3.

———."The Environment as a Musical Resource," n.d. http://www.resoundings.org/Pages/musical%20resource.html.

———. *Oscillating Steel Grids along the Brooklyn Bridge*, 1983. http://resoundings.org/Pages/Oscillating.html.

———. "The Relocation of Ambient Sound: Urban Sound Sculpture," n.d. http://www.resoundings.org/Pages/Urban%20Sound%20Sculpture.

———. *Sound Sculptures through the Golden Gate Bridge*, 1987. http://resoundings.org/Pages/Architectural_Sound_Sculptures.html.

Foucault, Michel. "Of Other Spaces: Utopias and Heterotopias." *Rethinking Architecture: A Reader in Cultural Theory*. Edited by Neil Leach, 330–36. New York: Routledge, 1997.

France, Anatole. *The Red Lily*. 1894. http://www.gutenberg.org/files/3922/3922-h/3922-h.htm.

Frank, Ellen Eve. *Literary Architecture: Essays Toward a Tradition: Walter Pater, Gerard Manley Hopkins, Marcel Proust, Henry James*. Berkeley: University of California Press, 1979.

Franks, Tim. "President Trump Releases 'Deal of the Century.'" BBC Newshour, January 28, 2020.

Frazer, Sir James George, ed. "Commentary on Book V." In Ovid, *Publii Ovidii Nasonis Fastorum Libri Sex* [The Fasti of Ovid]. Vol. 4. London: Macmillan, 1929.

———. *The Fear of the Dead in Primitive Religion*. Vols. 1–3. New York: Arno Press, 1977.

Freud, Sigmund. *Totem and Taboo: Resemblances Between the Psychic Life of Savages and Neurotics*. Translated by A. A. Brill. London: Routledge, 1919.

Frothingham, A. L. *Roman Cities in Northern Italy and Dalmatia*. London: J. Murray, 1910.

Fusaro, Maria, Colin Heywood, and Mohamed-Salah Omri, eds. *Trade and Cultural Exchange in the Early Modern Mediterranean: Braudel's Maritime Legacy*. London: I. B. Tauris, 2019.

Gadamer, Hans Georg. *Truth and Method*. 2nd rev. ed. Translated by Joel Weinsheimer and Donald G. Marshall. London: Continuum, 2004.

Galanti, Bianca Maria. "La leggenda del 'ponte del diavolo' in Italia." *Lares* 18, nos. 1–2 (1952): 61–73.

Gambacurta, Michael. *Autophones: Hearing with the Ears of the Bridge* [Hören mit Ohren der Brücke]. 2008.

———. "Autophones," n.d. http://www.gambacurta.ca/michael/projects/autophones.htm.

Gardet, Louis. *Islam*. Paris: Desclée de Brouwer, 1967.

Garrod, Sir Martin. Foreword to John Yarwood, *Rebuilding Mostar: Urban Reconstruction in a War Zone*. Liverpool: Liverpool University Press, 1999.

Germi, Pietro. *Seduced and Abandoned*. Film. 1964.

Gies, Joseph. *Bridges and Men*. New York: Grosset & Dunlap, 1963.

Gilot, Françoise, and Carlton Lake. *Life with Picasso*. New York: McGraw Hill, 1964.

Gnisci, Armando. *La letteratura italiana della migrazione*. Rome: Lilith, 1998.

Göktürk, Deniz. "Projecting Polyphony: Moving Images, Travelling Sounds." In *Orienting Istanbul: Cultural Capital of Europe?*, edited by Deniz Göktürk, Levent Soysal, and Ipek Türeli, 178–98. New York: Routledge, 2010.

———. "Sound Bridges: Transnational Mobility as Ironic Melodrama." In *European Cinema in Motion: Migrant and Diasporic Film in Contemporary Europe*, edited by Daniela Berghahn and Claudio Sternberg, 215–34. New York: Macmillan Palgrave, 2010.

Golson, G. Barry, ed. *The Playboy Interviews with John Lennon & Yoko Ono*, conducted by David Sheff. New York: Berkley Books, 1982.

Gölz, Sabine. "'Ponte Mirabeau . . . Waterloo Bridge': A Contrastive Reading of Apollinaire's 'Le Pont Mirabeau' and Ingeborg Bachmann's 'Die Brücken.'" In *"If We Had the Word": Ingeborg Bachmann, Views and Reviews*, edited by Gisela Brinker-Gabler and Markus Zisselsberger, 47–92. Riverside, CA: Ariadne Press, 2004.

Gomme, Alice Bertha. *The Traditional Games of England, Scotland, and Ireland*. London: Thames and Hudson, 1984.

Goody, Jack. *Islam in Europe*. Cambridge: Polity Press, 2004.

Gordon, Rosemary. *Bridges: Psychic Structures, Functions, and Processes*. London: Karnac Books, 1993.

Gorman, Christine and J. Madeleine Nash. "Sizing up the Sexes." *Time* (January 20, 1992): 36–43.

Gould, Rebecca. "Allegory and the Critique of Sovereignty: Ismail Kadare's Political Theologies." *Studies in the Novel* 44, no. 2 (Summer 2012): 208–30.

Graf, Bernhard. *Bridges That Changed the World*. Munich: Prestel, 2002.

Grégoire, M. Henri. *Recherches historiques sur les congrégations hospitalières des frères pontifes, ou constructeurs de ponts*. Paris: Baudoin Frères, Libraires, 1818.

Gregotti, Vittorio. *Il progetto per l'Università delle Calabrie e altre architetture/The Project for Calabria University and Other Architectural Works*. Edited by Italo Rota and Gabriella Borsano. Milan: Electa International, 1979.

Groddeck, Georg. *The Book of the It*. Mansfield Centre, CT: Martino, 2015.

"Groundbreaking Ceremony for Bridge over Dardanelles to Take Place on March 18." *Hürriyet Daily News*, March 77, 2017. http://www.hurriyetdailynews.com/groundbreaking-ceremony-for-bridge-over-dardanelles-to-take-place-on-march-18-110948.

Grundlehner, Philip. *The Poetry of Friedrich Nietzsche*. New York: Oxford University Press, 1986.

Haddon, Alfred C. *The Study of Man*. London: John Murray, 1908.

Haller, Dieter. "The Cosmopolitan Mediterranean: Myth and Reality." *Zeitschrift für Ethnologie* 129, no. 1 (2004): 29–47.

Hallett, Judith P. "'Over Troubled Waters': The Meaning of the Title *Pontifex*." *Transactions of the American Philological Association* 101 (1970): 219–22.

Hametz, Maura Elise. "Naming Italians in the Borderland, 1926–1943." *Journal of Modern Italian Studies* 15 (2010): 410–30.

Hammer, Langdon. "Hart Crane's View from the Bridge." *NYRDaily*, November 24, 2017. http://www.nybooks.com/daily/2017/11/24/hart-cranes-view-from-the-bridge/.

Hamon, Philippe. *Expositions: Literature and Architecture in Nineteenth-Century France*. Translated by Katia Sainson-Frank and Lisa Maguire. Berkeley: University of California Press, 1992.

Harrison, Daphne Duval. *Black Pearls: Blues Queens of the 1920s*. New Brunswick, NJ: Rutgers University Press, 1988.

Harrison, Thomas. "The Architectural Word." In *Inquieto pensare: Scritti in onore di Massimo Cacciari*, edited by Emanuele Severino and Vincenzo Vitiello, 271–82. Brescia: Morcelliana, 2015.

———. "Have I Been Understood? The Eternal Nowhere of Nietzschean Existence." In *Nietzsche in Italy*, edited by Thomas Harrison, 181–98. Saratoga, CA: Anma Libri, 1988.

———. "Istrian Italy and the Homeland: The Lessons of Poetry." *Forum Italicum: Italy from Without* 47, no. 2 (2013): 324–35.

———. "Offscreen Space, From Cinema and Sculpture to Photography, Poetry and Narrative." *California Italian Studies* 7, no. 1 (2017): 1–20. https://escholarship.org/uc/item/2w40187f.

———. "Without Precedent: The Watts Towers." *California Italian Studies* 1, no. 2 (2010): 1–16. https://escholarship.org/uc/item/3vo6b8jt.

Harvey, David. *The Condition of Postmodernity*. Oxford: Basil Blackwell, 1990.

Hearn, Lafcadio. *The Romance of the Milky Way and Other Stories*. New York: Houghton Mifflin, 1905. https://archive.org/details/romanceofmilkywaoohear.

Hedges, Christopher. *War Is a Force that Gives Us Meaning*. New York: PublicAffairs, 2014.

Heidegger, Martin. "Building Dwelling Thinking." In *Poetry, Language, Thought*, translated by Albert Hofstadter, 143–61. New York: Harper & Row, 1971.

———. *An Introduction to Metaphysics*. Translated by Ralph Manheim. New York: Doubleday, 1961.

———. "Letter on Humanism." In *Basic Writings*, edited by D. F. Krell, 213–65. London: Routledge, 1978.

———. *Phenomenology of Intuition and Expression*. Translated by Tracy Colony. London: Continuum International, 2010.

———. ". . . Poetically Man Dwells. . . ." In *Poetry, Language, Thought*, translated by Albert Hofstadter, 211–29. New York: Harper & Row, 1971.

———. "Who Is Nietzsche's Zarathustra?" In *The New Nietzsche: Contemporary Styles of Interpretation*, edited by David B. Allison, 64–79. London: MIT Press, 1985.

Heidegger, Martin, and Karl Jaspers. *The Heidegger-Jaspers Correspondence, 1920–1963*. Translated by Gary E. Aylesworth. Amherst, NY: Humanity Books, 2003.

Herczeg, Ferenc. *A híd* (The Bridge). Budapest: Singer és Wolfner, 1925.

Höfferer, Christina. *A Literary Journey to Rome: From the Sweet Life to the Great Beauty*. Newcastle upon Tyne: Cambridge Scholars, 2017.

Hölderlin, Friedrich. *Selected Poems*. Translated by Christopher Middleton. Chicago: University of Chicago Press, 1972.

Holland, L. A. *Janus and the Bridge*. Rome: American Academy in Rome, 1961.

Hollinrake, Roger. "A Note on Nietzsche's *Gondellied*." *Nietzsche-Studien* 4 (1975): 139–45.

Hood, Thomas. "The Bridge of Sighs." https://www.poeticous.com/thomas-hood/the-bridge-of-sighs.

Horden, Peregrine, and Nicholas Purcell. *The Corrupting Sea: A Study of Mediterranean History*. Malden, MA: Blackwell, 2000.

Howe, Susan. *My Emily Dickinson*. Berkeley, CA: North Atlantic Books, 1985.

Hudson, Mike. "Suicide Season." http://www.niagarafallsreporter.com/column366.html.

Irwin, John T. *Hart Crane's Poetry: "Appollinaire [sic] Lived in Paris, I Live in Cleveland, Ohio."* Baltimore: Johns Hopkins University, 2011.

Jackson, Buzzy. *A Bad Woman Feeling Good: Blues and the Women Who Sing Them*. New York: W. W. Norton, 2005.

Jadhav, Prakash. "Under Dadar Bridge." *Encyclopedia of Dalits in India*. Vol. 11, *Literature*. Edited by Sanjay Paswan and Pramanshi Jaideva, 147–49. Delhi: Kalpaz Publications, 2002.

Jakobson, Roman. "Two Aspects of Language and Two Types of Aphasic Disturbances." In *Fundamentals of Language*, by Roman Jakobson and Morris Halle, 69–96. The Hague: Mouton, 1971.

James-Raoul, Danièle. "Le pont dans les locutions: aperçu sur les langues européennes." In *Les Ponts au Moyen Âge*, edited by Danièle James-Raoul and Claude Thomasset, 291–318. Paris: PUPS, 2006.

James-Raoul, Danièle, and Claude Thomasset, eds. *Les Ponts au Moyen Âge*. Paris: PUPS, 2006.

Jay, Paul. *Global Matters: The Transnational Turn in Literary Studies*. Ithaca, NY: Cornell University Press, 2010.

Jordan, Jim. "More Than a Metaphor: The Passing of the Two Worlds Paradigm in German-Language Diasporic Literature." *German Life and Letters* 59, no. 4 (October 2006): 488–99.

Jorio, Piercarlo. *Acque, ponti, diavoli nel leggendario alpino*. Turin: Priuli & Verlucca, 1999.

Joyce, James. *Ulysses*. New York: Random House, 1934.

Juvenal [Decimus Iunius Iuvenalis]. *The Satires: A New English Translation*. Translated by A. S. Kline, 2011. https://www.poetryintranslation.com/PITBR/Latin/JuvenalSatires6.php.

Kadare, Ismail. "L'Adriatico visto dalla cittadella." *Venature Mediterranee. Dialogo con scrittori di oggi*. Edited by Costanza Ferrini, 159–64. Messina: Mesogea, 1999.

———. *The Three-Arched Bridge*. Translated by John Hodgson. New York: Arcade, 1997.

Kafka, Franz. "The Bridge." In *The Complete Stories*, edited by Nahum N. Glatzer, 411–12. New York: Schocken Books, 1983.

———. "The Judgment." In *The Sons*, edited by Arthur S. Wensinger, 1–16. New York: Schocken Books, 1989.

———. *The Trial*. Translated by Willa and Edwin Muir. New York: Vintage Books, 1969.

Kane, Brian. *Sound Unseen: Acousmatic Sound in Theory and Practice*. Oxford: Oxford University Press, 2014.

Kavanagh, Bernard J. "Pontifices, Bridge-Making and Ribezzo Revisited." *Glotta* 76, nos. 1–2 (2000): 59–65.

Keil, Andreas. *Pedestrian Bridges: Ramps, Walkways, Structures*. Translated by Christina McKenna. Munich: Edition Detail, 2013.

Keil, Charles. *Urban Blues*. Chicago: University of Chicago Press, 1991.

Kellett, James Andrew. "Fathers and Sons: American Blues and British Rock Music, 1960–1970." PhD diss., University of Maryland, College Park, 2008.

Kellman, Steven G. *The Translingual Imagination*. Lincoln: University of Nebraska Press, 2000.

Kezele, Michaela. *My Beautiful Country* (Die Brücke am Ibar). Film. 2012.

Klotz, Alfred. "Sexagenarii." In *RE* (*Realencyclopädie der classischen Altertumswissenschaft*). Vol. 2 A, 2 (1923): 2025–26.

Knight, G. A. Frank. "Bridges." *Encyclopaedia of Religion and Ethics*. Edited by James Hastings, 2:848–57. New York: Charles Scribner's Sons, 1910.

Koenig, Joseph. "Favored by Suicides." *New York Times*, June 30, 1991. http://fionnchu.blogspot.com/2009/05/jumping-off-golden-gate-bridge-two.html.

Kostka, Alexandre, and Irving Wohlfarth, eds. *Nietzsche and "An Architecture of Our Minds."* Los Angeles: Getty Research Institute Publications and Exhibitions Program: Issue and Debates, 1999.

Kövecses, Zoltán. *Where Metaphors Come From: Considering Context in Metaphor*. Oxford: Oxford University Press, 2015.

Kunze, Donald, and Wesley Wei. "The Vanity of Architecture: Topical Thinking and the Practice of Discontinuity." In *Via 8: Architecture and Literature*, edited by Muscoe Martin et al., 54–69. New York: Rizzoli, 1986.

Lakoff, George, and Mark Johnson. *Metaphors We Live By*. Chicago: University of Chicago Press, 2003.

Lanchester, John. "Flashes of Flora." *New York Review of Books*, December 17, 2009. https://www.nybooks.com/articles/2009/12/17/flashes-of-flora/.

Larkin, Philip. "Bridge for the Living." In *Collected Poems*, edited by Anthon Thwaite, 203–4. London: Faber & Faber, 1988.

Le Blévec, Daniel. "Une institution d'assistance en pays rhodanien: Les Frères pontifes." In *Assistance et charité, Cahiers de Fanjeux 13*, edited by Marie-Humbert Vicaire, 87–110. Toulouse: É. Privat, 1978.

Leavitt, David. *Florence: A Delicate Case*. New York: Bloomsbury, 2002.

Lenoir, J. B. *Alabama Blues*. CBS, 1965.

Lennon, John. *Walls and Bridges*. Apple, 1974.

Leontis, Artemis. "The Bridge Between the Classical and the Balkan." *South Atlantic Quarterly* 98, no. 4 (Fall 1999): 633–54.

Leopardi, Giacomo. "The Dialogue of Christopher Columbus and Pedro Gutierrez." In *Moral Essays/Operette Morali*, translated by Patrick Creagh, 158–62. New York: Columbia University Press, 1983.

———. "The Dialogue of a Physicist and a Metaphysician." In *Moral Essays/Operette Morali*, translated by Patrick Creagh, 85–90. New York: Columbia University Press, 1983.

———. "L'infinito," in *Canti: Poems/A Bilingual Edition*, translated by Jonathan Galassi (New York: Farrar, Straus and Giroux, 2010), 106–7.

———. "Ricordi d'infanzia e d'adolescenza." In *Tutte le poesie e tutte le prose*. Edited by Lucio Felici and Emanuele Trevi, 1100–1106. Rome: Newton Compton, 1997.

———. *Zibaldone: The Notebooks of Leopardi*. Edited by Michael Caesar and Franco D'Intino. London: Penguin Books, 2013.

Lewis, Bernard. *From Babel to Dragomans: Interpreting the Middle East*. Oxford: Oxford University Press, 2004.

Lewis, R. W. B. *The Poetry of Hart Crane: A Critical Study*. Princeton, NJ: Princeton University Press, 1967.

Lindow, John. *Norse Mythology: A Guide to the Gods, Heroes, Rituals, and Beliefs*. Oxford: Oxford University Press, 2002.

Little, Lester K. "Life and Afterlife of the First Plague Pandemic." In *Plague and The End of Antiquity: The Pandemic of 541–750*, edited by Lester K. Little, 3–32. Cambridge: Cambridge University Press, 2008.

Lodge, David. *The Modes of Modern Writing*. London: E. Arnold, 1977.

Lombardi-Diop, Cristina, and Caterina Romeo, eds. *Postcolonial Italy: Challenging National Homogeneity*. Basingstoke, UK: Palgrave Macmillan, 2012.

Lorenz, Ulrike. *Brücke*. Los Angeles: Taschen, 2008.

Lösel, F. G. "Nietzsche's 'Venice': An Interpretation." *Hermathena* 105 (1967): 60–73.

Luckert, Karl W. *Navajo Mountain and Rainbow Bridge Religion*. Flagstaff, AZ: Museum of Northern Arizona, 1977.

György [Georg] Lukács. "On Poverty of Spirit: A Conversation and a Letter." In *The Lukács Reader*, edited by Arpad Kadarkay, 42–56. Oxford: Blackwell, 1995.

———. *Soul & Form*. Translated by Anna Bostock, edited by John T. Sanders and Katie Terezakis, and with an introduction by Judith Butler. New York: Columbia University Press, 2010.

Maalouf, Amin. "Il viaggiatore delle due rive." In *Venature Mediterranee. Dialogo con scrittori di oggi*, edited by Costanza Ferrini, 207–17. Messina: Mesogea, 1999.

———. *In the Name of Identity: Violence and the Need to Belong*. Translated by Barbara Bray. New York: Arcade, 2000.

Maeder, Beverly. *Wallace Stevens's Experimental Language: The Lion in the Lute*. New York: St. Martin's Press, 1999.

Magherini, Graziella. *La sindrome di Stendhal*. Florence: Ponte Alle Grazie, 1989.

Makaš, Emily Gunzberger. "Representing Competing Identities: Building and Rebuilding in Postwar Mostar, Bosnia-Hercegovina." PhD diss., Cornell University, 2007.

Mancini, Loredana. "*Pietas* e *superstitio* nella decorazione dei ponti romani." In *I riti del costruire nelle acque violate. Atti del Convegno Internazionale Roma, Palazzo Massimo 12–14 giugno 2008*. Edited by Helga Di Giuseppe and Mirella Serlorenzi, 139–59. Rome: Scienze e Lettere, 2010.

Mandel, Ruth. "Sacrifice at the Bridge of Arta: Sex Roles and the Manipulation of Power." *Journal of Modern Greek Studies* 1, no. 1 (May 1983): 173–83.

Mansel, Philip. *Levant: Splendour and Catastrophe on the Mediterranean*. New Haven, CT: Yale University Press, 2010.

Maranelli, Carlo, and Gaetano Salvemini. *La questione dell'Adriatico*. Rome: Libreria della Voce, 1919.

Matvejević, Predrag. *Mediterranean: A Cultural Landscape*. Translated by Michael Heim. Berkeley: University of California Press, 1999.

———. *Mondo ex e tempo del dopo: Identità, ideologie, nazioni nell'una e nell'altra Europa*. Milan: Garzanti, 2006.

———. "Per una talassopoetica." In *Venature Mediterranee. Dialogo con scrittori di oggi*, edited by Costanza Ferrini, 255–56. Messina: Mesogea, 1999.

May, Rollo. *Psychology and the Human Dilemma*. New York: Norton, 1996.

McClary, Susan. *Conventional Wisdom: The Content of Musical Form*. Berkeley: University of California Press, 2000.

McCullough, David. *The Great Bridge*. New York: Simon and Schuster, 1972.

McGilchrist, Iain. *The Master and His Emissary: The Divided Brain and the Making of the Western World*. New Haven, CT: Yale University Press, 2012.

McGowan, Moray. "Brücken und Brücken-Köpfe: Wandlungen einer Metapher in der türkisch-deutschen Literatur." In *Die "andere" deutsche Literatur: Istanbuler Vorträge*, edited by Manfred Durzak and Niler Kuruyazici, 31–40. Würzburg: Königshausen & Neumann, 2004.

McStravick, Summer, and John Roos, with Martin Celmins and Bob Brunning. *Blues-Rock Explosion*. Mission Viejo, CA: Old Goat, 2002.

Mengaldo, Elisabetta. "Strategie di reticenza e demistificazione: Il trattino di sospensione negli aforismi di Friedrich Nietzsche." *Studi germanici* 43, nos.1–2 (2005): 25–48.

Merleau-Ponty, Maurice. *Signs*. Translated by Richard McCleary. Evanston, IL: Northwestern University Press, 1964.

Mesqui, Jean. *Le Pont en France avant le temps des ingénieurs*. Paris: Picard, 1986.

"Metaphor." *Dictionary.com Unabridged (v. 1.1)*. Random House, Inc. http://dictionary.reference.com/browse/metaphor.

Milward, John. *Crossroads: How the Blues Shaped Rock 'n Roll (And Rock Saved the Blues)*. Boston: Northeastern University Press, 2013.

Montale, Eugenio. *Collected Poems, 1920–1954*. Translated by Jonathan Galassi. New York: Farrar, Straus and Giroux, 1998.

———. *The Occasions*. Translated by William Arrowsmith. New York: Norton, 1987.

Morin, Edgar. *Vidal and His Family*. Sussex: Sussex Academic Press, 2009.

Motta, Giovanni, ed. *I Turchi, il Mediterraneo e l'Europa*. Milan: Franco Angeli, 1998.

Milutinović, Zoran. "Andrić's Strategy of Redemption." *Journal for the North American Society for Serbian Studies* 14, no. 1 (2000): 93–98.

Murray, Charles Shaar. *Crosstown Traffic*. New York: St. Martin's Press, 1989.

Murray, Peter, and Mary Anne Stevens, eds. *Living Bridges: The Inhabited Bridge, Past, Present and Future*. Munich: Prestel-Verlag, 1996.

Musil, Robert. *The Man Without Qualities II: "Into the Millennium"* and *"From the Posthumous Papers."* Translated by Sophie Wilkins, with editorial consultant Burton Pike. New York: Alfred A. Knopf, 1995.

———. "Towards a New Aesthetic. Observations on a Dramaturgy of Film." In *Precision and Soul*, edited and translated by Burton Pike and David S. Luft, 193–207. Chicago: University of Chicago Press, 1990.

The Muslim Jesus: Sayings and Stories in Islamic Literature. Edited and translated by Tarif Khalidi. Cambridge, MA: Harvard University Press, 2001.

Nafus, Chale. "Celluloid Connections: The Bridge in Cinema." http://historicbridgefoundation.com/?page_id=10.

Nagy, Gregory. *The Best of the Achaeans: Concepts of the Hero in Archaic Greek Poetry*. Baltimore: Johns Hopkins University Press, 1979.

Nancy, Jean-Luc. *Listening*. Translated by Charlotte Mandell. New York: Fordham University Press, 2007.

Natirbov, Patricia B. "*The World Is A Bridge*, by Christine Weston." *Middle East Journal* 4, no. 3 (July 1950): 364–65.

National Park Service. "Natural Bridges." http://www.nps.gov/nabr/index.htm.

Necipoğlu, Gülru. *The Age of Sinan: Architectural Culture in the Ottoman Empire*. London: Reaktion, 2011.

Nicoletti, L. J. "Downward Mobility: Victorian Women, Suicide, and London's 'Bridge of Sighs,'" http://www.literarylondon.org/london-journal/march2004/nicoletti.html.

Nietzsche, Friedrich. *The Anti-Christ*. In *"Twilight of the Idols" and "The Anti-Christ,"* translated by R. J. Hollingdale, 113–87. Harmondsworth, England: Penguin, 1968.

———. *Beyond Good and Evil: Prelude to a Philosophy of the Future*. Translated by Walter Kaufmann. New York: Vintage Books, 1966.

———. *Briefe/Letters*. Accessible online at the Nietzsche Source, http://www.nietzschesource.org/#eKGWB.

———. *Ecce Homo: How One Becomes What One Is*. In *Basic Writings*, translated and edited by Walter Kaufmann, 657–791. New York: Modern Library, 1968.

———. *The Gay Science*. Translated and edited by Walter Kaufmann. New York: Vintage Books, 1974.

———. *Human, All Too Human: A Book for Free Spirits*. Translated by R. J. Hollingdale. Cambridge: Cambridge University Press, 1986.

———. *Nachgelassene Fragmente/Posthumous Fragments*. Accessible online at the Nietzsche Source, http://www.nietzschesource.org/#eKGWB.

———. "On Truth and Lie in an Extra-Moral Sense." In *The Portable Nietzsche*, translated by Walter Kaufmann, 42–47. New York: Viking Press, 1968.

———. *Sämtliche Briefe: Kritische Studienausgabe*. 8 vols. Edited by Giorgio Colli and Mazzino Montinari. Munich: Deutscher Taschenbuchverlag and de Gruyter, 1988.

———. *Sämtliche Werke: Kritische Studienausgabe*. 15 vols. Edited by Giorgio Colli and Mazzino Montinari. Munich: Deutscher Taschenbuchverlag and de Gruyter, 1988.

———. *Thus Spoke Zarathustra*. In *The Portable Nietzsche*, translated by Walter Kaufmann, 103–439. New York: Viking Press, 1968.

———. *Thus Spoke Zarathustra (Selections): Also sprach Zarathustra (Auswahl)*. A Dual-Language Book. Edited and translated by Stanley Appelbaum. Mineola, NY: Dover Publications, 2004.

———. *Werke*. 3 vols. Edited by Karl Schlechta. Munich: Carl Hanser Verlag, 1954.

———. *The Will to Power*. Translated and edited by Walter Kaufmann. New York: Vintage Books, 1967.

———. *Writings from the Early Notebooks*. Edited by Raymond Geuss and Alexander Nehamas. Cambridge: Cambridge University Press, 2009.

Oudin, Antoine. *Curiositéz françoises, pour supplément aux dictionnaires*. Paris: Antoine de Sommaville, 1640.

Özdamar, Emine Sevgi. *The Bridge of the Golden Horn*. Translated by Martin Chalmers. London: Serpent's Tail, 2009.

Palazzo Ducale Fondazione per la Cultura. *Quella volta sul ponte*. Genoa: Erredi Grafiche Editoriali, 2018.

Palmer, Richard E. "The Liminality of Hermes and the Meaning of Hermeneutics." *Proceedings of the Heraclitean Society: A Quarterly Report on Philosophy and Criticism of the Arts and Sciences* 5 (1980): 4–11. https://edoc.site/the-liminality-of-hermes-and-the-meaning-of-hermeneutics-richard-palmer-pdf-free.html.

Paolini, Claudio. *Ponte Vecchio di pietra e di calcina*. Florence: Edizioni Polistampa, 2012.

Parati, Graziella. *Migration Italy: The Art of Talking Back in a Destination Culture*. Toronto: University of Toronto Press, 2005.

Parker, Patricia. "The Motive for Metaphor: Stevens and Derrida." *Wallace Stevens Journal* 7, nos. 3/4 (Fall 1983): 76–88.

Pascal, Paul. "Mediaeval Uses of Christianity," *Classical Journal* 61, no. 5 (February 1966): 193–97.

Pašić, Amir. *The Old Bridge (Stari Most) in Mostar*. Istanbul: Research Centre For Islamic History, Art, and Culture, 1995.

Pasqualotto, Giangiorio. *Il Tao della filosofia. Corrispondenze tra pensieri d'Oriente e d'Occidente*. Milan: Luni Editrice, 2017.

Pastré, Jean-Marc. "Se battre sur le pont, passer le pont ou s'en passer: de quelques ponts mythiques de la littérature européenne au Moyen Âge." In *Les Ponts au Moyen Âge*, edited by Danièle James-Raoul and Claude Thomasset, 119–36. Paris: PUPS, 2006.

Patch, Howard Rollin. *The Other World According to Descriptions in Medieval Literature*. Cambridge, MA: Harvard University Press, 1950.

Pater, Walter. "Conclusion" to *The Renaissance* (1873). In *Modernism: An Anthology of Sources and Documents*, edited by Vassiliki Kolocotroni, Jane Goldman, and Olga Taxidou, 111–14. Chicago: University of Chicago Press, 1998.

Paul, Sherman. "Lyricism and Modernism: The Example of Hart Crane." In *Hart Crane: A Collection of Critical Essays*, edited by Alan Trachtenberg, 163–79. Englewood Cliffs, NJ: Prentice-Hall, 1982.

Paulus, Nikolaus. *Indulgences as a Social Factor in the Middle Ages*. Translated by J. Elliot Ross. New York: Devin-Adair, 1922.

Pellegrini, Marco. *Gli xenodochi di Parma e provincia dagli inizi al 1471*. Parma: Parma nell'Arte, 1973.

Peretz, Eyal. *The Off-Screen: An Investigation of the Cinematic Frame*. Stanford, CA: Stanford University Press, 2017.

Perloff, Marjorie. *Unoriginal Genius: Poetry by Other Means in the New Century*. Chicago: University of Chicago Press, 2010.

Petacco, Arrigo. *A Tragedy Revealed: The Story of the Italian Population of Istria, Dalmatia, and Venezia Giulia, 1943–1956*. Translated by Konrad Eisenbichler. Toronto: University of Toronto Press, 2005.

Piazza, Francesco. *L'altra sponda adriatica*. Verona: Cfierre, 2001.

Pinza, Giovanni. "Conservazione delle teste umane e le idee ed i costumi coi quali si connette." *Memorie della società geografica italiana* 7:305–492. Rome: La Società Geografica Italiana, 1897–98.

Plant, Margaret. *Venice: Fragile City, 1797–1997*. New Haven, CT: Yale University Press, 2002.

Plato, *The Collected Dialogues, including the Letters*. Edited by Edith Hamilton and Huntington Cairns. Princeton, NJ: Bollingen Foundation, 1973.

Pliny the Elder, *Naturalis Historia*. http://penelope.uchicago.edu/Thayer/E/Roman/Texts/Pliny_the_Elder/home.html.

Pralon, Didier. "La Méditerranée des grecs anciens." In *La Méditerranée au temps du monde: #14 encontres d'Averroès*, edited by Thierry Fabre, 13–24. Marseilles: Parentheses, 2008.

Pupo, Raoul. *Il lungo esodo: Istria: Le persecuzioni, le foibe, l'esilio*. Milan: Rizzoli, 2005.

Radiohead. *Amnesiac*. XL, 2001.

———. *In Rainbows*. XL, 2007.

———. *The King of Limbs*. XL, 2011.

Rakić, Bogdan. "The Proof Is in the Pudding: Ivo Andrić and His Bosniak Critics." *Journal for the North American Society for Serbian Studies* 14, no. 1 (2000): 81–91.

Randel, Don Michael, ed. *The New Harvard Dictionary of Music*. Cambridge, MA: Belknap Press, 1996.

Ratzinger, Georg. *Geschichte der kirchlichen Armenpflege*. Freiburg im Breisgau: Herder, 1884.

Reed, Brian. *Hart Crane: After His Lights*. Tuscaloosa: University of Alabama Press, 2006.

Reill, Dominique Kirchner. *Nationalists Who Feared the Nation: Adriatic Multi-Nationalism in Habsburg Dalmatia, Trieste, and Venice*. Stanford, CA: Stanford University Press, 2012.

Reimbold, Ernst T. "Die Brücke als Symbol." *Symbolon* 1 (1972): 55–78.

Revill, David. *The Roaring Silence*. New York: Arcade, 1992.

Reynolds, Freddie. "Bridge to Nowhere: Exploring the Two Sides of the River Ibar in Mitrovica." *Compass Cultura* 10 (May 11, 2015). http://compasscultura.com/mitrovica-kosovo-bridge-nowhere/.

Richards, I. A. *The Philosophy of Rhetoric*. New York: Oxford University Press, 1936.

Ricoeur, Paul. "Listening to the Parables of Jesus." In *The Philosophy of Paul Ricoeur. An Anthology of His Work*, edited by Charles E. Reagan and David Stuart, 239–45. Boston: Beacon Press, 1978.

———. "Metaphor and the Main Problem of Hermeneutics." In *The Philosophy of Paul Ricoeur. An Anthology of His Work*, edited by Charles E. Reagon and David Stuart, 143–48. Boston: Beacon Press, 1978.

———. *The Rule of Metaphor: Multi-Disciplinary Studies of the Creation of Meaning in Language*. Toronto: University of Toronto Press, 1981.

Rimbaud, Arthur. *Illuminations*. Translated by Louise Varèse. New York: New Directions, 1957.

Rizzo, Tiziano. *Ponti di Venezia*. Rome: Newton Compton, 1986.

Robinson, Richard. *Narratives of the European Border: A History of Nowhere*. Basingstoke, UK: Palgrave Macmillan, 2007.

Roe, Albert S. *Blake's Illustrations to the Divine Comedy*. Princeton, NJ: Princeton University Press, 1953.

Rogers, Franklin R., with the assistance of Mary Ann Rogers. *Painting and Poetry: Form, Metaphor, and the Language of Literature*. Lewisburg, PA: Bucknell University Press, 1985.

Róheim, Géza. *Animism, Magic, and the Divine King*. London: Kegan Paul, 1930.

Rose, Jodi. "Project Outline." http://www.singingbridges.net/about/index.html.

———. *Singing Bridges*. https://singingbridgesmusic.bandcamp.com/.

Rossanda, Rossana. Preface to Matvejević, *Mondo ex e tempo del dopo: Identità, ideologie, nazioni nell'una e nell'altra Europa*. Milan: Garzanti, 2006.

Rossellini, Roberto. *Paisan*. Film. 1946.

Roth, Joseph. *The Legend of the Holy Drinker*. Translated by Michael Hofmann. London: Chatto & Windus, 1989.

———. *The White Cities: Reports from France 1925–39*. Translated by Michael Hofmann. London: Granta Books, 2005.

Rushdie, Salman. *Imaginary Homelands: Essays and Criticism, 1981–1991*. London: Granta Books, 1991.

Ruskin, John. *The Stones of Venice*. Vol. 2: *The Sea-Stories*. London: Smith, Elder, 1873.

Sail, Lawrence. "Bridge Passages." *Poetry Nation Review* 28, no. 4 (2002): 4–6.

Sainéan, Lazare. "Les Rites de la construction d'après la poésie populaire de l'Europe orientale." *Revue de l'histoire des religions* 45, no.1 (1902): 359–96.

Savi-Lopez, Maria. *Leggende del mare*. Florence: Ermanno Loescher, 1894.

Sayad, Abdelmalek. *The Suffering of the Immigrant*. Translated by David Macey. Cambridge, UK: Polity Press, 2004.

Schaeffer, Pierre. *Traité des objets musicaux*. Paris: Le Seuil, 1966.

Schafer, R. Murray. "The Soundscape." In *The Sound Studies Reader*, edited by Jonathan Sterne, 95–103. London: Routledge, 2012.

Schopenhauer, Arthur. *The World as Will and Representation*. Vol. 2. Translated by E. F. J. Payne. New York: Dover, 2000.

Schott, Robin May. "Sexual Violence, Sacrifice, and Narratives of Political Origins." In

Birth, Death, and Femininity: Philosophies of Embodiment, edited by Robin May Schott and Sara Heinämaa, 25–48. Bloomington: Indiana University Press, 2010.

Schwandner-Sievers, Stephanie, and Bernd J. Fischer, eds. *Albanian Identities: Myth and History*. London: Hurst, 2002.

Schwartz, Roberta Freund. *How Britain Got the Blues: The Transmission and Reception of American Blues Style in the United Kingdom*. Aldershot, UK: Ashgate, 2007.

Seguin, Roger. "Remarques sur les origines des pontifices romains." In *Hommages à Henri Le Bonniec: Res Sacrae*, edited by Danielle Porte and Jean-Pierre Néraudau, 405–18. Brussels: Latomus, 1988.

Sells, Michael. *The Bridge Betrayed: Religion and Genocide in Bosnia*. Berkeley: University of California Press, 1998.

Selz, Peter. *German Expressionist Painting*. Berkeley: University of California Press, 1957.

Seppilli, Anita. *Sacralità dell'acqua e sacrilegio dei ponti. Persistenza di simboli e dinamica culturale*. Palermo: Sellerio, 1977.

Serres, Michel. *Angels: A Modern Myth*. Translated by Francis Cowper and edited by Philippa Hurd. Paris: Flammarion, 1995.

———. *L'Art des ponts: Homo pontifex*. Paris: Éditions Le Pommier, 2006.

Seyhan, Azade. *Writing Outside the Nation*. Princeton, NJ: Princeton University Press, 2001.

Sigler, Amanda. "Crossing Folkloric Bridges: The Cat, the Devil, and Joyce." *James Joyce Quarterly* 45, nos. 3–4 (Spring–Summer 2008): 537–55.

Sillani, Tommaso. *Mare nostrum*. Milan: Editori Alfieri e Lacroix, 1918.

Simek, Rudolf. *Dictionary of Northern Mythology*. Cambridge: D. S. Brewer, 1993.

Simmel, Georg. "Bridge and Door," translated by Mark Ritter. In *Rethinking Architecture: A Reader in Cultural Theory*, edited by Neil Leach, 66–69. London: Routledge, 1996. The essay has also been very well translated by Michael Kaern, with a substantial introduction, again as "Bridge and Door," in *Qualitative Sociology* 17, no. 4 (1994): 397–413. An excellent and earlier (unidentified) translation lies in *Lotus International* 47 (1985): 52–56.

Singleton, Charles S. "The Vistas in Retrospect." *MLN* 81, no. 1 (January 1966): 55–80.

Sitz, Walter. "Hölderlin's 'Ode to Heidelberg.'" *Germanic Review* 37 (January 1962): 153–60.

Siviero, Enzo. *Il ponte umano. Pensieri e ricordi in libertà*. Edited by Roberto Morese. Venice: Libreria Cluva Editrice, 2014.

Sloterdijk, Peter. *Spheres*. Vol. 1: *Bubbles, Microspherology*. Cambridge, MA: MIT Press, 2011.

———. *You Must Change Your Life: On Anthropotechnics*. Translated by Wieland Hoban. Cambridge: Polity Press, 2013.

Sluga, Glenda. *The Problem of Trieste and the Italo-Yugoslav Border*. Albany: State University of New York Press, 2001.

Smith, Merril D., ed. *Cultural Encyclopedia of the Breast*. London: Rowman and Littlefield, 2014.

Soja, Edward. *Thirdspace: Journeys to Los Angeles and Other Real-and-Imagined Places*. Oxford: Basil Blackwell, 1996.

Sproul, David Kent. "A Bridge Between Cultures: An Administrative History of Rainbow Bridge National Monument." http://www.nps.gov/archive/rabr/adhi/adhi5b.htm.

St. Catherine of Siena. *A Treatise of Discretion*. Translated by Algar Thorold. Potosi, WI: St. Athanius Press, 2014.

St. Ephrem the Syrian. "Homily on Our Lord." In *Selected Prose Works*, translated by

Edward G. Mathew and Joseph P. Amar and edited by Kathleen McVey, 277–80. Washington, DC: Catholic University of America Press, 1994.

Stanesco, Michel. "Du pont de l'épée au pont eschatologique: Le 'passage périlleux' dans l'imaginaire folklorique roumain." In *Les Ponts au Moyen Âge*, edited by Danièle James-Raoul and Claude Thomasset, 163–78. Paris: PUPS, 2006.

Starr, Kevin. *Golden Gate: The Life and Times of America's Greatest Bridge*. New York: Bloomsbury Press, 2012.

Steel, Eric. *Bridge*. Film. 2006.

———. "Interview, Part I." YouTube, 2007. https://www.youtube.com/watch?v=ADxUFAD6eBU&playnext=1&list=PL9E1479F536BDF580.

Steinman, David B., and Sara Ruth Watson. *Bridges and Their Builders*. New York: G. P. Putnam's Sons, 1941.

Stevens, Wallace. *The Palm at the End of the Mind: Selected Poems and a Play*. Edited by Holly Stevens. New York: Random House, 1990.

Strack, Daniel C. "The Bridge Project: Research on Metaphor, Culture and Cognition," *University of Kitakyushu Faculty of Humanities Journal* 68 (2004), 19–45. https://www.dcstrack.com/pdf/strack%20-%20the%20bridge%20project.pdf.

———. "When the Path of Life Crosses the River of Time: Multivalent Bridge Metaphor in Literary Contexts," *University of Kitakyushu Faculty of Humanities Journal* 72 (2006): 1–18. https://www.dcstrack.com/pdf/strack%20-%20when%20the%20path%20of%20life%20crosses%20the%20river%20of%20time.pdf.

Sturluson, Snorri. *Edda*. Translated and edited by Anthony Faulkes. London: Dent, 1995.

Sugg, Richard P. *Hart Crane's "The Bridge": A Description of Its Life*. Tuscaloosa: University of Alabama Press, 1976.

Sweetman, John. *The Artist and the Bridge, 1700–1920*. Brookfield, VT: Ashgate, 1999.

Tang, Huan Cheng. "Philosophical Basis for Chinese Bridge Aesthetics." In *Bridge Aesthetics Around the World*, edited by Committee on General Structures, Subcommittee on Bridge Aesthetics, 167–76. Washington, DC: Transportation Board Research Board, 1991.

Tate, Allen. "On the 'Intensity of Sensation.'" In *Hart Crane: Comprehensive Research and Study Guide*, edited by Harold Bloom, 102–4. Philadelphia: Chelsea House, 2003.

Tawada, Yoko. *Facing the Bridge*. Translated by Margaret Mitsutani. New York: New Directions, 2007.

———. "I Did Not Want to Build Bridges." In *Germany in Transit: Nation and Migration, 1955–2005*, edited by Deniz Göktürk, David Gramling, and Anton Kaes, 416. Berkeley: University of California Press, 2007.

Teel, Mary Lou, producer. *Sunday Morning*, "Encyclopedia Britannica Is Turning 250—Look It Up!" Aired December 30, 2018, on CBS News. https://www.cbsnews.com/news/encyclopedia-britannica-is-turning-250/.

Theroux, Alexander. "Letter to the Editor." *New York Times*, May 26, 1991. http://www.nytimes.com/1991/05/26/books/l-the-enigma-of-suicide-579991.html.

Thomasset, Claude. Introduction to *Les Ponts au Moyen Âge*, edited by Danièle James-Raoul and Claude Thomasset, 7–15. Paris: PUPS, 2006.

———. "La Construction du pont médiéval dans deux romans contemporains." In *Les Ponts au Moyen Âge*, edited by Danièle James-Raoul and Claude Thomasset, 19–41. Paris: PUPS, 2006.

Thoreau, Henry David. *I to Myself: An Annotated Selection from the Journal of Henry D. Thoreau*. Edited by Jeffrey A. Cramer. New Haven, CT: Yale University Press, 2007.

Tomizza, Fulvio. *Alle spalle di Trieste*. Milan: Bompiani, 2000.

———. *Materada*. Milan: Bompiani, 2015.

Trachtenberg, Alan. *Brooklyn Bridge: Fact and Symbol*. Chicago: University of Chicago Press, 1979.

Trinchese, Stefano, ed. *Mare nostrum. Percezione ottomana e mito mediterraneo in Italia all'alba del '900*. Milan: Guerini, 2005.

Troy, Una. *The Other End of the Bridge*. London: Heinemann, 1960.

Tucci, Tina, and Anna Chiarini. *A chi appartiene l'Adriatico? Italia e Balcani. Gli stereotipi e la realtà nel '900*. Imola, Italy: La Mandragora, 1999.

Tutaev, David. *The Man Who Saved Florence*. New York: Coward-McCann, 1967.

Ungaretti, Giuseppe. *Vita d'un uomo. Tutte le poesie*. Edited by Leone Piccioni. Milan: Mondadori, 1977.

Valéry, Paul. *The Art of Poetry*. Translated by Denise Folliot. Princeton, NJ: Princeton University Press, 1989.

———. *Oeuvres I*. Edited by Jean Hytier. Paris: Gallimard, 1957.

Valussi, Giorgio. *Il confine nordorientale d'Italia*. Nuova Edizione a cura di Pio Nodari. Gorizia: Istituto di Sociologia Internazionale Gorizia, 2000.

van Haeperen, Françoise. *Le collège pontifical (3ème s.a.C.—4ème s.p.C.): Contribution à l'étude de la religion publique romaine*. Brussels: Institut historique belge de Rome, 2002.

Vargyas, Lajos. "The Origin of the 'Walled-Up Wife.'" In *Researches into the Medieval History of Folk Ballad*, 173–233. Budapest: Akadémiai Kiado, 1967.

Vattimo, Gianni. "Cristianesimo senza verità." In *Inquieto pensare: Scritti in onore di Massimo Cacciari*, edited by Emanuele Severino and Vincenzo Vitiello, 203–10. Brescia: Morcelliana, 2015.

Vernant, Jean-Pierre. *Myth and Tragedy in Ancient Greece*. Translated by Janet Lloyd. New York: Zone Books, 1990.

Villalba, Maria López. "Arches of Discord, Streams of Confluence: The Building of Bridges in the Balkans." In *Greece and the Balkans: Identities, Perceptions and Cultural Encounters since the Enlightenment*, edited by Dimitris Tziovas, 141–54. Burlington, VT: Ashgate, 2003.

von Beit, Hedwig. *Symbolik des Märchens*. Bern: A. Francke, 1957.

Wallace-Hadrill, Andrew. *Rome's Cultural Revolution*. Cambridge: Cambridge University Press, 2008.

Watson, Wilbur J., and Sara Ruth Watson. *Bridges in History and Legend*. Cleveland: J. H. Jansen, 1937.

Wheeler, Mark. "Hyperactivity in Brain May Explain Multiple Symptoms of Depression," *UCLA Newsroom*, February 27, 2012. http://newsroom.ucla.edu/releases/hyperactivity-in-brain-may-explain-228954.

Weil, Mark S. *The History and Decoration of the Ponte S. Angelo*. University Park: Pennsylvania State Press, 1974.

Weil, Simone. "The Great Beast." In *Selected Essays, 1934–1943: Historical, Political, and Moral Writings*, translated by Richard Rees, 89–144. Eugene, OR: Wipf and Stock, 2015.

———. "Human Personality." In *An Anthology*, edited and translated by Siân Miles, 49–78. New York: Grove, 1986.

Weizman, Eyal. *Hollow Land: Israel's Architecture of Occupation*. London: Verso, 2007.

———. "The Politics of Verticality: 10. Roads—; over and under." *Open Democracy Net*. April 30, 2002. https://www.opendemocracy.net/en/article_809jsp/.

Westerhausen, René, Frank Kreuder, Sarah Dos Santos Sequeira, et al. "Effects of

Handedness and Gender on Macro- and Microstructure of the *Corpus Callosum* and Its Subregions." *Cognitive Brain Research* 21, no. 3 (2004): 418–26.

Wilbur, Richard. *New and Collected Poems*. New York: Harcourt, Brace and Jovanovich, 1988.

Wilder, Thornton. *The Bridge of San Luis Rey*. New York: Harper Collins, 2003.

———. *Conversations with Thornton Wilder*. Edited by Jackson R. Bryer. Jackson: University Press of Mississippi, 1992.

Wittgenstein, Ludwig. *Philosophical Investigations*. Translated by G. E. M. Anscombe. New York: Macmillan, 1968.

Worringer, Wilhelm. *Abstraction and Empathy*. New York: International Universities Press, 1958.

Wright, Chantal. "Writing in the 'Grey Zone': Exophonic Literature in Contemporary Germany." *GFL: German as a Foreign Language* 3 (2008): 26–42.

Yardley, William. "Alvin Lee, Guitarist of Ten Years After, Dies." *New York Times*, March 6, 2013.

Yarwood, John. *Rebuilding Mostar: Urban Reconstruction in a War Zone*. Liverpool: Liverpool University Press, 1999.

Yates, Frances Amelia. *The Art of Memory*. Chicago: University of Chicago Press, 1966.

Yeats, W. B. *Per Amica Silentia Lunae*. In *Mythologies*, 317–69. New York: Macmillan, 1959.

———. *A Vision*. New York: Collier Books, 1966.

Yeşiltepe, Demet, and Ayşe Sema Kubat. "The Effect of Bridges on the Spatial Dimension of Cities: The Golden Horn, Istanbul Case." Proceedings of the 11th Space Syntax Symposium, 2017. http://www.11ssslisbon.pt/docs/proceedings/papers/120.pdf.

Yıldız, Yasemin. *Beyond the Mother Tongue: The Postmonolingual Condition*. New York: Fordham University Press, 2012.

Ziółkowski, Adam. "Ritual Cleaning-Up of the City: From the Lupercalia to the Argei." *Ancient Society* 29 (1998–99): 191–218.

Zurawsky, Stephen. User Review, "Nirvana, Nevermind." *AllMusic Review*, October 2, 2018. http://www.allmusic.com/album/nevermind-mw0000185616.

INDEX

Page numbers in boldface refer to figures.